Industrial Renaissance:
New Business Ideas for the Japanese Company

Industrial Renaissance: New Business Ideas for the Japanese Company

Edited by Kappei HIDAKA

with contributions by
Yoshihiro INOUE
Nobuyuki TOKORO
Masatoshi YAMADA
Youngjin SON
Kota SHIMAUCHI
Takeshi SEGUCHI
Hyunjung JUNG
Kanako NEGISHI

Research Series 39
The Institute of Business Research Chuo University

CHUO UNIVERSITY PRESS
TOKYO, 2017

Research series 39
The Institute of Business Research
Chuo University

Edited by
Kappei Hidaka

Industrial Renaissance:
New Business Ideas for the Japanese Company

Published by Chuo University Press
742-1 Higashinakano, Hachioji-shi,
Tokyo, 192-0393 Japan

Distributed by Japan Publications Trading Co., Ltd.
P. O. Box 5030 Tokyo International,
Tokyo 100-3191, Japan

ISBN 978-4-8057-3238-0

Copyright © 2017 by Kappei Hidaka

All rights reserved. No part of this publication may be reproduced or transmitted in any form or by any means, electronic or mechanical, including photocopy, recording, or any information storage and retrieval system, without permission in writing from the publisher.
Printed in Japan

Preface

These research results were published for the Institute of Business Research at Chuo University, which was founded in 1979 to conduct theoretical and empirical research into companies and businesses.

At this Institute, joint teams of researchers specializing in fields such as business administration, accounting, commerce, finance, and economics, and visiting fellows and assistant researchers, come together to conduct research activities. Their research findings are made public through such publications as Kenkyu Sosho (Research Series) and the periodical Kigyo Kenkyu (Corporate Research Reports). Many of the Institute's public lectures and research meetings are attended by a large number of people. The Institute has an active program of international exchange that covers international collaborative research, accepting foreign researchers, and exchanging papers with overseas research facilities.

Our team attempted to scientifically analyze several economic, industrial, corporate and business problems in Japan that the country faces as it reaches a turning point due to the progressive and dramatic ageing of its population, and strong earthquakes have occurred frequently since the Great East Japan Earthquake of 2011.

We are grateful to have been able to publish the results of our research to date in a relatively short span of time. The Great East Japan Earthquake occurred at the time of this research unit's foundation. The serious impact of the resultant tsunami also critically damaged the Fukushima Daiichi Nuclear Power Plant, and at this point in time, all we can say is that it is still not clear how this situation will turn out.

Japanese society is facing unprecedented ageing and thus must confront an acute shortage of labor. This reduction of the workforce is accompanied by lower productivity in all industries, and has also resulted in more registrations of foreign workers, all of which means major changes to Japanese-centered economic structures and production systems in the near future, although exactly how these impacts will affect Japanese industrial structures and their international competitiveness remain unclear.

As these changes will mean the creation of new social structures in Japan, now in the 21st century, it has become important to break away from the old mass production and mass consumption economy in Japan and in the whole global village. Thus, with this shared sense of crisis facing Japanese society, each member of our research team wrote articles printed in this book.

The fundamental and alarming problems in Japanese society are closely connected with the aging population. This coupled with the emergent problems in the world economy have driven the Japanese government to enact policies to develop human resources to further globalize Japanese society. However, since Japanese society is mostly a monoculture, it is very difficult for Japan to find ways to deal with these various issues. Nevertheless, it is imperative that Japan find ways to successfully deal with these issues in its own unique way.

Following are summaries and keywords on articles printed in this book.

A Turning Point in the Automotive Business and the Japanese Market

Kappei HIDAKA
Chuo University

Keywords
Ageing society, Automotive industry architecture, Remarkable diversified markets, Triple Bottom Line, Intelligent system and electronic controls

Summary

The industrial structure of the Japanese economy is at a turning point. The time has come to get serious about the ageing society and its accompanying decrease in working population. These are serious current and ongoing problems that will continue to greatly impact the Japanese society and economy going forward.

First of all, we look at the serious reduction in the workforce, then we discuss how the reduction of the workforce in Japan is bringing a decline in productivity in all industries and increased foreign worker registrations. These facts are bringing drastic changes to Japanese economic structures and production systems, although the near future impacts on these industrial structures and Japanese international competitiveness are still unknown.

Fundamental problems closely linked to the ageing population are beginning to emerge. As well as that, the 2011 Tohoku earthquake and tsunami seriously damaged the Fukushima Daiichi Nuclear Power Plant, which has resulted in heated debates about the stable procurement of electric power, despite the fact that development in the electric power business does not properly take the future into account.

Meanwhile, there is widespread and conspicuous deterioration of social infrastructure; for example, problems with such things as motorways, bridges and harbors, problems with utilities such as gas and water supplies, and lax housing design with regards to earthquake durability.

Japan's leading industry is currently its automotive industry. To date, the automotive and consumer electronics industries have led in terms of acquisition of foreign money, since they had export-oriented strategy. Being internationally competitive, these industries account for about 50% of Japan's trade surplus. The automotive industry currently ships 47 trillion yen worth of products, which represents a solid 16.4% of all exports from Japanese manufacturing industries.

However, the possibility of the appearance of a new powertrain in the near future could fundamentally change the automotive industry. While this is a serious threat, it could also present a business opportunity for Japanese companies.

This paper examines the historical approaches to business environments in the Japanese automotive industry, and then analyzes the dramatic business model changes in the global automotive industry in connection with changes in the Japanese automotive market and Japanese society.

The automotive industry is entering a historical turning point. Automotive makers are under pressure to overcome a range of impacts. For example, principal markets are shifting from developed countries such as United States, Japan, and the EU to emerging countries such as BRICs. Expansion of sales is always welcomed by automotive makers, although they must face the challenges of developing and supplying cars for various markets in a greater variety of ways.

Environment-friendly car design is the most important an immediate issue facing the global automotive industry. The CO_2 reduction goal itself is common to all, and a range of technological solutions have already been developed. These solutions include hybrid and plug-in hybrid vehicles produced mainly by Japanese makers, downsized and improved efficiency with gasoline and diesel engines mainly by European makers, and R&D into electric car seating and building the required new infrastructure. In addition, all automotive makers are developing fuel cell vehicles to survive during this major competition. These new low-pollution vehicle approaches are necessary to gain the support of governments in terms of subsidies and preferential tax systems.

Innovative technologies such as electronic devices, Artificial Intelligence (AI) and the Internet of Things (IoT) are bringing dramatic changes to modern and future vehicles. Nevertheless, the principal causes of these changes are not only technological factors, but also social factors. Especially in the Japanese market, as previously stated, one of the most important things for automotive makers is to work out how to handle these changing social factors.

Conditions for Sustainable Management: Traditional Succession and Risk Awareness

Yoshihiro INOUE
Kobegakuin University

Keywords
  Long-lived company, Brand value, Integrity of management,
  Systematic disgraceful affair, Trust obligation

Summary

The business environment of modern companies is severe. Managers are challenged by stiff price competition and intense demand pressure. Even in this economic environment, there are many companies in Japan that have existed for over 200 years now. Why do so many long-lived companies thrive in Japan?

As an example, two long-lived companies are considered in this paper. The first is Kongougumi, a company in the temple and shrine construction industry. This company was established in the Asuka period and entered the apartment house construction business in the 2000s. As a result, price competition with other house construction companies became severe, and the management of this company changed.

The second case is that of Toraya, established during the Muromachi period. This was a traditional company that missed the sweets boom at the beginning of the 2000s.

Both companies overcame an operational crisis using management integrity and traditional succession, raising brand value in society, which should be considered an important factor in business continuation.

Brand value and positive crisis evasion assists risk management. Management integrity is also a factor in risk management, as is prompt correspondence, the second form of risk management. The third risk management tool is to learn from the lessons of the past.

Thus, management characteristics and trust in long-lived companies are considered in this paper.

Value Creation through Co-creation: The Case of a Smart City

Nobuyuki TOKORO
Nihon University

Keywords
Value Creation, Co-creation, Ba, Emergence, Synthesis
Summary

As globalization accelerates, competition among corporations is becoming more severe. To overcome competition in the marketplace and capture competitive advantage, corporations must create new value. The problem they face is how to go about creating new value. This paper presents the hypothesis that co-creation by corporations in different industries can create new value, and it attempts to verify the hypothesis through an investigation of actual conditions. Existing theories on competitive advantage have been built on the premise of "competition with other companies" where companies search for ways to beat the competition, and their fundamental recognition was that they had to pursue value creation on their own.

More recently, however, the idea of open innovation has been gaining attention and corporations are becoming more interested in creating new value in cooperative efforts with other companies. This paper develops this idea, suggesting that new value is created when companies of various industries exchange, combine, and resonate their knowledge and know-how and that this new value enables them to build competitive advantage. As a theoretical framework for verifying this approach through an investigation of actual conditions, this paper presents the three concepts of "Ba" (shared context in motion), "emergence", and "synthesis". These concepts are all necessary components for realizing co-creation among corporations of different industries. Value creation is assumed to occur when these three components function effectively and are organically linked.

An investigation into actual conditions was conducted in this paper to verify the theory described above. The subject of this investigation was Fujisawa Sustainable Smart Town (Fujisawa SST) that Panasonic is currently constructing in Fujisawa City in Kanagawa Prefecture, Japan. Along with utilizing ICT to use electric power effectively and build a city with a low carbon footprint, this next-generation smart city also has the potential to create new value in such areas as mobility, security, and healthcare. Since corporations from a variety of different industries-including electronics, automotive, housing, real estate, gas, and finance-are participating in the construction of this smart city, new trials in fields of technology and services are continually being conducted.

The author of this paper verified the co-creation of value among corporations of different industries through detailed interviews with personnel at Panasonic, which is leading the Fujisawa SST project. These interviews resulted in a number of valuable findings. One of the findings was the autonomy of Ba and the existence of a leader of Ba. Fujisawa SST is a project led by Panasonic, and other participating corporations are referred to as partners. Essentially, the project follows guidelines put forward by Panasonic. On the other hand, however, Panasonic makes attempts to reflect the knowledge of partner corporations, and autonomy is ensured in the Ba that is formed in the project. As a leader of the Ba, Panasonic manages the Ba so that the knowledge and know-how of partner corporations can be exchanged, combined, and resonated, and takes on the role of linking it to the creation of value. In other words, the system that has been functioning in the Fujisawa SST project is one that co-creates value with corporations of different industries while skillfully combining both top-down and bottom-up styles of management.

Ecological Modernization of Business Management: The Innovation of Environmental Management for Changing into Sustainable Society

Masatoshi YAMADA
Tamagawa University

Keywords
Environmental management, Sustainability, Weak ecological modernization, Strong ecological modernization, Gradual innovation

Summary
In this paper, we will study ecological modernization of business management, which is practiced under environmental management and incorporating

the concept of sustainability, corporate social responsibility (CSR), and creating shred value (CSV), with an example of the group-wide environmental management by Ricoh Company Ltd. (hereafter referred to as Ricoh). To do so, we can examine the existing state of environmental management and examine how business administration and the competitiveness of a firm combine to create a sustainable society.

The modernization of capitalist society since the Industrial Revolution has transformed production from handicrafts and cottage industries, into mass-produced products, and factory-based industries with global division of labor. In the process of modernization, the focus on economic rationality of mass production and mass consumption has brought about an ecological crisis since the end of the 20th century. Today, businesses and societies are challenged to find solutions for the ecological crisis. Globally, governments and environmental managers at individual firms have planned and implemented policies seeking a transformation into a sustainable society. These policies and environmental management, aiming for a "green" economy, comprise the process of ecological modernization.

There are weak and strong versions of ecological modernization. Weak ecological modernists assume that we can achieve sustainability by modifying the existing socio-economical structure, rather than radical changing of it. Strong ecological modernists insist on the necessity of overcoming mass production and mass consumption to solve the ecological crisis. Under the present circumstances, without radically changing the existing structure of mass production and mass consumption, individual firms such as Ricoh has positively integrated the concepts of sustainability, CSR, CSV into their business management to establish environmental management which can combine economic and ecological rationalities. However, many observers see little improvement in the ecological crisis to date.

What type of environmental management can combine both economic and ecological rationalities? In this paper, we present seven typologies of environmental management and a new concept, "gradual innovation", to explain the development process of environmental management. In addition, we will review Ricoh as a case study, and discuss the features of its existing environmental management and future directions.

How Japanese Paper Manufacturers Resolving Social Desire: Evaluating a Japanese Paper Manufacturer's Waste Paper Usage Condition

Youngjin SON
Nippon Materio Co., Ltd.

Keywords

Creating shared value (CSV), CSR, Paper manufacturer, Waste paper

Summary

This study argues the need of expanding the CSV concept by evaluating a Japanese paper manufacturer's waste paper usage condition showing a clear trade-off relationship between economics and sociality.

In general, paper manufacturers use pulp from wood chips and 'waste paper' as main raw materials. The ratio of these two materials determines the product cost and the pollution production of a company.

This paper considers the response of a paper company to environmental issues, and analyzes the status of waste paper recycling including the released paper produced from waste gypsum board.

Waste paper recycling (the released paper of waste gypsum board) needs to progress further through the cooperation among paper companies, waste-paper collection related companies, and consumers. In particular, the efficient and active usage of waste paper can be a driving force to resolve social issues. Moreover, the improvement of wastepaper utilization coefficient can be a way to maximize the economic benefit of paper companies as well as to take social responsibilities.

The objective of this paper is to identify the correlation between the response of paper companies to social issues and the economic benefit of companies. The responses of paper companies to social issues are associated with the competitiveness of companies such as innovations in production facilities and the sales of society friendly products. However, the environmental problems as social issues and the economic value of companies pursuing profit cannot always show the form exceeding the trade-off relationship. (In other words) it is not conclusive to say that an environmental plan of a company cannot be directly related to the competitiveness of the company. This paper analyzes the relationship between industrial waste treatment companies producing the released paper of waste gypsum board and paper companies shows the traditional trade-off relationship between sociality and economics clearly. In other words, this paper concludes that the paper industry still widely believes that conducting environmental measures is a right thing to do but it can induce negative effects on the normal business activities. This problem is consistent with the skepticism of a group, which has been studied and practiced CSR, on the CSV concept. We are not free from the criticism that the CSV concept remains in naïve condition without fully reflecting the realistic conditions of companies and CSV ignores the tensions between social and economic goals. Therefore, we need to evaluate the CSV concept thoroughly. Furthermore, we need to expand and develop the concept.

Employment Management Reform and the Japanese Production System: The Experience of Japanese Manufacturers During the "Lost Decade"

Kota SHIMAUCHI
Takushoku University

Keywords
Employment portfolio management, Non-regular employee, Japanese production system, Skill formation, Competitiveness

Summary
In the early 1990s, Japanese companies faced a long recession after the burst of Japan's economic bubble and the intensification of global competition, and looked to employment management reform to promote business recovery. The employment portfolio management (EPM) system that the Japan Federation of Employers' Associations (Nikkeiren, currently Nippon Keidanren) proposed in 1995 then had an impact on the employment management reform among many Japanese companies.

In this chapter, we seek to clarify the effects of employment management reform among Japanese manufacturers on their production systems and skill formation practices which are major sources of competitiveness, focusing on the period from the 1990s to the 2000s (the so-called "lost decade").

In order to achieve the objective, firstly, we consider the features of EPM introduced by many Japanese companies. Then, we illustrate the features of the Japanese production systems and skill formation practices which are the sources of Japanese manufacturers' competitiveness. Finally, in order to clarify the effects of employment management reform on the Japanese production system and skill formation practice, we analyze the case of Toyota.

In its conclusion, this chapter shows that employment management reform during this period was focused on cutting personnel costs as well as maximizing workforce flexibility, and resulted in the widespread use of non-regular employees and in a reduction of domestic consumer demand, which is essential to business success. Moreover, this chapter shows that the reform caused damage to the skill formation practice as the infrastructure supporting production system which is major source of Japanese strength.

These conclusions suggest that a management style pursuing cost reduction and employment adjustment depending on the use of non-regular employees is an unsustainable solution.

How Lexus Has Utilized Culture in the Japanese Market: Content and Discourse Analysis of its Brochures

Takeshi SEGUCHI
Kagoshima Prefectural College

Keywords
Market strategy of Lexus, Content and discourse analysis, Cultural factors, Cultural platform, Cultural apparatus, Representation

Summary
The purpose of this chapter is to understand how Lexus, the luxury brand of Toyota, has utilized Japanese culture in its market strategy through a content and discourse analysis of its brochures from 2006 to 2013.

Contemporary multinational companies (MNCs) have to face intense global competition. To avoid commoditization and the consequent price competition MNCs try to create added values which are able to appeal to their customers and at the same time sustainably differentiate themselves from rivals. This chapter casts a spotlight on cultural meaning as the potential added value mentioned above, and on the market strategy that utilizes it. This strategy comprises two meanings: utilizing "cultural factors" and creating a "cultural platform" for customers. The former provides a product with cultural signs and articulates it to attract customers to the brand, while the latter forms conceptual or interpretive frameworks for customers by adopting a diverse cultural apparatus. A brochure is a twofold media that, on the one hand, represents particular meanings and makes a product meaningful; on the other hand, it becomes an expression of a cultural apparatus, providing a cultural platform for readers.

Toyota built the Lexus brand for the American market in 1989. Later, it introduced the brand into the Japanese market in 2005 by integrating the existing models into one brand. Several studies argued that Lexus used Japanese culture as one of its competitive advantages. Therefore, we analyzed brochures in terms of the cultural factors that Lexus utilized, how Lexus has represented aspects of its products, what differences exist in car models, and how its market strategy using culture has changed across time.

As a result of content analysis, we revealed three ways in which Lexus has been using Japanese culture. The first group includes brochures for the ISF, CT200h, and HS250h models and features oniy a limited a mount of cultural factors. The second group of cars has been introduced in the Japanese market in 2005, at the beginning, and includes GS, IS, and SC, in addition to RX. Although the brochures for these models used many cultural factors in the early stage, the contribution of these factors gradually reduced over time. The third group correspond to the LS series. This group utilized more cultural factors than others in its brochures, but the number of cultural factors also decreased over time. In other words, Japanese culture has been used in the high-grade model of Lexus to add value to the brand.

Moreover, we discuss which cultural factors were used and how cultural factors were utilized through discourse analysis. Certain factors, such as "Japanese culture", "takumi", and "omotenashi" have been used to represent brand identity, elegance of interior, precision of painting process, and sometimes to differentiate its engine or design from its rivals.

Hyundai Motor Company's Alliance with Ford Motor Company in the Founding Period

Hyunjung JUNG
Graduate school of Commerce,
Chuo University

Keywords

Alliance, Hyundai Motor Company, Ford Motor Company, Technical Assistance, Direct Sales System

Summary

This chapter contains descriptions and evaluations of studies and interpretation of alliance effects associated with Hyundai Motor Company at the outset. Its purpose is to present the effects of Hyundai-Ford alliance; how is the alliance related to Hyundai Motor Company's operations at that time and what did it gain from Ford?

The automobile industry has witnessed the formation of alliances to acquire technologies. Hyundai Motor Company, the leading automobile maker in the Korean automobile industry, was founded in 1967 and signed an Overseas Assembler Agreement with Ford to obtain their technologies. Hyundai Motor Company through the acquisition of packed foreign technology from Ford took the shortest time to achieve its first commercial production, with their vigorous efforts to learn systems of Ford. But some of the systems transferred from Ford didn't fit the circumstances of Korea and made it difficult for Hyundai Motor Company to acquire them, due to no modification.

Ford's role in Hyundai, however, is not limited to technical assistance for automobile manufacturing. This chapter highlights the need to go beyond the current knowledge about Hyundai-Ford alliance and reveals significant other effects of the alliance. That is, Hyundai recognized the importance of after-sales service as well as automobile production technologies. Ford emphasized operation of the sales system completely before vehicle production and market entry. By exploring the managerial difficulties, Hyundai Motor Company reinforced the sales systems, and tried to modify its own direct sales forces gradually. Although it was influenced by the sales system of Ford, it was remodeled to adapt to the situation in Korea. That's when the current direct sales system of Hyundai Motor Company, which is known as a rare system in the global community, was formed.

Multinational Enterprises' Global Supply Chain: Study of the Global Reporting Initiative and United Nations Global Compact

Kanako NEGISHI
National Institute of Technology,
Ube College

Keywords
   Corporate Social Responsibility, Rating of delisting, Developing countries, United Nations Global Compact, Global Reporting Initiative.

Summary
   This study explores the environment with regard to multinational enterprise (MNE) sustainability. In particular, it focusses on relationships between firms, international institutions, and non-governmental organizations

(NGOs). Although sustainability of the global supply chain is a vital issue for MNEs, certain aspects of the environment have been institutionalized by them. Therefore, this study examines how firms use the Global Reporting Initiative (GRI) guidelines and the 10 principles of the United Nations Global Compact (UNGC). This paper shows not overall trend of ranking but analyzes data on firms from Japan and some developing countries. Certain studies have demonstrated that sustainability initiatives have progressed further in Western advanced countries than in developing countries that have more serious social problems. Analysis results based on GRI and UNGC data show that not all firms from Western advanced countries but from Japanese, the other Asian countries firms and even small and medium sized enterprises (SME) use GRI guidelines and participate with the UNGC and their agendas that certain firms are led to the delisting from UNGC database because of failure to submit their reports. The ratio of delisting of SMEs from developing countries and Japan is relatively higher than the other size and from advanced countries firms. The result also suggests the agendas of MNEs global supply chain. This study contributes to the literature by highlighting certain features of the environment that effect MNEs' global strategy.

Lastly, we would like to thank all members of our research unit and colleagues, Prof. Toshihiko Miura, the head of Institute of Business Research at Chuo University, Ms. Michiko Miyakawa, the secretary of Institute of Business Research at Chuo University, and Ms. Mizuho Kobayashi, the proofreader of Chuo University Press.

Kappei HIDAKA
Chairman of research unit
The Institute of Business Research, Chuo University

Contents

Preface

I. A Turning Point in the Automotive Business and
the Japanese Market　　　　　　　*Kappei Hidaka*　　1

II. Conditions for Sustainable Management:
Traditional Succession and Risk Awareness　　*Yoshihiro Inoue*　　23

III. Value Creation through Co-creation:
The Case of a Smart City　　　　*Nobuyuki Tokoro*　　49

IV. Ecological Modernization of Business Management:
The Innovation of Environmental Management for
Changing into Sustainable Society　　*Masatoshi Yamada*　　71

V. How Japanese Paper Manufacturers Resolving Social
Desire: Evaluating a Japanese Paper Manufacturer's
Waste Paper Usage Condition　　　*Youngjin Son*　　99

VI. Employment Management Reform and the Japanese
Production System: The Experience of Japanese
Manufacturers During the "Lost Decade"　　*Kota Shimauchi*　　137

VII. How Lexus Has Utilized Culture in the Japanese Market:
Content and Discourse Analysis of its Brochures
　　　　　　　　　　　　　　　　　Takeshi Seguchi　　159

VIII. Hyundai Motor Company's Alliance with Ford
Motor Company in the Founding Period　　*Hyunjung Jung*　　187

IX. Multinational Enterprises' Global Supply Chain:
Study of the Global Reporting Initiative and
United Nations Global Compact　　*Kanako Negishi*　　211

About the authors

Kappei HIDAKA   Chuo University

Yoshihiro INOUE   Kobegakuin University

Nobuyuki TOKORO   Nihon University

Masatoshi YAMADA   Tamagawa University

Youngjin SON   Nippon Materio Co., Ltd.

Kota SHIMAUCHI   Takushoku University

Takeshi SEGUCHI   Kagoshima Prefectural College

Hyunjung JUNG   Graduate school of Commerce, Chuo University

Kanako NEGISHI   National Institute of Technology, Ube College

1.
A Turning Point in the Automotive Business and the Japanese Market

Kappei HIDAKA

1. Big changes of business circumstances in the Japanese market

The Japanese economy and industrial structures are at a turning point. Crucially, the ageing of society, and the decrease in the working population are becoming serious. The total population of Japan is 127,110,000 people, 33,920,000 are 65 years and over: (male 14,660,000 people, female 19,260,000), which accounts for 26.7% of the population. In the same way, the population of the 65–74 age group is 17,520,000 people (13.8%), while the 75 and over age group is 16,410,000 (12.9%). Compared to other developed countries, Japan had low-level aging in 1980s, medium-level in 1990s, and then reached the highest level in 2005.

The 65 and over age group will peak at 38,780,000 people in 2042, and will accounts for 39.9% of the total population, or one out of 2.5 people. The average life span of the Japanese in 2014 was 80.50 years for males and 86.83 years for females, and by 2060, these figures are expected to rise to 84.19 years for males and 90.93 years for females. From a 110.656 trillion yen total for social security expenses in 2013, which was 30.56% of the national income, 68.4% of that, or 75.642 trillion, accounted for social security expenditure on the aged. (based upon statistics by Japanese government and the UN. *World Population Prospects: The 2015 Revision.*)

The seriousness of this ageing society is having major impacts on the Japanese society and economy. First of all, we discuss the serious reduction in the workforce. The workforce of Japan reached its highest level in 2000 with 67.66 million people. This consisted of 15.88 million aged 15~29 years, or

23.5%, 42.60 million aged 30–59 years, or 63.0%, 4.26 million aged 60–64 years, or 6.3%, and 4.93 million aged 65 years and over, or 7.3%. The workforce of Japan is estimated to shrink to 61.80 million by 2030, consisting of 10.19 million aged 15–29 years, or 16.5%, 38.87 million aged 30–59 years, or 62.9%, 5.86 million aged 60–64 years, or 9.5%, and 6.86 million aged 65 years and over, or 11.1%. (based upon statistics from the Ministry of Internal Affairs and Communications.)

Secondly, the reduction of the Japanese workforce is bringing declining productivity in all industries, and increasing foreign worker registrations, which will bring dramatic changes to the Japanese-centric economic structures and production systems in the near future. However, how these factors will impact on Japanese industry and international competitiveness remains unclear. For example, "the strategy on the restoration of Japan" (revised in 2014) lays great emphasis on making the best use of foreign workers. This entails making good conditions for reception of foreign workers, reconsideration of the technical internship programs, taking in workers for housework in special economic zones, and enforcement of policies to support international students in the field of nursing care.

While there are fundamental problems closely linked with the ageing population, many problems have begun to surface. For example, the 2011 Great East Japan Earthquake and tsunami seriously damaged the Fukushima Daiichi Nuclear Power Plant, which brought about heated debates on the stable procurement of electric power, even though developments in electric power business do not look ahead to the future.

Meanwhile, there is widespread and conspicuous deterioration of social infrastructure problems with such things as motorways, bridges and harbors, problems with utilities such as gas and water supplies, and lax housing design with regards to earthquake durability. Such social infrastructure was built during high economic growth and has reached the end of its service life. Hence, it is hoped that the Japanese government will make plans that fit with the rate of economic growth.

Japan's leading industry is currently its automotive industry. To date, the automotive and consumer electronics industries have led in terms of acquisition of foreign money, since they are export-oriented. Being internationally competitive, these industries account for about 50% of Japan's trade surplus. The automotive industry currently ships 47 trillion yen worth of products, which represents a solid 16.4% of all exports from Japanese manufacturing industries. The total sum of Japanese exports is currently 289 trillion yen.

There are 5,480,000 people working in the automotive industries, which accounts for 8.8% of the workforce.

The ministry of economy, Trade and Industry has identified the importance of the automotive industry to the Japanese economy.

As a flagship of Japanese business, the automotive industry can be described as a national industry or national brand. Hence, development of the Japanese automotive industry is pivotal to reviving the Japanese economy. (The Ministry of Internal Affairs and Communications and the Ministry of Economy, Trade and Industry.)

Japanese companies in the consumer electronics industry have been impacted by a new manufacturing system called "The Lego Model of production", as described by MIT. As Apple Computer or Samsung have made the best use of these new production systems, Japanese business models in consumer electronics have reached their limitations in terms of competitiveness. In contrast, the Japanese automotive industry remains a leading and internationally competitive industry.

The rise and fall of both these industries can be explained by their architectures. The modern consumer electronic industry encourages standardization of parts and modularity in production systems. Standardized interfaces such as those used with large-scale integration (LSI) have enabled production system modularization, which has become the general architecture in the global consumer electronic industry. Japanese companies lag behind the Apple and Samsung business models that employ these new production systems.

Tough competition from new players like Koreans and Southeast Asians made companies more sensitive to labor costs as well as to the cost of capital. Companies started looking for way to hive off the labor-intensive parts of their operations. The new competitive pressures in the international economy were the drivers of the shift toward a modular system in which companies would carry out fewer and fewer of the functions in the production process within their own walls.

What made this transformation possible in a wide range of industries across the economy were the new digital technologies coming on line in the 1990s. In other words, these new information technologies, involving both design and production, are the enablers of modularity. (Berger, S. and the

MIT Industrial Performance Center (2005), p. 74)

Modular production in electronics started to take off in the 1990s. New software made it possible to provide digital instructions ("codification") so that companies could give supplies exact information on how to carry out parts of production. In the past, companies drew on the tacit knowledge and experience of engineers to link one phase of the production process to the next. But as soon as engineers learned to write disital code specifying how to translate designs into production specifications, the "hand-off" between one function and the next no longer required having the designers and the production people in the same facility working out problems together. Now the engineers who lays out the circuit-board design can write specifications in software that tell the technicians making the board or the chip exactly what to do. (Berger, S. and the MIT Industrial Performance Center (2005), p. 76)

On the other hand, the architecture of the automotive industry has adopted the integral approach. A standard vehicle is made with about 30,000 parts which are assembled using these integrated design methods. For example, to realize a smooth ride, automotive makers have to integrate various technologies and material to form on-board seating, suspension systems, body durability and tire technologies. Japanese automotive makers lead with their engineering techniques using these integrated designs.

Takahiro Fujimoto, a Professor at Tokyo University and leading expert on the Toyota production systems, explains why Toyota maintains in-house control over every stage of its production processes.

Take the example of three functional elements (handling, ride, fuel efficiency) and three structural elements (body, chassis, power train of an automobiles). Engineers know that the characteristics of the product's handling are determined by a subtle orchestration of body, chassis, and power-train designs, and likewise in the cases of ride and fuel efficiency ..... Each component is functionally incomplete and interdependent with other components functionally and/or structurally ..... Mix and match is difficult, and so is the use of many common components without sacrificing functionally and the integrity of the total product. (Berger, S. and the MIT Industrial Performance Center (2005), p. 61)

However, the possibility of the appearance of a new powertrain in the near future could fundamentally change the automotive industry. While this is a serious threat, it could also present a business opportunity for Japanese companies.

This paper examines the historical approaches to business environments in the Japanese automotive industry, and then analyzes the dramatic business model changes in the global automotive industry in connection with changes in the Japanese automotive market and Japanese society.

2. The dawning of Japanese automotive businesses and American motor companies

2-1. The beginning of the automotive industry and the Japanese market

The automotive industry began in Europe. Notably, the Nikolaus August Otto's 1876 development of the 4-stroke (Otto cycle) engine was a turning point. Then, the first successes in the industry were achieved by Karl Benz with his gasoline-powered three-wheeled motor vehicle in 1885, which he patented the following year, and Gottlieb Daimler's gasoline-powered four-wheeled motor vehicle. However, industrialization of the automotive business was achieved later by Henry Ford who was the first to mass-produce automobiles.

In 1898, automobiles made their first appearance in Japan. Then in 1904, Torao Yamaba completed the Yamaba steam engine in Okayama, and then made the first Japanese car. In 1905, bus services began in Hyogo Prefecture, and the automotive industry slowly began to take root in Japan.

In 1911, the first automotive company in Japan was established at Azabu in Tokyo, and was called "Kaisinsya Jidousya Kojyo (the Kaishinsha Motor Company). In 1914, Masujirou Hashimoto established this company to produce automobiles for the domestic market, which he named DAT.

After that, Hakuyosha Iron Works established by Junya Toyokawa manufactured first full-scale automobile called Otomo-Go in 1923. Toyokawa studied in America from 1913 to 1915, and had developed both 4-cylinder water-cooled and 4-cylinder air-cooled engines by 1920. Notably, his air-cooled engine technology was original at the time.

2-2. Incorporation of the Toyota Motor Corporation and American motor companies

The Toyota Motor Corporation was founded in 1937. However, this story begins with Sakichi Toyoda, the father of founder Kiichiro Toyoda. Sakichi was became well-known as the inventor of Japan's first Automatic Looms.

In 1895, Sakichi and his business partner opened a company called Toyoda Shoten in Nagoya. Sakichi built 60 power looms and contributed them as his investment in this new partnership. Then In 1898, Sakichi and his new partner opened a textile mill fitted with steam-powered looms.

Although the older a hand powered looms could only be operated one at a time, two or three of Sakichi's powered looms could be operated simultaneously. Hence, productivity increased fourfold at the new mill, and costs decreased by over 50%. These factors, coupled with the high quality of the product, spurred the rapid growth of the new company. (Toyota Motor Corporation (1988), p. 27)

Kiichiro Toyoda majored in mechanical engineering at the Faculty of Engineering at Tokyo Imperial University. In the fall of 1929, The Toyoda Automatic Loom Works was on the verge of signing an agreement with Platt Brothers to use the patent for the G-type Automatic Loom.

Kiichiro traveled to England via the United States to conclude the negotiations, but on the way he wanted to see for himself how far the automotive industry had developed, and thus spent time visiting auto assembly plants and parts makers in the United States and Great Britain.

At the time, the American automotive industry was using a mass production conveyor system to turn out over 5 million vehicles a year. Particularly, the Ford Motor Company, founded in 1903, was enjoying spectacular growth with its mass-produced, mass-marketed Model T. (Toyota Motor Corporation (1988), p. 39)

Meanwhile, the Japanese automotive industry was still in its infancy. The number of vehicles owned by Japanese exceeded 12,000 units in 1923 and grew rapidly thereafter, but the majority of these were European or American imports.

In the aftermath of the Kanto Earthquake of September 1, 1923, eight hundred Ford truck chassis were imported to be used for building buses as an emergency measure in Tokyo, whose transit system had been destroyed. The transport efficiency of these vehicles inspired public awareness of automobiles practically overnight, and American automotives soon began coming into the country in great numbers.

After studying the Japanese market, Ford entered it in 1925 by establishing Ford Motor Company of Japan (Ford-Japan) and building an assembly plant in Midori-cho in Yokohama. This company was capitalized with forty-thousand yen, and all stocks were held by the company. The Ford-Japan

Chronology on Henry Ford and Ford Motor Company

1863 (Jury 30) Henry Ford is born in Greenfield Township, Wayne Country, Michigan.
1903 Incorporates the Ford Motor Company and launches the Model A.
1908 (October 1) The Model T is introduced.
1910 Builds an automotive plant in Highland Park, Michigan.
1913 Introduces the modern assembly line for mass production of his Ford automobiles. Opens plants in Canada and Britain.
1914 Established profit-sharing program with employees and Five-Dollar Day.
1917 Constructs the Rouge factory near the Rouge River in Dearborn.
1927 Model T production ends. The second Model A is launched at the River Rouge plant.
1947 Henry Ford dies of cerebral hemorrhage at the age of eighty-three.

Source: Michele Wehrwein Albion, *The Quotable Henry Ford*, University Press of Florida, 2013, pp. xxiii~xxv.

organization consisted of general affairs, stock, service, sales, customs and accounting departments, and purchase, transport, inspection, assembly and factory refurbishment sections, 5 section in total.

The outputs of the first year recorded was 3,437 units, 8,677 in 1926 and then 7,033 in 1927, the year that GM set up General Motors of Japan (GM-Japan) and built an assembly plant in Osaka. Both were huge knockdown assembly plants that far exceeded the output capacity of the Japanese automotive industry. The Ford plant turned out 8,000 units a year, and GM's plant 10,000 units, and the number of vehicles on Japanese roads grew from 50,000 in 1927 to 80,000 in 1929. (Toyota Motor Corporation (1988), p. 41)

The opening of the Ford-Japan and GM-Japan assembly plants also gave rise to domestic manufacturers who supplied parts to both companies, and a trend toward improved quality became apparent. (Toyota Motor Corporation (1988), p. 42)

Table 1: Japanese market 1916~1935 (Units)

Year	Import cars	Domestic Cars	Knockdown	Knockdown Ford-Japan	Knockdown GM-Japan	Knockdown Kyoritu (chrysler)
1916	218					
1917	860					
1918	1,653					
1919	1,579					
1920	1,745					
1921	1,074					
1922	752					
1923	1,938					
1924	4,063					
1925	1,765		3,437	3,437		
1926	2,381	245	8,677	8,677		
1927	3,895	302	12,668	7,033	5,635	
1928	7,883	347	24,341	8,850	15,491	
1929	5,018	437	29,338	10,674	15,745	1,251
1930	2,591	458	19,678	10,620	8,049	1,015
1931	1,887	436	20,199	11,505	7,478	1,201
1932	997	880	14,087	7,448	5,893	760
1933	491	1,681	15,082	8,156	5,942	998
1934	896	2,247	33,458	17,244	12,322	2,574
1935	934	5,094	30,787	14,865	12,492	3,612

Source: Sato, M., *Yokohama-sei Ford, Osaka-sei America Sha*, 230 club, 2000, p. 91.

Table 2: Volume of imports on automotive and auto parts (Japanese-yen)

Year	Import car	Auto parts	Total
1916	386	826	712
1917	1,569	1,097	2,666
1918	4,524	3,136	7,660
1919	5,531	5,750	11,281
1920	4,865	5,613	10,478
1921	3,261	4,805	8,066
1922	2,216	5,093	7,309
1923	4,955	8,527	13,482
1924	8,772	12,413	21,185
1925	4,600	7,061	11,661
1926	5,324	10,391	15,715
1927	8,063	10,218	18,281
1928	13,770	18,474	32,244
1929	9,545	31,182	40,727
1930	4,896	19,765	24,661
1931	3,378	16,654	20,032
1932	2,894	11,927	14,821
1933	1,864	12,006	13,870
1934	3,357	28,945	32,302
1935	3,302	29,387	32,689

Source: Sato, M., *Yokohama-sei Ford, Osaka-sei America Sha*, 230 club, 2000, p. 117.

Table 3: Japanese-domestic Suppliers for Ford-Japan

Supplier	Site	Auto part's name
Dunlop (Far East Dept.)	Kobe	Tire, Tube
Bridgestone	Kurume(Fukuoka)	Tire, Tube
Mitsui Bussan	Tokyo	Battery
Okura syoji	Tokyo	Battery
Shibaura seisakusyo	Yokohama	Electric Dynamo, Electric Motor
Tokyo denki	Tokyo	Electric Bulb
Nissan jidosya	Yokohama	Tools
Nippon SKF kogyo	Tokyo	Bearings
Daido denki Seikosyo	Tokyo	Springs
Izumi seisakusyo	Tokyo	Springs for seat
Hasegawa syoten	Tokyo	A sort of glass

Source: Sato, M., *Yokohama-sei Ford, Osaka-sei America Sha*, 230 club, 2000, p. 145.

3. The hurricane of structural change in the modern automotive business

The global auto industry is gradually developed its capacity to become a leading industry in the 20th century. Facing steep Gasoline price rises, global auto industry overcame obstacles by developing weight saving technologies, improving aerodynamic characteristics and innovating for greater combustion efficiency. However, the global auto industry has arrived at a turning point, and is under pressure to reconstruct its traditional business models. This is largely due to the following 4 complicating factors.

3-1. Remarkable market diversification

The first factor is the maturing of markets in developed countries and remarkable market diversification in developing countries. Generally speaking, the main auto makers have preferred to develop and supply the markets in developed countries such as the United States, the EU, and Japan. This is basically exemplified by the history of mass production for mass consumption, in which marketing strategies such as planned obsolescence and dishonest business practices constantly caused customer dissatisfaction.

These mass consumption structures were put in place by GM in the 1920s. Alfred Chandler wrote that Henry Ford refused to take seriously these fundamental changes in the market, although Ford made a fuss about production of Model T with its low price and high labor costs, and switched from the simple Model T to polished and elegant new models. In other words, Ford switched to develop new models that were market-oriented.

However, modern markets in developed countries have matured, which is putting pressure on global automakers to development of new markets. This phenomenon has also resulted in downsizing, while vehicle maneuverability is beginning to far exceed the driving capabilities of humans, which means automatic vehicle-control systems will become even more necessary in the future if makers want to improve vehicle maneuverability even further. However, automatic vehicle-control systems detract from the "Fun to drive" aspect of vehicles.

Hence, moving into markets in developing countries such as China and Russian is a crucial issue for global automakers in their struggle for survival.

Auto sales in Asian markets except Japanese market in 2010 accounted for about 35% of the global market, whereas sales volumes in the triad US, EU and Japanese markets was 51% (United States 19%, Japan 7%, EU 25%).

J.D.Power and Associates estimate that sales in Asian markets except Japan in 2018 will grow to about 43% of the global total, centered on China, which is the biggest market in the world. The Chinese market is estimated to grow to about 3 billion units by 2018.

In addition, there are emerging structural changes in each market. As a consequence of the globalized economy, all markets including those in developed and developing countries are moving toward polarization of the kind of people who buy passenger cars. Thus, to maintain business model stability, automakers have to develop luxury cars for the rich and low price cars for the masses.

3-2. Society's demands for CO_2 emission reductions

The second factor is the demand for reduction of CO_2. Obviously CO_2 reduction is a central issue with regards to global warming, and the automotive industry has a particular duty to reduce CO_2 to help build societies that inflict little damage on the environment.

All this travel and shipping add up when it comes to global warming. The production and use of fuel for transportation in the United States is directly responsible for more than 2 billion metric tons of carbon dioxide and other heat-trapping emissions annually. That puts the U.S. transportation system second to power plants as the biggest contributors to the nation's global warming emissions---producing about 30 percent of the total, and more than one-third (36 percent) of all carbon dioxide emissions.

The biggest transportation sources of heat-trapping emissons are light-duty vehicles (including cars, SUVs, pickups, and minivans), which account for more than 60 percent of transportation's total, and about one-fifth of the nation's total. Next in line are medium- and heavy-duty vehicles at 18 percent, followed by air at 10 percent, and then shipping, rail, military, and other uses. (Cleeyus, R., Clemmer, S. and Friedman, D. (2009), p. 93)

The demands that society is making for CO_2 reductions are forcing technological switchover from the internal combustion engine to new forms of propulsion such as those in electric and fuel cell vehicles, and in fact, automotive companies, venture companies, and research institutions are vigorously accelerating next-generation power train developments.

Nevertheless, until next-generation fuel cell power trains and so forth fully come into being, various types of power train will have to coexist. In the Japanese market, hybrid vehicles account for 20% in the passenger car market, although the proportion of these vehicles in the American market is only 3%, and only 1% in the EU. Cleaner Diesel engine developments and downsized gasoline engine have priority over hybrid vehicles in EU markets. In the developing countries, the Chinese government promotes electric vehicles as a state strategy, while diesel-powered vehicles are mainstream in Indian market, and ethanol flex vehicles are mainstream in Brazil. Hence, the dominant power trains different in each market because of different driving conditions or government energy policies.

Thus, demands and diversification of markets are both business chances and threats to traditional automotive businesses. New concepts have strong appeal for new customers in maturing markets, which useful to bear in mind to deal successfully with the mature markets in developed countries.

3-3. Practicing the Triple Bottom Line

The third factor is the major changes to standards for judging businesses and industries in the automotive industry and industry in general. The right attitude and special efforts to meet demands is immediately effective in acquiring money from social investors.

Practicing the Triple Bottom Line, a word coined by a consultancy firm in Great Britain, is crucial in all industries and all businesses.

Originally, the phrase "Triple Bottom Line" implied a social change benchmark to measure the future potential of an enterprise, not only in terms of its profitability but also its environmental and social performance, and hence provided an excellent opportunity for many companies to enhance the image of themselves. Of course, profitability and economic efficiency are core obligations imposed on companies, although conventional corporate management with its either/or thinking on profitability versus social performance can no longer meet the needs of the times.

3-4. From mechanical engineering to intelligent electronic control systems

The mainstay power train at present is the internal-combustion engine. Whether gasoline or diesel-powered, these engines are very good at moving heavy weights such as automobiles. However, this represents the forth factor in this historical turning point in the modern automotive industry. The architecture and manufacture of automobiles is undergoing a revolution with a shift away from the traditional mechanically-engineered hydraulically-operated technologies to intelligent electronic control system technologies. Modern vehicles are propelled by engines controlled with microcomputers and stop using electronically controlled braking systems. These intelligent systems also make the best use of intelligent transportation systems on motorways and in urban areas.

The computerization of automobiles began in the 1970s, during which time demands for development of emission-controlled and fuel-efficient vehicles rose globally.

Then in the 1980s, intelligent electronic control technologies began to be adopted in earnest. These technologies were adopted to solve urban traffic problems in developed countries, especially in some European countries and in the United States. For example, the Prometheus Program (Program for a European Traffic with Highest Efficiency and Unprecedented Safety) came into being in 1986. This program was aimed at creating safety and uninterrupted traffic systems to reducing traffic congestion, reduce the load on the environment and improve economic efficiency. Building on this, communication devices and driver support systems were developed such as Dedicated Road Infrastructure for Vehicle safety in Europe (DRIVE).

These were combined into the European Road Transport Telematics Implementation Coordination Organization (ERTICO) in 1991, and in the same year, governments of United States started a similar program named the Intelligent Vehicle/Highway Systems (IVHS), while Japanese government launched the Advanced Safety Vehicle (ASV) system.

Various programs and driver support systems such as head-up displays, intelligent cruise control and warning devices to prevent the driver from falling asleep at the wheel were developed. Crucially, improvements over the long term in electronics, electronic control systems and intelligent systems are indispensable for their potential in the development of next-generation vehicles and transportation systems.

Thus, these four interweaving factors are driving change in traditional business models of the global auto industry, and modern automakers must face the challenge of abolishing their old-styled business models and designing completely new ones to adjust to social change.

4. What does Ford's withdrawal from the Japanese market mean?

4-1. Ford's withdrawing from the Japanese market

Early in the 2016, the Ford Motor Company decided to withdraw from the Japanese and Indonesian markets. New imported vehicle registrations to Japanese in 2015 were Mercedes Benz with 64,001 vehicles (19.60%), Volkswagen with 50,333 vehicles (15.41%), BMW with 47,158 vehicles (14.44%) and Ford with only 4,477 vehicles (1.37%).

Ford expressed that since the Japanese market remains sluggish, it is not confident about the profitability of future investments, and hence withdraw all its business from the Japanese market. This entailed closing its down dealer businesses, cancellation of agency contracts and severance of the import and supply of Ford and Lincoln -branded vehicles.

Ford Japan was incorporated in 1974, and is presently staffed by 292 employees with 52 dealerships. Ford Japan has a rich history and a substantial dealership network. Ford invested in Mazda with the aim of getting better results. The company secured management rights with an investment rate of 33.4%. Despite that, Ford's business changed for the worse after the Lehman Brothers collapse, and the company disposed of all its stocks in Mazda.

4-2. The closed nature of the Japanese market or Ford's major blunders ?

Why did Ford decided to withdraw from the Japanese market? Ford makes repeated claims that the closed nature of the Japanese market was the source of its troubles. One Ford publicity agent says that Japan is the most closed country among the advanced countries that have the automotive industries, as it only imports 6% of all its cars to sell in the Japanese market each year. The Associated Press reports that Ford has accused the Japanese government of protecting the domestic automotive industry, and The Wall Street Journal says also that American automotive companies are dissatisfied with the Japanese market.

The Wall Street Journal continues that executives at American automotive companies have a grievance about non-tariff barriers such as regulations for imported vehicles.

There is no doubt that Japanese companies have a monopoly in the domestic market, and Ford has had a tough time selling its Fiesta (subcompact car), Mustang (Sports car) and Explorer (SUV) products.

However, Ford's grievance about the closed nature of the Japanese market does not explain the reason for the expanding sales of German automotive

Table 4: New registration of import car; including Truck&Bus, in the Japanese market

(Units,%)

Year	2015 2015.4–2016.3	2014 2014.4–2015.3	2013 2013.4–2014.3	2012 2012.4–2013.3	2011 2011.4–2012.3
Mercedes-benz	64,001(19.60%)	61,832(19.08%)	59,774(16.51%)	42,838(13.33%)	36,520(12.37%)
VW	50,333(15.41%)	62,439(19.27%)	72,157(19.93%)	57,626(17.94%)	55,671(18.86%)
BMW	47,158(14.44%)	43,339(13.37%)	50,256(13.88%)	41,635(12.96%)	36,814(12.47%)
Audi	27,760(8.50%)	30,821(9.51%)	30,222(8.35%)	25,188(7.84%)	22,348(7.57%)
BMW MINI	21,640(6.63%)	18,831(5.81%)	17,163(4.74%)	15,903(4.95%)	16,027(5.43%)
Nissan	20,035(6.13%)	21,480(6.63%)	33,123(9.15%)	38,276(11.91%)	51,535(17.46%)
Toyota	14,991(4.59%)	15,595(4.81%)	16,329(4.51%)	17,895(5.57%)	16,685(5.65%)
Volvo	14,087(4.31%)	12,615(3.89%)	18,223(5.03%)	14,051(4.37%)	13,083(4.43%)
Jeep	7,279(2.23%)	6,802(2.10%)	5,596(1.55%)	4,956(1.54%)	3,721(1.26%)
Porsche	6,802(2.08%)	5,408(1.67%)	5,301(1.46%)	4,667(1.45%)	3,913(1.33%)
Fiat	6,502(1.99%)	6,171(1.90%)	8,357(2.31%)	5,417(1.69%)	6,235(2.11%)
Peugeot	6,393(1.96%)	5,515(1.70%)	6,152(1.70%)	5,576(1.74%)	6,323(2.14%)
Renault	4,955(1.52%)	4,859(1.50%)	4,285(1.18%)	3,292(1.02%)	3,055(1.04%)
Suzuki	4,873(1.49%)	517(0.16%)	753(0.21%)	1,336(0.42%)	2,844(0.96%)
Ford	4,477(1.37%)	4,544(1.40%)	4,570(1.26%)	4,009(1.25%)	3,662(1.24%)
Mitsubishi	3,847(1.18%)	4,693(1.45%)	9,771(2.70%)	17,997(5.60%)	720(0.02%)
Land Rover	3,245(0.99%)	3,130(0.97%)	3,425(0.95%)	2,356(0.73%)	1,101(0.37%)
Smart	2,301(0.70%)	846(0.26%)	1,345(0.37%)	1,453(0.45%)	1,105(0.37%)
Alfa Romeo	2,146(0.66%)	2,452(0.76%)	3,194(0.88%)	4,288(1.33%)	2,301(0.78%)
Citroën	1,981(0.61%)	2,041(0.63%)	2,887(0.80%)	3,595(1.12%)	3,367(1.14%)
Jaguar	1,754(0.54%)	1,042(0.32%)	1,019(0.28%)	1,015(0.32%)	1,005(0.34%)
Total	326,588(100%)	324,087(100%)	362,052(100%)	321,292(100%)	295,149(100%)

Source: Japan Automobile Manufacturers Association.

Table 5: New registration of import car in the Japanese market

(Units)

Year	2015 2015.4–2016.3	2014 2014.4–2015.3	2013 2013.4–2014.3	2012 2012.4–2013.3	2011 2011.4–2012.3	2010 2010.4–2011.3	2009 2009.4–2010.3
Passenger car	281,073	280,487	300,394	243,733	221,168	180,936	164,835
Truck	903	1,200	1,558	1,872	2,049	1,802	1,715
Bus	103	79	66	74	55	91	54
Total	282,079	281,766	302,018	245,679	223,272	182,829	166,604

Source: Japan Automobile Manufacturers Association.

Table 6: New registration of Ford car in the Japanese market

(Units, %)

Year	2015 2015.4–2016.3	2014 2014.4–2015.3	2013 2013.4–2014.3	2012 2012.4–2013.3	2011 2011.4–2012.3	2010 2010.4–2011.3	2009 2009.4–2010.3
Passenger car	4,374 1.56%	4,385 1.56%	4,314 1.44%	3,609 1.48%	3,211 1.45%	2,531 1.40%	2,551 1.55%
All (including Truck&Bus)	4,477 1.37%	4,693 1.45%	4,570 1.26%	4,009 1.25%	3,662 1.24%	3,082 1.28%	3,078 1.68%

Source: Japan Automobile Manufacturers Association.

companies. Ford's models and sales methods look bad in comparison to the German companies. For example, Ford does not provide left-hand drive vehicles for the Japanese market and its consumers.

While Ford may well have management problems, the more pressing issue is the falling demand in the Japanese market, as Japanese society is rapidly ageing. The outlook for car sales is thus seriously bleak, which is an issue common to all automotive companies doing business in Japan.

4-3. Car sales in the Japanese market and its own unique characteristics

4,215,899 units were sold in Japan in 2015. 1,354,541 passenger cars were sold, 1,349,944 small commercial vehicles were sold, and 1,511,404 subcompact cars were sold. 4,699,591 cars were sold in 2014. Thus, compared with the previous fiscal year, this was only an unfortunate 89.7%. To date, the best year for sales was 1990, when 5,102,659 vehicles were sold. Since then, there has been a marked downward trend in the market, which is a serious problem for the Japanese automotive industry.

Young people have lost interest in cars, and smaller cars have become popular among the old people in a graying society. The reasons for the former

Table 7: Car Sales in the Japanese market, 1970~2015 (Units)

Year	Passenger car	Small-sized commercial car	Subcompact car	Total	Ratio to a year earlier %
1970	9,068	1,652,899	717,170	2,379,137	116.8
1975	49,125	2,531,396	157,120	2,737,641	119.7
1980	71,931	2,608,215	174,030	2,854,176	94.0
1985	73,539	2,869,527	161,017	3,104,083	100.3
1990	467,490	3,839,221	795,948	5,102,659	115.9
1995	889,260	2,654,291	900,355	4,443,906	105.6
2000	770,220	2,208,367	1,281,265	4,259,872	102.5
2005	1,271,349	2,089,992	1,387,068	4,748,409	99.6
2006	1,225,867	1,908,267	1,507,598	4,641,732	97.8
2007	1,299,168	1,654,025	1,447,106	4,400,299	94.8
2008	1,250,987	1,549,677	1,426,979	4,227,643	96.1
2009	1,160,175	1,480,137	1,283,429	3,923,741	92.8
2010	1,419,909	1,507,693	1,284,665	4,212,267	107.4
2011	1,139,910	1,246,126	1,138,752	3,524,788	83.7
2012	1,411,700	1,602,951	1,557,681	4,572,332	129.7
2013	1,399,407	1,472,704	1,690,171	4,562,282	99.8
2014	1,437,589	1,422,883	1,839,119	4,699,591	103.0
2015	1,354,541	1,349,944	1,511,404	4,215,889	89.7

Source: Japan Automobile Manufacturers Association.

are various, but we are positive that young people are very concerned about their present and their future.

In the long term, Japanese society is projected to experience problems of chronic labor shortages. At this point in time, it remains unclear exactly how these situations will turn out, although, job insecurity and lower earned income will impact on car sales. The young will be especially hesitant to buy cars.

Automotive companies are trying to improve these situations. For example, companies hold family events at racing circuits and amusement facilities. Japan has several racing circuits, and automotive companies invite parents and their children to these circuit events so they can have a first hand experience for motor sports. As a result, there is a strong image that the users of the future will grow up alongside these automotive companies. In contrast, unlike Japanese and European companies, American automotive companies don't take these initiatives. The promotional activities of the American automotive companies are very important for their brand image.

On the other hand, a unique market force in Japan is the downsizing of cars to suit the elderly. The main sales in the Japanese passenger car market are the subcompact cars and eco-cars with hybrid engines. Subcompact cars have a long history with makers specializing in them such as Suzuki and Daihatsu. These vehicles are carefully designed for narrow streets and small parking lots. The subcompact car market grew by degrees after end of the high economic growth and the bubble economy of the late 1980s. This category now has s deep-rooted popularity due to the convenient size and a fuel-efficiency of its vehicles.

Subcompacts are special vehicles produced for Japanese road conditions, although market expansion for eco-cars with hybrid engines has been a winner for Toyota as the Japanese government has priority policies for low-pollution cars, such as eco-car tax cuts.

Sales of subcompact and hybrid eco-cars in Japan are also driven by consumer incentives. Automotive companies in Japan develop and sell cars after carefully considering these consumer incentives. For example, Honda sells hybrid eco-cars, Nissan sells electric cars, Mazda sells clean diesel cars, and the German automotive companies also promote sales of their low-pollution vehicles. In this regard, American automotive companies have completely fallen behind with the exception of Tesla. As well as the issue of no left-hand-drive vehicles, American automotive companies do not develop cars with these sorts of consumer incentives.

Historically, Adam Opel and Hyundai motors under the GM umbrella also decided to withdraw from the Japanese market. In the end, Hyundai was unable to establish its own brand in the Japanese market. But in the case of Ford, it did not have a well-defined sales strategy, which is a tendency observed in other American automotive companies and some European automotive companies.

5. Considerations and future prospects

The automotive industry faces a historical turning point. All automotive makers are under pressure to solve a combination of problems. For example, principal sales markets are shifting from developed countries such as the United States, Japan and the EU to emerging countries such as BRICs. While expansion of sales markets is welcomed by automotive makers, they have to develop and supply vehicles suitable for various markets through a variety of means.

Car design compatible with global environmental conservation is the most pressing issue for the automotive industry to solve. CO_2 reduction is a common goal and strategies to develop technological solutions are progressing. Japanese makers focus on developing hybrid and plug-in hybrid vehicles, and European makers focus on downsizing and improving efficiency for gasoline and diesel engines, and researching and developing electric cars and their required infrastructure. The final stage will be the development of fuel cell vehicles by all automotive makers so that they can survive during this fierce competition. These new approaches are necessary to support to low-pollution vehicles. Governments also provide support with automotive industry subsidies and preferential tax systems.

New automotive concepts are bringing new technologies and solutions to protect the global environment. Electric and hybrid cars have existed since the dawning of automotive industry - Ferdinand Porsche created the first hybrid vehicle called the "Lohner-Porsche". This vehicle was a two-wheel drive, battery-powered electric vehicle with two front wheel hub-mounted motors. A supposed later version was a series hybrid using hub-mounted electric motors in each wheel powered by batteries and gasoline-engine generator.

However, modern electric and hybrid cars are the result of remarkable technological progress with electronic control systems. Modern vehicle systems have integrated technological innovations in these electronic control systems and applied them to automotive engineering. Consequently, modern changes in automotive concepts entail switching the automotive industry to a new industrial structure with fundamentally different design, development and manufacturing processes.

For example, since the 1990s, Toyota has engaged in automated driving technology R&D aimed at contributing to the complete elimination of traffic casualties, and delivering freedom of mobility for everybody including senior citizens and others who require extra support. Furthermore, in 2016, Toyota established a new company, the Toyota Research Institute Inc. (TRI) in Silicon Valley, California, as a base to boost research and development into Artificial Intelligence (AI) technology and will invest some 1 billion US dollars in this institute over the next 5 years. (Toyota Motor Corporation Website (2016))

Innovative technologies including electronic devices, Artificial Intelligence (AI), Internet of Things (IoT) are dramatically changing both modern day and future vehicles. However, the principal causes of these changes are not only technological factors, but also social factors. Especially in the Japanese market, as previously stated, one of the most pressing issues facing automotive makers is to work out countermeasures against social factors.

References

Journals, books and articles
■ English
Albion, M.W. (2013), *The Quotable Henry Ford*, University Press of Florida.
Alvarez, M.A. (ed.) (2011), *Tire Industry Changes, Competition and Globalization*, Nova Science Publishers: New York.
Batchelor, R. (1994), *Henry Ford: Mass Production, Modernism and Design*, Manchester University Press: Manchester and New York.
Beeton, D and Meyer, G. (eds.) (2015), *Electric Vehicle Business Models: Global Perspectives*, Springer International Publishing Switzerland.
Berger, S. and the MIT Industrial Performance Center (2005), *How We Compete: What Companies Around The World Are Doing To Make It In Today's Global Economy*, Doubleday.
Bloomfield, G.T. (1990), *Locational Processes at Work: The Ford Car Assembly Plant at ST Thomas, Ontario*, University of Guelph.
Burgdoerfer, C.D. (ed.) (2010), *Cars, Climate and the EPA: Issues in Regulating Greenhouse Gas Emissions*, Nova Science Publishers: New York.
Calabrese, G. (ed.) (2012), *The Greening of the Automotive Industry*, Palgrave Macmillan.
Chandler, Jr., A.D. (1964), *Giant Enterprise: Ford, General Motors, and the Automobile Industry*, Harcourt, Brace & World.

Ciravegna, L. (ed.) (2012), *Sustaining Industrial Competitiveness after the Crisis: Lessons from the Automotive Industry*, Palgrave Macmillan.
Clark, K.B. and Fujimoto, T. (1991), *Product Development Performance: Strategy, Organization, and Management in the World Auto Industry*, Harverd Business School Press: Boston, Massachusetts.
Cleeyus, R., Clemmer, S. and Friedman, D. (2009), *Climate 2030: A National Blueprint for A Clean Energy Economy*, Union of Concerned Scientists: Citizens and Scientists for Environment Solutions.
Curcio, V. (2013), *Henry Ford*, Oxford University Press.
Cusumano, M.A.(1985), *The Japanese Automobile Industry: Technology & Management at Nissan & Toyota*, The Harvard University Press.
Doody, A.F. and Bringaman, R. (1988), *Reinventing the Wheels: Ford's Spectacular Comeback*, Ballinger Publishing: Cambridge, Massachusetts.
Filho, W.L. and Kotter, R. (eds.) (2015), *E-Mobility in Europe: Trends and Good Practice*, Springer International Publishing Switzerland.
Galman, P.G. (2011), *Green Alternatives and National Energy Strategy: The Facts behind The Headlines*, The Johns Hopkins University Press.
Goods, C. (2014), *Greening Auto Jobs: A critical Analysis of the Green Job Solution*, Lexington Books.
Hoffmann, P. (2012), *Tomorrow's Energy: Hydrogen, Fuel Cells and the Prospects for a Cleaner Planet*, The MIT Press.
IAEA International Peer Review Mission On Mid-And-Long-Term Roadmap Towads The Decommissioning Of TEPCO's Fukushima Daiichi Nuclear Power Station Units 1-4, 9-17 February 2015.
Japan Association for Comparatives Studies of Management (2007), *Business and Society*, Bunrikaku publisher.
Jones, D., Roos, D. and Womack, J.P.(1990), *The Machine that Changed the World*, Macmillan Publishing.
Kenney, M. and Florida, R. (1993), *Beyond Mass Production: The Japanese System and its Transfer to the U.S.*, Oxford University Press.
Kewley, S.J. (2002), *Toyota's French Connection: Trends in Japanese—European Automotive Relations*, Royal Institute of International Affairs: Great Britain.
Lewis, D.L. (1987), *Ford Country: The Family, The Company, The Cars*, Amos press.
Magee, D. (2003), *Turnaround: How Carlos Ghosn Rescued Nissan*, Harper Collins Publishers.
Maxton, G.P. and Wormald, J. (2004), *Time for a Model Change: Re-engineering the Gobal Automotive Industry*, Cambridge University Press.
Mikler, J. (2009), *Greening the Car Industry: Varieties of Capitalism and Climate Change*, Edward Elgar.
National Research Council of The National Academies (2013), *Transitions to Alternative Vehicles and Fuels*, The National Academies Press: Washington, D.C..
Rae, J.B. (ed.)(1969), *Henry Ford*, Prentice-Hall.
Sandalow, D.B. (ed.) (2009), *Plug-In Electric Vehicles: What Role for Washington?*, Brooking Institution Press: Washington, D.C..
Snow, R. (2013), *I Invented the Modern Age: The Rise of Henry Ford*, Scribner.
Studer-Noguez, I. (2002), *Ford and the Global Strategies of Multinationals: The North America Auto Industry*, Routledge.
The Economist (2012), *Megachange: The World in 2050*, The Economist Newspaper Ltd..

Toyota Motor Corporation (1988), *TOYOTA; A History of the First 50 Years*, Toyota Motor Corporation.
Ward's Automotive Group (2012), *Ward's Automotive Yearbook 2012*, Ward's Automotive Group: A Division of Penton Media.
Welfens, P. (ed.) (2011), *Cluster in Automotive and Information & Communication Technology: Innovation, Multinationalization and Networking Dynamics*, Springer.
Wells, P.E. (2010), *The Automotive Industry in an Era of Eco-Austerity: Creating an Industry as if the Planet Mattered*, Edward Elgar: Cheltenham, UK.
Werling, D.P. (2000), *Henry Ford: A Hearthside Perspective*, Society Automotive Engineers.
Wik, R.M. (1972), *Henry Ford and Grass-Roots America*, The University of Michigan Press.
Wilkins, M. (1964), *Amrican Business Abroad: Ford on Six Continents*, Wayne State University Press: Detroit.
Womack, J.P. and Jones, D.T. (1996), *Lean Thinking: Banish Waste and Create Wealth in Your Corporation*, Simon & Schuster.
Yates, B. (1983), *The Decline and Fall of the American Automobile Industry*, Empire Books: New York.
Young, S.T. & Dhanda, K.K. (2013), *Sustainability: Essentials for Business*, SAGE Publications.

■ German
Eckermann, E. (1981), *Vom Dampfwagen zum Auto,* Japan UNI Agency.

■ Japanese
Sato, M. (2000), *Yokohama-sei Ford, Osaka-sei America Sha*, 230 club.

Websites
Toyota Motor Coporation (2016), Retrieved July 27, 2016, from http://www.toyota.co.jp

II.
Conditions for Sustainable Management: Traditional Succession and Risk Awareness

Yoshihiro INOUE

1. Introduction

Business interactions between a company and a consumer can be based either on contracts or on trust. For the former, trust can be an issue when exchanging detailed information. But once the consumer trusts the company, deals can often be approved. With this trust, the consumer can accept the goods and services offered by the company.

Management that accomplishes the trust obligation is related to the brand power and the experience value creation of the enterprise, and they are big factors of a long-term continuing. In this paper, it looks back on the management of the long lived enterprise from the aspect of trust obligation. And, from the case with the enterprise that causes the systematic disgraceful affair, the importance of the accomplishment of faithful obligation and attention obligation is discussed. It is connected with the trust obligation to be integrity and to defend the tradition. It is a business model of the long lived enterprise.[1]

Many Japanese companies have been in business for over a century. National industry policies facilitated companies during the Meiji period, and many companies were founded in this era. The Edo period, approximately 200 years ago, witnessed a development of commerce in Edo, Osaka, and Kyoto. In addition, the development of highway and marine transportation

---

1) The content of this paper is an evolution edition of the following paper. Inoue, Yoshihiro (2014), "Sustainable Management of a Long Lived Company", *The Journal of Business Management (Japan Business Management Association)*, No. 4, pp. 69-75.

infrastructures contributed to the expansion of commerce, as shown in Figure 1.

The number of Japanese companies more than 200 years old totals 3,886 and the number is the first places in the world. 2nd place is Germany. This number is about halves of Japanese company. The company in European nations has accomplished the trust obligation in the field such as a traditional glass technology, the skin work, the clock, the beer, and wine. Therefore, there are comparatively a lot of numbers of long lived companies. The oldest companies in Europe are in the fields of glass, skin fur clocks, beer, and wine.

2. Framework of long-lived company research

2-1. Managerial characteristics of long-lived companies in Japan: Traditional succession and diversification

Long-lived companies in Japan generally value business traditions. Kongougumi was established during the Asuka Period by Kongou Shigemitsu, who received instruction in Shitennouji construction from Shotoku Taishi, and was invited by Kudara. The carpenter who came from Kudara with him had the mission of defending Shitennouji, and this has become a tradition, handed down by word of mouth.[2] A specialized technique is necessary for temple and shrine restoration. The master posed a difficult restoration challenge to the apprentice, which forced the apprentice to grow. In carpentry, training usually takes place directly from master to apprentice.[3]

However, it entered the 2000s, and Kongougumi that had kept defending the tradition of the temples and shrines construction entered the apartment house construction.[4] In the temples and shrines construction, it took long time to make arrangements with those who supported it. And, it took long time from the order for construction to the collection of bill. On the other hand, if it is an apartment house, the period from construction to the collection of bill is short. And, if it is large-scale construction, the income that enters by one contract is large. Therefore, Kongougumi entered concrete construction, and developed the apartment house construction especially.

As a result, Kongougumi has despised the tradition where construction has existed till then for the profit of the viewpoint. In the apartment house con-

---

2) Kongou, Toshitaka (2013), *Sougyo 1400 nen* (*1400 from Establishment: Teaching of 16 Succeeded by the Oldest Company in the World*), Diamondosha, p. 49.
3) *Ibid.*, p. 19.
4) *Ibid.*, p. 122.

struction, the cost consideration became important, and opposite work was needed with a gorgeous construction to which energies had been devoted till then. Naturally, in the major construction company that had specialized in the apartment house construction, there was domination on a large amount of material procurement and the cost side, and Kongougumi that was a late-started participator became a loser. Kongougumi fell into the operating crisis after six years the entries into the apartment house construction.

Takamatsu Construction, the primary general contractor in Osaka, mitigated this crisis, and Kongougumi's tradition created brand value for Takamatsu Construction. Also, support from Takamatsu Construction facilitated a debt waiver.

In a competitive business world, evasion of such an operating crisis is unusual. Why did Takamatsu Construction assist Kongougumi? And why did the creditors renegotiate their claims? The tradition of Kongougumi, particularly their construction of temples and shrines, certainly was an important element in this restructuring.

After this crisis, Kongougumi consolidated its business, centering on the construction of temples and shrines. Kongougumi also makes good use of apartment house construction technology and builds kindergarten and social welfare facilities. Such flexibility is a strong point of long-lived companies. What is the charm of a long-lived company, which allows it to expand and be flexible during periods of change in the economic environment?

Yuasa Trading, established by Yuasa Shokuro in 1666, took over the charcoal business in Kyoto and became a company in 1919.[5] A battery-producing company, with 12 generations of experience, under present master Yuasa Shichizaemon in Sakai City, Yuasa Trading was a mother's company of GS Yuasa. Afterwards, Yuasa Trading expanded to the air conditioning, machine tool, building site equipment, pipe and house equipment, and construction materials businesses. Yuasa Trading's traditions have benefited many, while also reforming various business conditions.

According to Darwin's theory of evolution, the person who adjusts to the environment has the best chance of survival.

Kamei industrial HD in Chigasaki City establishment was 1890."Kameigumi" that was the antecedent of the Kamei industry established the architectural construction industry. Former Kameigumi managed the inn and the public bath by the name of "Hoteiya". Kamei, Yousuke who was the adopted son

---

5) *Toyokeizai Weekly* (2010), No. 6294, p. 62.

of "Hoteiya" advanced diversification. One was the sales of the gravel paved on the road. The building and repairs of the construction work was started with it. The Kamei industry did the labor to construction, road works, and occupation troops for years. The turning point of the Kamei industry was the 1990s. A private order has decreased gradually. Kamei, Nobuyuki, the vice president at that time was thought that the building trade was futureless.

And, he looked for the business that was able to propose originality in the field without the competition. It was management of "Super-public bath" that he had hit on at that time. Kamei, Nobuyuki assumed the position of the fourth generation president, and he brought up the hot spring of the day trip business to the second pillar of the Kamei industry in 1999. And, in 2010 when it establishes and 120 years were received, Kamei, Nobuyuki thought something about the contribution to local in addition. As a result, they paid attention to many elderly persons embarrassed because the place to go was lost. Then, Kamei, Nobuyuki has advanced to the nursing care for elderly people business. The Kamei HD will aim at the reformation in the following four areas in the future. They are ①engineering works, an architectural businesses, ②construction materials manufacturing sales, the recycling businesses, ③bathing health relaxation businesses, and ④nursing care for elderly people businesses.

2-2. Business characteristics of long-lived companies

According to the Teikoku Data Bank, in September, 2013, more than 26,000 Japanese companies were at least 100 years.[6] By industry, the ranking is: 1. sake manufacturing, 2. retail trade of sake, 3. kimono and cloth sales, and 4. inns and hotels.

Zengoro in Ishikawa is the oldest inn registered in the Guinness Book of World Records. Zengoro is on sacred ground, although it began as a watering hole. During the Nara period, people used the hot spring there to treat illnesses. Moreover, the Japanese considered this hot spring inn a resort. Additional hot spring inns more than 800 years old include the Nishiyama Inn, established in 705, the Koman Inn, established in 717, Hotel Sakan, established in 1184, and Goshobo, established in 1191.

Like Kongougumi, many long-lived Buddhist companies exist, such as Buddhist altar fitting shops, which are the property of temples and shrines. Long-lived companies can make use of the technology and the knowledge

---

6) Teikoku Data Bank homepage, http://www.tdb.co.jp/lineup/publish/pdf/tr92_summary.pdf (last access December, 28, 2016).

base that has been handed down for centuries. Please refer to Table 1.

The order of the long lived company appearance rate is shown in Table 2. The type of business with the highest appearance rate is 59.6% in the sake manufacturing. Hereafter, it is a ranking of manufacturing of the soy sauce manufacturing and the fermented soybean paste. These three types of business are the manufacturing of the eating and drinking goods based on the fermentation technology spread to Japan from of old. Sake appeared in the Harimanokuni regional chronicle that had been compiled the 700s. The same content as a modern manufacturing method was described in the Engishiki compiled at the Heian period, and sake was established to Japan from of old. The long lived company appearance rate is high in the type of business of this sake.[7]

Soy sauce is a seasoning suitable for the Japanese gastronomic culture. The brewing of soy sauce originated at Kikkoman, Yamasa, and Higashimaru, in the Edo period. Brewing of fermented soybean paste was used as food during the Warring States Period, since the Revolt in Ounin, and it was used as a protein source in various places.[8] Miso brewing was started by "Kakukyu" and "Maruya" in the Edo period in Okazaki. This "Haccyo miso" is part of the gastronomic culture in the Nagoya region.

2-3. Geographic characteristics of long-lived companies

Many long-lived companies exist in Tokyo, according to the investigation of the Teikoku Data Bank, because has Tokyo prospered as a central city in Japan since the Edo period. However, most long-lived companies originated in Kyoto. Kyoto was a capital city and a center of Japanese culture, with numerous temples and shrines.[9] The following regions are Yamagata, Shimane, and Niigata, on the Sea of Japan. The Kitamaebune carried goods from Matsumae in Hokkaido to the Kinki region by way of the Sea of Japan. Therefore, in these regions, companies that loaded goods near the port were important. The company that assumes such a business to be an origin is

---

7) Teikoku Data Bank Shiryokan, Sangyochosabu (ed.) (2009), *100nen tsuzuku kigyou no jouken*, (*The condition of the company which continues for 100 years*), Asahishinbun Publisher, p. 60.
8) *Ibid.*, p. 59.
9) Teikoku Data Bank home page, http://www.tdb.co.jp/lineup/publish/pdf/tr92_summary.pdf (last access December, 28, 2016). A whole number is the corporate numbers registered in the database named COSMOS2. The 6th place following are the orders such as Fukui, Nagano, Toyama , Mie , and Nara. Five regions are the Sea of Japan sides in top 10. Three regions are the vicinity regions in Ohmi merchant's trading area.

reflected in the height of a modern long-lived company appearance rate. Shiga, in fifth place, was Ohmi merchant's accumulation ground. Ohmi merchants carried goods from Tsuruga, the base port of the Kitamaebune, in the vicinity of Biwako. Goods stocked there were sold nationwide. Because Ohmi merchants were required to visit the same regions continuously, they practiced good management integrity.

3. Ohmi merchant's management philosophy

3-1. Ohmi merchant's triple-win management

Long-lived companies in Japan value harmony and contribute to regional society. This integrates with these companies' outlook on business ethics. During the Edo period, Ohmi merchants provided profits to sellers, purchasers, and other individuals, which we call a "triple-win" management. This contrasts with the standard business arrangement, whereby profits accrue only to the seller. An even better strategy is to offer some gain to the purchaser as well. To improve a company's social responsibility, a wider distribution of profits and capital accumulation is desirable. Ohmi merchant had placed the profit to the people requested by managing the present age at the center of the management in Edo period.

Many of Ohmi merchants approached Kyoto, and there was a base in four counties. In Gamou, Kanzaki, Aichi, and Sakata, Tokaido, Higashiyamado, and Hokurikudo concentrated. Geographic characteristics in these regions were the locations of distributing point of goods to Kyoto.[10] In addition, they have expanded the business. They had the shouldering pole, and peddled various places of Hokkaido, Tohoku, Kanto, Chugoku, and Kyushu. Thus, it was called a Product turning of various countries to send various places the product, and to fill local person's demand.

Ohmi merchant's forms of company were advanced at that time. The method of business of Ride sharing trade that was a joint company of the partnership form was taken so that Ohmi merchant might attempt diffusion of risks when the kind of their business included many things.[11] In a word, Ohmi merchant's base was the vicinity of the Ohmi country. And, they have expanded the business in managing the large area intention in cooperation with

---

10) Genma, Akira and Kobayashi, Toshiharu (supervision), Nihontorishimariyakukai (ed.) (2006), *Edo ni manabu kigyou rinri (Corporate ethics studied to Edo)*, Seisansei Publisher, p.116.

11) *Ibid.*, p. 118.

the capital in foreign countries. This was a novelty on the forms of companieside. Because Ohmi merchant who was unnamed cooperates with a local merchant outside the country, their business became smooth.

3-2. Ohmi merchant's idea of "profit after the previous right"
In the durability descent trade,[12] Ohmi merchants tried to satisfy and make local people happy by means of business. Fairness in a sales transaction, with both the seller and the purchaser profiting, was an important concept that benefited many regions. Transactions aided sellers, buyers, the region, and society in general. This management idea was expressed by the words "secret virtue happy thing".

Thus, advantages accrued to both the seller and the customer, in such diverse areas as school construction, the installation of streetlights, and bridge repair. This mode of business ethics is a model for a modern, socially responsible company. This idea of "profit after the previous right" belongs in the 21 century.[13] Ohmi merchant's ethics have been passed on to many other companies, including: Takashimaya, Itochu Business Affairs, Nishikawa Industries, Nippon Lived Insurance, and Toyono.

The profit supremacy principle of an company influences how workers approach their jobs. Imitation food displays in prestigious hotels are a classic example. By selling cheaper food at a high price, a certain hotel disregarded its trust obligation with the customer. Moreover, the customer believed the displayed items were real imitations. This act led to the failure of this fashionable hotel. This approach to business is quite different from the idea of an Ohmi merchant's "profit after the previous right."

4. Business of tradition and reformation

4-1. Continuity and change of a long-lived company
Generally, because the long-lived company does valuing the profession, and clings to the tradition, a lot of people think that the development of the business is scarce of them. However, though the long lived company has continued to live in a kaleidoscopic society, They firmly succeed to the tradi-

---

12) In the durability descent trade, the final product such as Kimono, fancy goods, and the medicines was sent from Ohmi to the provinces. Raw silk, safflower and the potato, etc. were sent from the provinces to Ohmi oppositely.
13) Yokozawa, Toshimasa (ed.) (2012), *Shinisekigyou no kenkyu (Research of long-lived companies)*, Seisansei Publisher, p. 208.

tion, and have continued a tough reformation. Oppositely, they might not exist as a long lived company now if there is no bold reformation. The long-lived company has the reformation matched at the period at the same time as succeeding to the tradition that doesn't change and it has two clear sides of always doing. A slight balance during succession and the reformation of the tradition is secrets of the management of the long-lived company.

One tradition that has not changed is "customer creed", "steady management of the dominant constraint", "quality standards", "succession of the manufacturing method", "valuing employees," and "maintenance of corporate philosophy", according to Yokozawa Toshimasa's questionnaire.[14] These traditions can become part of a long-lived company's set of principles and values, which often do not change over time. The basic philosophy of a long-lived company is not only to maximize profit, but also to expand sales and stockholder profit.

Yokozawa, Toshimasa notes other important corporate aspects: "Satisfy customer needs concerning commodity and service", "Posture in which it goes the half step of the period ahead", "Sales channel matched at the period," and "Interpretation of the family creed matched at the period".[15]

Ongoing reformation is indispensable for long-lived companies, and the most important is the pursuit of high customer satisfaction, which can be achieved by maintaining professional quality. There are many long-lived companies to stick to the business field where the technology and the market were well informed.

Changes made by long-lived companies differ according to the period in question. In a word, the ideas of continuity and change are valued. In sake manufacturing, operating results of many small businesses have declined because of decreasing demand, even though manufacturing methods for sake have been passed down from generation to generation.

In manufacturing sake, aspergillus and brewers invented methods for smelling and tasting sake. JFLA: Japan Food & Liquor Alliance structured corporate governance of sake warehouses in various places, as shown in Figure 2. Morita Asset Management in Nagoya supported this cartel with capital, to defend the tradition of sake. The two sides of sake reformation are tradition and corporate governance.

---

14) *Ibid.*, p. 104.
15) *Ibid.*, p. 107.

4-2. Tradition of Toraya

Toraya, which is more than 480 years old, represents the succession and reformation of tradition.[16] Toraya has managed confectionery in Kyoto since the Muromachi period. The first Court order that Toraya supplied was a cake to the emperor Goyouzei (1568–1611), a tradition that continued thereafter. In the Meiji period, Toraya transferred capital and opened a liaison office in Tokyo, continued the Court order, and widened sales in the vicinity of Marunouchi. Toraya also opened department stores, starting with the Tobu Department Store in Ikebukuro. Toraya is a long-lived company that transformed itself from making cake for royalty to baking for the general public.

One corporate principle of Toraya is "eat delicious cake",[17] an idea shared by all employees and practiced through the process of cake-making.[18] Therefore, the idea is expressed by a comprehensible, simple objection. To the achievement of the idea of "Eat pleasing a delicious cake", the cake should be delicious. All employees examine the material closely, and a good cake making is pursued for that. And, they are doing the highest serving to the customer. When the customer eats the cake, the effort for the guest to feel delicious is practiced through the process of the cake-making.[19] In relation to this idea, Faith of Toraya is seriousness to clumsiness that manufacturing becomes a starting point. There is a strong will that keeps pursuing the highest to the end one in word "Manufacturing is a starting point".[20]

The word "dexterity" means "action that behaves shrewdly, and well". Clumsiness makes integrity foundation on the other hand. It contains the meaning of advancing the thing ahead stepping on a correct procedure even if points are bad. The customer satisfactorily leads to the accomplishment of this idea though it is nature. The idea of such a customer valuing is shared in the employee of Toraya. In a word, the customer valuing is directly connected to the seriousness to clumsiness in manufacturing in a long history of Toraya. Well, though it is Toraya to which such an honest idea hangs, the business became severe because of an increase in the western-style cakes preference of the young person. Then, the conception of the reformation of making the cafe from Toraya arose. This reformation is on the extension wire of the

---

16) Kurokawa, Mitsuhiro (2005), *Toraya : wagashi to ayunda 500 nen (Toraya : 500 years where it walked with Japanese-style confection)*, Shincho-shinsho, pp. 3–4.
17) Kawashima, Yoko (2008), *Toraya brand monogatari (Toraya : brand story)*, Toyokeizaishinposha, p. 106.
18) *Ibid.*, p. 164.
19) *Ibid.*, p. 164.
20) *Ibid.*, p. 153.

tradition.

4-3. Reformation management by Toraya

A Toraya cafe is located facing Keyaki Street in Roppongi Hills. This cafe sells cake to young people. This is an example of Toraya's reformation management. This Toraya cafe transcends the principles of Japanese-style confection making by selling a new type of cake that uses butter, chocolate, and whipped cream. The theme of this Toraya cafe is "another cake that Toraya makes." The cafe also debuted a sweet jelly cake, made from bean jam and cacao, which combines Japanese and Western cake styles. Also, coffee is not the only drink offered in the Toraya cafe; it also sells Japanese and Chinese tea. This is truly a cultural hybrid type of cafe.

Toraya's Tokyo midtown branch opened in 2007. In this store, tea is sold, and a gallery shop, selling Japanese-style confections, was established as an annex. Here a key concept was to pass on the culture surrounding Japanese-style confections. The shape of an old-fashioned cake was imitated, and both original and powdered green tea were offered in the store. These goods are made by the original branch in Tokyo.[21]

Two business conditions of Toraya, that is, Toraya cafe and Toraya Tokyo Midtown branches are reformative diversification for Toraya that has poured the majority of the energy into the japan-style confection manufacturing and sales. It is "eat pleasing a delicious cake" that the reformation ties to the success that is the idea of Toraya. The idea of Toraya has influenced the commodity of a new cake or gallery shop. Therefore, Toraya is able to increase trust from the customer further.

The Japanese-style confection is a cultural asset spread to Japan. Having contributed to the development of this cultural asset is Toraya. The seriousness to clumsiness of the Toraya, in a word, integrity of management gives the satisfaction to not only Japan but also the customer in the world. Only this integrity of management is a secret of sustainability of the long lived company. Toraya has carried out integrity by the process of a very long history of 480 years or more.

---

21) *Ibid.*, p. 156.

5. What is the family business?

5-1. Continuity of family business

In the family business, the family takes part in a formal decision making concerning management. The influence of this family can be exercised by a legal property right and the stockholding. Substantial managerial participation of the family is an important requirement for the family business. The president as the representative of the family seizes real power by deciding Managing Board. And, two or more family members take part in a formal side and respect of managerial participation.

The difference between a family business and a general company is shown in Table 3. In the family business, the disagreement of interests caused among the stockholder and managers is not caused. Therefore, the cost to prevent the disagreement is not caused. Because the stockholder is corresponding to the manager, the stockholder need not observe the manager. And, the incentive to the manager of special reward cannot leave consideration.

The alliance of the family business with a long business continuance is Les Hénokiens. The admission to Les Hénokiens is as follows. ①Establishment is 200 years ago and more. ②The founding family must own a company, or they own the stocks of large majority. ③At least one founding family or more is involved in management or it is member of Managing Board. ④Financial affairs must be excellent. Present registration companies are about 30 companies around the Europe. Eight Japanese companies join in Les Hénokiens, as shown in Table 4. A technology and the creativity of the creator of these companies are evaluated high. Les Hénokiens companies have succeeded to the pride in one's craftsmanship importantly as corporate culture.

5-2. Clerk management

The merchant of Edo period was chiefly accepting the indented apprentice in childhood. New face's indented apprentice did for coarse of the merchant. And, they took the training of reading, writing, arithmetic. They become independent clerks as a salesclerk at about the age of 16. And, receipts and disbursements, the buying and selling, and the delivery of goods became their work. In addition, they became clerks in the first half 30 years old, and became representatives in the shop. The clerk became a large clerk afterwards, and supported the merchant as master's right arm and manager's member.

In the family business of Europe and America, only the successor with the pure blood succeeded to the business. The indented apprentice brought up by the apprentice service system is located as merchant's family in Japan. They came to participate in management as a member of the family back.

The clerk function as the assistance post is important for the long lived company.

Toyata family and Ishida, Taizo, Mastushita, Kounosuke and Takahashi, Kotaro, Honda, Soichro and Fujisawa, Takeo, they were in the relation such as founding families and clerk. Clerk's function is to supplement top manager's weak point as a member of the family, to admonish the wrong, to supplement the decision making and the decision, and to reduce the load.

In the management of the present age, the sociality of the company named compliance and CSR is paid to attention. The function of the clerk of preventing the failure of the manager who does the arbitrary decision proceeding for the company that aims at the long life beforehand is requested.

6. Trust obligations

6-1. Disregard for tradition

Recently, the railway company reported a false safety and security inspection. The company providing food to the railroad was mixing agricultural chemicals with frozen food. These events were preventable accidents, exacerbated by a lack of corporate ethics at all levels as well as poor management awareness. Specifically, Snow Brand Milk Products Co., Ltd. shipped milk mixed with bacillus, causing large-scale food poisoning. Mitsubishi Motors concealed the situation, which was clearly a severe ethical lapse that compromised the safety of passengers.

Snow Brand Milk Products Co., Ltd., which originated as a Hokkaido dairy farming sales association in the Taisho period, influenced the development of Hokkaido. The food poisoning case occurred at the end of June, 2000.[22] The consumer who drank the milk shipped by the Osaka factory appealed for an answer. The food poisoning did not originate in the Osaka factory; the cause was dried skim milk produced in the Daiju factory in Hokkaido. A power failure in this Daiju factory on March 31 stopped the production line, and during this power failure the cooling function was lost. As a result, toxic bacillus prolivedrated. The dried skim milk made on March 31

---

22) Fujiwara, Kunitatsu (2002), Y*ukijirushi no rakujitsu (Setting sun of Yukijirushi)*, Ryokufuu Publisher, pp. 22-34.

was dissolved in water at the Daiju factory, and skim milk was made. Bacillus was detected by voluntary inspection of this recycled dried skim milk. The inspection revealed that the dried skim milk was tainted, and at this point, Snow Brand Milk Products Co., Ltd. was cited as violating two ordinances.

The company's first mistake was to have overlooked the risk related to the power failure. The second mistake was to recycle infected dried skim milk with the bacillus and to conceal the first mistake. Ultimately, the situation was not clarified until more than a month after the accident. Poor preparation by the government's crisis-management system expanded the risk of this type of event. Unfortunately, consumer trust in Snow Brand Milk Products Co., Ltd. disappeared after this event.

The domestic camouflage event of the imported beef by Snow Brand Food comes to light in 2001, and the snow brand is damaged again[23]. Snow Brand Food was making an excuse of their having shipped the import cow putting up the domestic beef seal because a stock increase due to the mad cow disease event had fueled employee's uneasiness for the event. The common feature of the event concerning these two foods is disregard of safety to the food that the person eats. In logic in the company, it is guessed that the disregard of safety passed. The disregard of safety expanded the risk, and the company was continued dangerously. This also clearly shows blatant disregard for consumers' health and safety.

After an inspection in July, Mitsubishi Motors was indicted by the Ministry of Transport for a recall issue.[24] The final deficit of Mitsubishi Motors at the period on September, 2000 became the worst 75.6 billion yen ever. The cost that hung by the recall relation became 21.5 billion yen.[25] This systematic scandal has despised the safety of the car as a result. The result contradicted the idea of three diamonds. Three diamonds means expected service (Contribute for the society), a conduct oneself thing light (Take the positive immature car action), and an active trade (Act in the international scope). It hangs there out the idea on which it should work naturally as an company. In the concealment of such recall, there was a speculation said that it offended neither Mitsubishi Industries nor The Mitsubishi Bank over which the group reigned in the top. And, there was an idea of not defending, and not making

---

23) *Ibid.*, p. 224.
24) Sankeishinbun shuzaihan (2007), *Brand wa naze ochitaka (Why did the brand collapse?)*, Kadokawa-bunko, p. 342.
25) *Ibid.*, p. 343.

the tradition of the Mitsubishi group dirty in the speculation. However, such an idea was a good conception of the convenience of Mitsubishi Motors. It is a conception of disappointing if it sees for the consumer. The consumer's expectation was trust to Mitsubishi Motors that makes it for the track and army vehicles. It was trust in the safety that should be observed naturally. The concealment of recall by persistence in the tradition became the result of clouding the shine of three diamonds.

Several corporate scandals also have occurred in the United States.[26] To describe them, Mitchell, L. E. uses the term "irresponsible management." An American company prioritizes maximization of its stock value. In the process, consumer safety and the working environment may be compromised. Do profit maximization and management integrity conflict? As understood from the cases of Snow Brand Milk Products Co., Ltd. and Mitsubishi Motors, both accountable management and the pursuit of profit were necessary. Long-lived companies, such as Toraya and Kongougumi, have maintained management integrity, which has bolstered stakeholders' trust.

In a competitive period, the company has the possibility of causing the systematic disgraceful affair. However, the management is not irresponsible if providing with the action plan when the company foresees the possibility of the risk ahead, and the systematic disgraceful affair has been caused. The idea of risk management to evade irresponsible management is considered by the following clause.

6-2. What is the management risk?

The corporate misdoing becomes an important risk cause of connecting directly with the business crisis. Though the systematic disgraceful affair can be prevented when the company is excellent, the heavy competition obstructs management, and it becomes a social problem. The systematic disgraceful affair depends on sense of values in management. The attempt to save one's own neck in management causes the systematic disgraceful affair. For instance, window-dressing is an act of betraying the stake-holder. Reckless driving in management causes the systematic disgraceful affair. Though the financing of the enterprise is covered by the equity capital and the borrowed capital, the systematic disgraceful affair of using this capital for a usage personal management is a problem. Systematic injustice becomes scandalous, too. The distortion of the value criteria to safety in management

---

26) Mitchell, L. E. (2001), *Corporate Irresponsibility*, Yale University Press, p. 23.

negatively affects employee's behaving. Because the company is trusted as existence that improves the society by a systematic activity, a systematic scandal betrays the consumer, and the crisis of the company arises as a result. The risk management is necessary to evade these systematic disgraceful affair.

The aim of the risk management is to observe the law, and to avoid penalty by the law violation. By the comparison between the system condition and the observance situation provided in the law, the approach that understands the gap as a risk is risk management.

It is important to accomplish information disclosure to the stake-holder integrity at an unexpected situation.

The increase of the corporate value and the maintenance of the stability of the enterprise are the risk management. This stage is risk management of the attack. Communications with the stake-holder are concretely made active, and the information that the enterprise sends is passed on correctly. For the food manufacturing company, if the indication of source of the food material becomes clear, the risk management of the attack is strengthened.

In assumption that there must be a risk in management, if the best risk management rugged is constructed, the damage to the company by the risk is reduced.

Thus, the technique of risk management is a critical tool for the enterprise that tries to survive in a complex business environment. A lot of long lived companies consider "Eyes" of the society, and practice the conversation with a positive society. The management of the act on one's own authority of the company don't lead to the stake-holder's support.

6-3. Necessity for risk management

Risk management necessitates risk awareness, and emphasizes preparation.[27] Risk management also involves minimizing damage after a scandal. After a problem comes to light, a company must acknowledge its accountability.

The first stage of risk management is for all constituent members of a company to have "risk awareness."[28] In the company, various people are working. And the company has the chance to contact various customers and the societies. If the awareness of occurring without fail has spread in the

---

27) Nakajima, Shigeru (2013), *Saikyo no risk kanri (The strongest risk management)*, Kinyuzaiseijijoukenkyukai, p. 11.
28) *Ibid.*, p. 11.

entire company as for the systematic disgraceful affair, that company can immediately evade it.

In the second stage of the risk management, a past case study and the preservation are performed.[29] If corporate culture has not changed, the same accident as the past often happens under the same situation. The event similar to 2000 of Snow Brand Milk Products Co., Ltd. had occurred to 1955. Snow Brand Milk Products Co., Ltd. has violated the same error. If the preservation temperature of milk is mistaken, the bacillus breeds innumerably at once. The president of Snow Brand Milk Products Co., Ltd. 45 years ago had already recognized that.[30] Snow Brand Milk Products Co., Ltd. did not analyze a past event, and the content was not preserved. The failure became the beginning of a new event. A past failure occurs again. The corporate leader should recognize that. And, it is necessary to record the failure as a property.

The third stage of the risk management is to establish the method of collecting the risk information.[31] Concretely, the top of the company should enact the risk management regulations. When the fact that might do the company damage is discovered, all workers owe the obligation to report to the risk management post at once. As a result, the expansion of the problem generation is evaded. Let's assume the case where the reporter is taking part in the risk matter. Even if it is a case where it transgresses against the rules, the disposal of the person who offered voluntarily is reduced. If such regulations are enacted, the mistake with the possibility of developing into the weighty subject is prevented from spreading.

Even in a case in which the reporter is involved in the transgression, if his punishment is reduced, there is a greater possibility that the problem will not spread.

Risk management within a company is influenced by the trust and faithful obligation of workers, described in the next section.

6-4. Trust obligation and business ethics

The relationship between an company and the consumer is divided into the contract and trust. In a contract, people can pursue only profit goals, which encourage the exchange of information.[32] At the same time, contracts generally protect participants against unfair actions, by compensating for damages if

---

29) *Ibid.*, p. 11.
30) Sankeishinbun shuzaihan (2007), *op. cit.*, p. 76.
31) Nakajima, Shigeru (2013), *op. cit.*, p. 12.
32) *Ibid.*, p. 14.

the contract is broken.

In the relation of the reality between dealings, the contract of the person concerned who has the information of this level mutually is a rare case. Dealings are conducted though the difference of the information has been left among persons concerned. The concept of passing dealings with the information divide left is a trust.[33] In the trust relation, the received duty person must not act the first own profit by thinking. Trust person's profit is given priority to the received duty person in compliance with the trust person. In a word, the trust side owes faithful obligation to the trusted side in the trust relation. For instance, in food manufacturing, the buyer should be able to assume that the food he purchases is safe to eat. The meaning of integrity is to mean the act of damaging the trust of the camouflage of the home camouflage and the best-before date is not done.

If a person violates a promise in a contract, protective clauses in the contract often resolve problems. On the other hand, if an agreement is based solely on trust, the responsibility rests with the provider of the goods or services. For instance, if a railway company runs trains while ignoring safety restrictions, this breaks the bond of trust with the consumer. If the railway company does not establish Automatic Train Stop (ATS) because of cost reductions, and a derailment accident occurs, this company is also not accomplishing its attention obligation.[34]

Although they may examine available information, not all the information is indicated, most consumers do not search for detailed manufacturing when they buy milk. Thus, the consumer trusts the company, because he makes purchases without complete information. Therefore, the active conduct of this business relates to trust. To continue a business based on trust, the companies should answer for this trust. And the entrepreneur should be cautious.[35]

6-5. Germination of new social businesses

Modern companies can contribute to social problems. People who are called social entrepreneurs develop new concepts to answer social needs, using a profitable future business model.[36]

A social entrepreneur rushes into action, to achieve his mission, and to

---

33) Taka, Iwao (2013), *Business ethics*, Nihonkeizaishinbun Publisher, p. 479.
34) *Ibid.*, p. 481.
35) *Ibid.*, p. 488.
36) Porter, M. E. and Kramer, M. R. (2011), "Creating Shared Value", *Harvard Business Review*, January-February, p. 23.

regenerate society.[37] They firmly build an economic foundation, becoming independent, while at the same time considering social targets.[38] In a word, entrepreneurs create social value and economic merit.

Characteristics of a social entrepreneur, according to Saito (2004), are as follows[39]:

① While answering various regional and larger needs, they apply business techniques.
② Though their capital strength is weak, their organizations overflow with ideas and creativity that are adopted by the next generation.
③ They value partnerships that share their values and organically relate to their organizations.
④ They believe that labor is not a means only for income but also for self-actualization.
⑤ They are willing to consider a developing country as a stakeholder, and they provide products and services that express their sense of values.
⑥ They value long-term effects. Even if short-term profits are sacrificed, they are convinced that stakeholders appreciate a long-term approach.

Thus, a social entrepreneur has long-term ideas and an important network, is aware of his stakeholders, and shares their sense of values.

Fields with many active social entrepreneurs include medicine, welfare, education, the environment, and culture. Especially, it adds to the field invented depending instead of public service. Demand for industry for the senior citizen grows in Japan that received aging society. The policy in the country to such a business has been faced to the problem of not functioning enough because of the increase of the cost of social security expense. Appearing here is a social entrepreneur. Because a social entrepreneur is having both the consideration of the private company base, it is cost-conscious of them. And, they are excellent in the ability to accomplish work efficiently. In addition, a social entrepreneur who does labor with the sense of purpose offers the user the quality service. Therefore, the user can share each value with a social entrepreneur.

The other leading part that composes the new economy is a net entrepreneur. They are inventing value of improving relations between a dull person

---

37) Saito, Maki (2004), *Shakaikigyouka (Social entrepreneur)*, Iwanamishinsho, p. 7.
38) *Ibid.*, p. 27.
39) *Ibid.*, pp. 28-29.

and the person at the present age. A social entrepreneur is acting like good at creation of sympathy, and widening the circle of this sympathy as much as possible. It is a net entrepreneur to support sympathy that such a social entrepreneur originates. Common value is invented by their cooperation of labors. This common value is social capital that ties people's minds. Money plays the role as the mediation of the accumulation means of value and the exchange. Money forms a capital market where the convertibility of value in the society is pursued. Money unifies the standard of value as an economic blood stream.

In the economic arena, money underlies the capital market, where the convertibility of value in the society is pursued.

The market economy gives universality to value by price. Anything "extra", without monetary value is rounded down. This "extra" is the social entrepreneur's domain.

One of the techniques for pressing the innovation and economic growth is a Creating Shared Value (CSV). The supporter who invents this CSV is a social entrepreneur who works on the social task. These economic agents do not catch the action on an economical gain and a social problem with the relation of the trade-off as mentioned above. Answering the social task becomes new needs, and it becomes the source of the profit acquisition. The innovation is invented by piling such an activity, and economic growth is promoted.

CSV is fundamentally different from CSR (Corporate Social Responsibility). The latter means any contribution to society that excludes assisting the company itself. The former aims for a better society, as part of the business's role, while the latter can operate by means of external pressure, the former is a more integrated strategy that helps firms compete.

A paper by Porter, M. E. and Kramer, M. R. defines social value and the economic merit of CSV. They insist that the pursuit of CSV is an important part of a firm's strategy. Meeting social needs should be an integral part of a manager's role. For this reason, new entrepreneurs will ultimately evolve to become managers of long-lived companies.

Because companies are centers of society, it is impossible for managers to disregard society's demands. We can assume that companies will defend the law and corporate ethics: so in the future, the most promising companies will be the ones that contribute to social development.

7. Conclusion

Although the United States is an economic power, it ranks ninth in Figure 1. Does economic development lead to a long-term continuing the company? The relation doesn't actually exist. In the basis of the capitalism of the United States, there is a stockholder supreme principle. Therefore, the United States company is requesting immediate profit by a short-term intention. In a word, the United States company does not perceive an important aspect for management like founder's entrepreneurship and a traditional corporate philosophy. On the other hand, the United States company is going forward on the maximization of the stockholder value. The management fulfilled to the maximum proposition for the long-term continuing company in the United States company is not practiced.

Does economic development lead to long-term business success? The relationship does not actually exist. In U. S. capitalism, stockholders reign supreme. Therefore, U. S. companies often have a short-term profitability focus. This means that management's attention is diverted from entrepreneurship, traditional corporate philosophies, and long-term value.

Ohmi merchant obtained a large sum of gain because of business, and saved the local person who suffered poorly. Action with such morality was a key of the triple win management. In a word, the spirit of Ohmi merchant who pursued such the people stopping accelerated the cycle when their management was good. Because, such a good doing has improved social stability in the region. As a result, the reputation of the business that was the profession rose. The idea like Ohmi merchant's morality has infiltrated the modern company. A social company that starts making the society better appears from the aspect like the environment in the society, labor, human rights, and the corruption prevention. Such a social company is a leading part of the contemporary society. And, the significance of existence of the company that has both the economy and the sociality is closed up. In a word, such a company is accomplishing the trust obligation to the whole society. Especially, the triple win management of Japan passes also in foreign countries where a social request is strong.

When considering wellbeing from the Ohmi merchant's perspective on business ethics and the succession of tradition by Toraya, sustainability is directly connected with the establishment of trust between the company and its stakeholders. Companies also should strongly consider the two following trust obligations[40]: ①a company should think about its benefit to society and act in a faithful manner, and ②a company should improve its risk awareness. After fulfilling these obligations, a company should investigate the integrity of its management.[41] Even if a company recites wonderful corporate principles, an insincere management will not to be able to practice them. A company cannot make a formal ethical contract with stakeholders: therefore, only the consistent application of wholesome corporate principles by management, and its integrity, will sustain a company over a long period of time.

---

40) Taka, Iwao (2006), *Seijitsusa wo tsuranuku keiei (Management through integrity)*, Nihonkeizaishinbunsha, p. 49.
41) *Ibid.*, p. 51.

Figure 1: The number of companies which has passed for more than 200 years from foundation

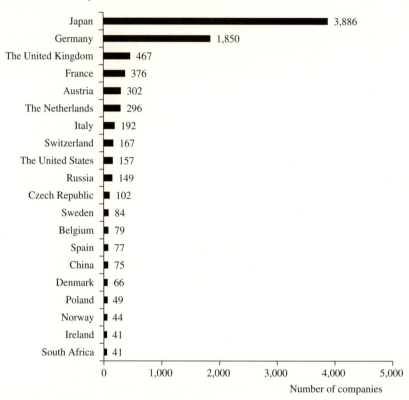

Source: *Toyokeizai Weekly* (2010), No. 6264, p. 43.

Table 1: Main long-lived companies which has passed more than 800 years from foundation

The name	Foundation	Location	Business status
Kongougumi	578	Osaka	Temple and shrine architecture
Nishiyama hot spring Keiunkaku	705	Yamanashi	Japanese-style inn with a hot spring
Koman	717	Hyogo	Japanese-style inn with a hot spring
Zengoro	718	Ishikawa	Japanese-style inn with a hot spring
Genda paper trade	771	Kyoto	Mizuhiki strings and paper
Tanaka,Iga butsugu store	889	Kyoto	Buddhist image and garden lantern
Sudo Honke	1141	Ibaraki	The oldest sake cellar
Tsuuin	1160	Kyoto	Japanese tea
Hotel Sakan	1184	Miyagi	Japanese-style inn with a hot spring
Ito blacksmith	1189	Yamagata	Cast and Special valve
Gosyobo	1191	Hyogo	Japanese-style inn with a hot spring
Shirasagiyu Tawaraya	1190	Ishikawa	Japanese-style inn with a hot spring

Source: Teikoku Data Bank Shiryokan, Sangyochosabu (ed.) (2009), *100nen tsuzuku kigyo no jouken, (The condition of the company which continues for 100 years)*, Asahishinbun Publisher, p. 53.

Table 2: Appearance rate of the long-lived companies (according to business category)

The business category	The number of the long-lived companies	The whole number	The appearance rate (%)
1. Sake	637	1,069	59.6
2. Soy sauce	136	347	39.2
3. Fermented soybean paste	94	251	37.5
4. Distilled liquor and Mixed liquor	93	261	35.6
5. Gunpowder and Fireworks	15	47	31.9
6. Saccharide	10	32	31.3
7. Department store	31	106	29.2
8. Ordinary bank	33	127	26.0
9. Gunpowder wholesale	39	151	25.8
10. Japanese Barrel	3	12	25.0

Source: Teikoku Data Bank Shiryokan, Sangyochosabu (ed.) (2009), *100nen tsuzuku kigyo no jouken, (The condition of the companies which continues for 100 years)*, Asahishinbun Publisher, p. 59.

Figure 2: JFLA Group

Source: Writer making.

Table 3: Family business and general business: the comparison

	Family business	General business
Stockholder and proprietor	Agreement (Many cases)	Disagreement (A stockholder entrusts management to a proprietor.)
The interest of the stockholder and the proprietor	Agreement	Disagreement (A proprietor often becomes selfish.)
Monitoring system	Unnecessary	Necessary (It's necessary to prevent own-oriented profit of the proprietor.)
Incentive	Unnecessary	Necessary (It's necessary to raise proprietor's morale.)

Source: Goto, Toshio (ed.) (2012), *Family business*, Hakuto shobou, p. 35. (Modification by Writer)

Table 4: Les Hénokiens (8 Japanese companies)

Company name	Business category	Foundation
Zengoro (Hoshi)	Japanese-style inn with a hot spring	718
Toraya	Japanese confection production and sale	1520
Gekkeikan	Sake brewing	1637
Yamasa	Soy sauce	1645
Okaya-kouki	General trading company	1669
Zaiso-lumber	Wood processing	1690
Akafuku	Japanese confection production and sale	1707
Nakagawamasashichi-Shoten	Hempen fabric	1717

Source: Les Hénokiens homepage, http//www.henokiens.com/index_gb.php (last access, December 28, 2016)

III.
Value Creation through Co-creation: The Case of a Smart City

Nobuyuki TOKORO

1. Introduction

As globalization accelerates, competition between corporations is also becoming more severe. Sharp, a major Japanese electronics manufacturer that once led the world in liquid crystal (LC) technology, has run into financial trouble and made news headlines when it decided to be acquired by Hon Hai Precision Instrument Co., Ltd. of Taiwan. The case of Sharp brought to mind Christensen's "innovator's dilemma" (Christensen, 1997). This debate over how successful companies have difficulty thinking beyond their experience of success and are slow to respond to new, disruptive innovations is remarkably applicable in the case of Sharp. A similar case can be seen where Sony established its position as an innovator when it released its Walkman to the world in the 1980s but then later lost ground to Apple when Apple developed the iPhone, an innovation that caused Sony to enter a long period of financial difficulties.

To overcome the cutthroat competition, it is important for companies to consider how to create new value. In the case of Hon Hai and Apple, the content and nature of the value they created are different, and they became winners because they both produced new value that differed from the existing value. This paper proposes the concept of "value creation through cocreation" from the standpoint of an approach whereby corporations of different industries exchange and combine technologies, know-how, and knowledge to create new value. The case of a smart city is presented as an embodiment of "value creation through co-creation", and a theoretical verification is conducted.

2. Corporate activity and value creation

Corporate activity and value creation are inseparably related. In short, corporate activity is nothing other than the creation of value through products and services. In the area of competitive strategy theory, value creation is interpreted to be synonymous with "differentiation". Companies use some method of differentiation to generate value for their own products or services compared with the products and services of competitors. Normally, that differentiation is expressed in price, performance, or quality. If value creation is successful and the market supports it, the firm can capture competitive advantage in the marketplace. Value creation is thus an endeavor aimed at capturing competitive advantage. An overview from the perspective of value creation concerning Positioning View and Resource-based View, two representative theories of competitive advantage, is presented next.

2-1. Positioning View and value creation

A representative theory presented by Porter concerning the competitive advantage of a corporation is known as Positioning View (Porter, 1980, 1985). The feature of the Positioning View approach is that it focuses on the external environment of the corporation, structural barriers in particular, and is linked to capturing competitive advantage by selecting a market that has desirable structural barriers from the viewpoint of corporate profits. Normally, structural barriers that exist in a market are those that block free economic activity or free competition, and it is normal to think that they should be removed. High tariffs on imported goods is a typical example. The Positioning View, however, maintains that it is exactly these markets with structural barriers that firms should choose to operate in. This is because structural barriers act as breakwaters, preventing other firms from entering the market and therefore allowing certain firms to enjoy stable profits. This unique approach of the Positioning View is based on the theory of industrial organization, an area of economics. In this theory, it can be seen that the idea of industries being profitable due to the existence of structural barriers in the market should be eliminated, but the Positioning View reverses this viewpoint and states that being protected by structural barriers is desirable for corporations and that when corporations position themselves in such market environments, they are able to capture competitive advantage.

The Positioning View focuses on five forces as structural barriers in the market: "Industry rivalry", "Threat of new entrants", "Threat of substitute products and services", "Bargaining power of suppliers", and "Bargaining power of buyers". If the extent of these five forces is low, it will be easier for companies to be profitable. Conversely, if the extent of these forces grows higher, corporate profits will decline. In industry rivalry, for example, if there are many companies within an industry, competition intensifies, companies scramble for market share, and profitability declines. In such a market, it is not easy for companies to achieve stable profits or capture competitive advantage. On the other hand, if there are only a few companies in an industry and they all coexist, the companies can achieve stable profits. Which marketplace a company will choose is self-evident.

The Positioning View thus focuses on structural barriers in the marketplace and emphasizes the point that when companies position themselves in markets where there are high structural barriers and stable profits are possible, differences between the companies become clearer, and that this then affects their competitive advantage. When this idea is seen from the viewpoint of value creation, marketplace selection and the positioning of the company in that marketplace become tied to the company's value creation. The Positioning View, however, focuses only on the company's external environment and does not touch on its internal environment. A theoretical weakness of the Positioning View is that it cannot explain differences between companies in the same external environment. This idea also focuses on how a company can capture a more advantageous position compared to other companies in the marketplace, and it assumes that value creation is something that companies pursue on their own in order to come out ahead in the competition with other companies.

2-2. Resource-based View and value creation

Along with the Positioning View, the Resource-based View is another representative theory concerning the competitive advantage of corporations (Wernerfelt, 1984, 1995; Rumelt, 1984, 1991; Barney, 1986, 1991). The Resource-based View emerged from the process of overcoming the theoretical weaknesses of the Positioning View. In other words, as mentioned above, the Positioning View sought the competitive advantage of companies in the structural forces of the external environment but was unable to explain what caused the differences in competitive advantage between companies positioned in the same external environment. A new theory, that focuses on the internal resources and competencies of companies rather than external structural forces, and links those differences to differences in competitive advantage between companies, has therefore emerged. In other words, the Resource-based View focuses on the internal resources of companies and argues that the resources, knowledge, and competencies that companies have accumulated internally are the source of their competitive advantage.

What specifically are the internal resources that are tied to companies' competitive advantage according to the Resource-based View? The following features can be identified:

(1) Rarity
(2) In-imitability
(3) Uniformity with customer value

Rarity indicates that the company's internal resources are scarce and it would be difficult for other companies to obtain those resources. For example, if a company has extremely advanced technology, even if other companies knew that this technology was a source of competitive advantage for that company, it would be difficult for other companies to obtain that technology, because the company that has this technology has black-boxed it.

In-imitability refers to the difficulty of other companies to imitate the internal resource of a company that they perceive as giving that company competitive advantage and to obtain the same level of competitive advantage as that company. A typical example is the just-in-time production system of Toyota Motors. It is widely known that Toyota's just-in-time production system is one of the sources of the company's competitive advantage, and many companies have imitated this system and adopted it in the management of their own company. Even if they have adopted it, however, it cannot be said that they have all been able to achieve the same level of competitive advantage that Toyota has. The reason for this is that many of these companies simply understood just-in-time as a how-to approach aimed at rationalization, while for Toyota, just-in-time is not at all a how-to system but a deeply-rooted organizational culture that thoroughly minimizes any waste. This culture is rooted in Toyota's DNA and other companies cannot easily understand and imitate it.

Uniformity with customer value refers to the efforts of a company to tie its internal resources to value sought by customers. No matter how rare a company's resources are and no matter how difficult it might be to imitate them, if those resources are not tied to value sought by customers, they cannot contribute to competitive advantage. Japanese companies in recent years, especially electronics manufacturers with superior technologies for high-resolution televisions, are struggling to survive despite these resources, and this is happening because these technologies have not been tied to value that customers want.

According to the Resource-based View, if a company's internal resources have rarity, in-imitability, and uniformity with customer value, they become sources of competitive advantage. Seen from the viewpoint of value creation, the act of accumulating the resources of rarity, in-imitability, and uniformity with customer value within the company is the very act of creating value. In this case as well, however, the assumption is that in order to come out ahead in the competition with other companies, a company must create this value on its own; the idea that value can be co-created with other companies is very rare.

3. Creating value through co-creation

Next comes a discussion on the act of creating value through co-creation between companies. As mentioned above, whether the theory concerning existing competitive advantage is the Positioning View or the Resource-based View, they both focus on how a company can come out ahead in the competition with other companies and in principle assume that companies create value on their own. Even if a company did work with another company to create value, it was generally thought to be a limited, mutually complimentary value. However, a company's act of creating value did not always follow this pattern. There are also cases in which companies with superior dynamic capabilities exchange, combine, and resonate their knowledge and know-how to create new value. Discussions on "open innovation" (Chesbrough, 2003, 2006) in particular have been active in recent years, stimulating further interest in value creation and co-creation among corporations.

3-1. What is co-creation?

What does co-creation, the act of joint creation, actually mean? This term has been used more frequently in a variety of fields in recent years, but it has not always been used in the context of a clear definition. While the act of creating new value has generally been thought to be dependent on the specific qualities of talented individuals, the actual situation is quite different. As an example, the story of Isaac Newton, considered the father of modern science, who came up with the law of gravity when he observed an apple falling from a tree, is well known, but he did not suddenly come up with the law of gravity from nowhere. Newton was already aware of scientists before him who had built an established font of knowledge about the force of gravity and planets in orbit, and it was on this basis that he established the new law of gravity. The general idea about the discovery of gravity has been that Newton was a genius who happened to discover it on his own as one of his great achievements. In reality, however, this discovery was the result of knowledge co-creation between Newton and scientists who preceded him.

Brilliant inventions, discoveries, and innovative ideas are not generated by individual geniuses out of nowhere but come from some sort of intellectual exchanges with other people, whether in real time or after a series of events over time. Thus, to create new value, it is important to establish a mechanism or system for co-creating with others.

In recent years, research into co-creation has made considerable strides particularly in the field of marketing. In the field of service marketing, the idea of Service-Dominant Logic (S-D Logic) was espoused as an approach for "value co-creation with customers" in the area of services, and the traditional concept of service is changing. S-D Logic, presented by Vargo and Lusch (2004), stresses that the value creation of companies is changing from the traditional model based on product price to a model that focuses on service systems and logic.

There is also research conducted by Prahalad & Ramaswamy (2003, 2004) into value co-creation with customers. These authors argue that the competitive advantage of companies in 21st-century marketplaces depends on value co-creation with customers, and they brought the concept of co-creation into the field of competitive advantage. According to these researchers, the creation of value in marketplaces up to the 20th century was mainly the work of companies, and customers existed only to purchase at a fair price the value that the company created, whereas in marketplaces of the 21st century, value is co-created by both companies and customers, and marketplaces are not only places where products and services are bought and sold but also function as places where companies and customers co-create value.

Research into co-creation is not limited to the field of marketing, as interest in the mechanism of co-creation has also been growing in recent years in fields of natural science. The Research into Artifacts, Center for Engineering at the University of Tokyo, for instance, established the Co-Creation Engineering Research Division and analyzes the mechanisms of co-creation from the approach of engineering. According to Ueda, et al. (2004), the aims of co-creation engineering are altering the co-creative relationship between humans and human artifacts, and the approach method is not the top-down analysis type that follows the optimization theory or the control theory, which are orthodox methods in fields of engineering, but the bottom-up synthesis type.

This paper refers to the perceptions of existing research concerning co-creation and defines co-creation as follows: "Co-creation, under a particular shared objective, is the act of creating value that could not be created by a single entity individually and is therefore created by a number of entities working together." The difference between co-creation and collaboration should also be clarified here. Generally, the terms co-creation and collabora-

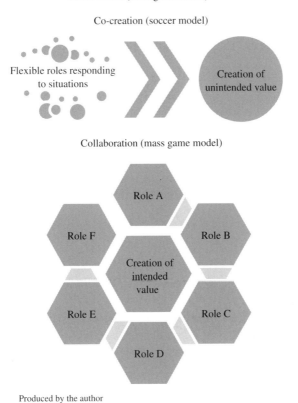

Figure 1: Conceptual diagram of co-creation (soccer model) and collaboration (mass game model)

Produced by the author

tion are often used in the same context and the difference between them has not been very problematic, but in this paper, the difference needs to be clarified. To explain, the author uses the metaphor of soccer and mass games (massed gymnastics). Soccer is a team sport with 11 players, and except for the goalkeeper whose role is to protect the goal, the roles of the others players are not clear. While there is a general division of roles between offense and defense, all players need to exercise flexibility in how they respond to situations during the flow of the match. If a defensive player sees an opportunity, they may participate in an offensive attack, and in the rhythm of the flow, they might score a beautiful goal. This sport has a highly co-creative character. The situation is different, however, with mass games, another team sport. In mass games, the role of each participant is strictly defined, and they must act following predetermined patterns. The sort of flexibility that soccer players have in responding to situations is not allowed in mass games. When each participant performs their predetermined role faithfully, the result is a beautiful overall performance of highly-skilled mastery. The patterns of mass games are the product of collaboration.

3-2. Three components generating co-creation

A structure is required when different entities interact and create value from their mutual efforts. For example, at conferences it is common for participants to have different opinions and clash, but new value is not created when each participant only stresses the correctness of their own opinion and attacks others. If someone can take the lead to amalgamate the different opinions and achieve more constructive ideas, the possibility of creating new value increases. The three components of "Ba", "emergence", and "synthesis" are therefore presented here as a structure for co-creation.

3-2-1. "Ba"

The term "Ba" (shared context in motion) appears frequently in our daily life. It is used in a variety of situations such as a Ba for a meeting, a Ba for learning, and a Ba for relaxation. This Ba is not simply a physical place such as a meeting room but also encompasses concepts of broader relationships including mental space, such as a virtual space where unacquainted people in remote locations exchange information over the Internet, or a spiritual bond between people sharing thoughts on a book.

While the presence of Ba is indispensable for different entities to interact and engage in mutual endeavors, for it to function as a Ba for co-creation, a number of conditions must be met. The first condition is the presence in this Ba of some sort of shared objective. If a shared objective is not present, the Ba simply turns into a spatiotemporal realm of chaos. A train station, for instance, is a Ba where large crowds of people cross paths, but there is no shared objective among all these people there. Some people came to get on a train, others came to meet someone, and still others came to buy something at a shop inside the station; the fact that they are all in this Ba at the same time is merely coincidental. In this case, there is no exchange of psychological energy or knowledge among these people participating in this Ba. The situation is different, however, among people who are participating in a gathering in front of the station. These people are interested in the agenda of the gathering and a shared objective is present there. Exchanges of psychological energy such as sympathy, backlashes, or anger occur among the people, and it is possible that new value will be created from it.

The second condition is that the Ba should be equipped with autonomy. Members participating in the Ba must be guaranteed freedom to interact, express their opinions and ideas, and engage in intellectual assimilation, without being subject to external restrictions or restraints. If the autonomy of Ba is lost due to the presence of constraints on interests or a number of powerful entities and the spontaneous actions of participants are restricted, it will be difficult to achieve co-creation. The degree of autonomy that is required of the Ba, however, may vary with the details of the shared objective and the relationships among participants. For example, if the Ba is equipped with a high level of autonomy and the relationships among participants are flat, there is a danger that participants' opinions will clash and conflicts of interest will worsen beyond control.

The third condition is that the leader of the Ba conduct appropriate Ba management. This third condition is closely related to the problem of Ba autonomy described in the second condition. In other words, autonomy at the Ba is necessary for participants to achieve co-creation, but if autonomy is over-emphasized, and the leader's presence at the Ba is weakened and appropriate management of participants is insufficient, it is possible that conflicts of interest will emerge and control will be lost. It is thus important that the leader of the Ba be able to exercise leadership when necessary while preserving the autonomy and spontaneity of participants, and manage the Ba as it achieves co-creation.

3-2-2. "Emergence"

The term "emergence" refers to the process where local movements originally conducted at the margins of an organization grew to become large movements over time and became activities that would ultimately move the overall organization. In other words, it expresses the act of evolving from the parts to the whole. Mintzberg (1973, 1978, 1990) espoused the idea of "emergence" in the field of strategic theory. He stated that strategy was not something that was conceived and proposed at the top and then executed from the top down but was formed through a process of trial and error during practical applications in the field. To achieve that end, the organization had to have freedom, and strategic ideas that emerged from the middle and lower levels had to be accorded greater significance.

The act of co-creation that is the subject of analysis in this paper has an extremely high affinity with "emergence". In other words, co-creation is an act that is generated from the process of emergence. If a specific entity (top management, for instance) proposes a plan in advance and follows through with the plan after establishing clear divisions of roles for other entities, it is questionable whether co-creation could occur. The general perception is that there is little possibility co-creation can occur under such circumstances. The reason in this case is that each entity is expected to faithfully play their own pre-determined role and they are not expected to do anything beyond that. If someone does anything beyond their pre-determined role, that person is deemed to have overstepped their authority and could be penalized for it. This closely corresponds with the mass games described above. Mass games are carefully planned in advance, each player's role is clearly defined, and the games are successfully played when each player faithfully follows their own particular role. If players act beyond the division of roles set out for them in advance, it becomes impossible for overall discipline to be maintained and the mass game fails. In other words, the beauty of a mass game is in the reproduction of value that was planned in advance, a value that was intended.

However, a value that is planned in advance – an intended value – is different from co-creation. A co-created value cannot be intended. A co-created value is instead akin to soccer, where players respond flexibly to situations as they enfold during the match; it is created through a process where players' abilities resonate with each other. It is thus necessary for "emergence" to occur when value is co-created.

3-2-3. "Synthesis"

The term "synthesis" is a concept referring to comprehensiveness or integration and is often contrasted with "analysis". In scientific fields, "analysis", as opposed to "synthesis", is used as the method of analysis and there is little familiarity with "synthesis". Since "analysis" and "synthesis" are inverse vectors, an understanding of "synthesis" can be improved through an understanding of "analysis".

"Analysis" is an approach based on reductionism whereby a complex system is understood by analyzing the individual parts that make up the system and investigating their character and relationships so the overall system can be understood. The "analysis" method has been used to achieve significant results in fields of natural science from the origin of the universe to the structure of micro-organisms. So-called scientific approaches indicate this sort of "analysis" approach.

"Synthesis", on the other hand, refers to the act of connecting individual elements to create something. What appear at first glance to be unrelated elements are connected by adding some sort of force or mechanism, which results in a large force, and this act produces some sort of creation or value that was not anticipated. While "analysis" follows the whole-to-the-parts vector, "synthesis" follows the parts-to-the-whole vector.

When analyzing the act of co-creation, it is not appropriate to follow the "analysis" approach used in the natural sciences. This is because the creative act of co-creation does not aim to understand the structure of a given creation by disassembling it into its various parts but to connect and integrate individ-

Figure 2: Relationship between Ba, Emergence, and Synthesis

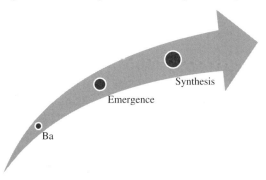

Produced by the author

ual parts to produce some sort of creation. It is therefore key to analyze the sort of mechanism that causes this act to take place. For example, looking at the relationship between the two components of "Ba" and "emergence" mentioned above, when autonomy is accorded to a Ba, it is easier for emergence to occur among members participating in the Ba. Even when various types of emergence occur, the Ba must be appropriately managed so that they can be connected, integrated, and lead to the creation of new value. In other words, the leader of the Ba must exercise appropriate leadership and control the Ba during the process from "emergence" to "synthesis". When these mechanisms work well, it is possible for value to be produced through co-creation.

4. Smart city construction and value co-creation

This chapter is devoted to an analysis of a case study in value creation based on the theoretical discussions in the previous chapters. The subject of this case study analysis is the smart city construction project. A smart city is an environmentally-friendly city where the infrastructure of urban life, such as electric power, water supply, communications, transportation and other areas, has been optimized through ICT with the aim to reduce energy consumption and carbon-dioxide emissions. The construction of smart cities also holds promise as a solution to urban problems such as population growth, aging society, and declining safety.

Interest in smart cities started in 2009 when the Obama administration in the United States came out with the smart grid concept, a next-generation electric power network that would utilize ICT to intelligently adjust demand for electricity and take the place of the existing power network that was aging. This stimulated the launch of smart city projects at various locations around the world. The largest number of smart city construction projects is currently underway in China. Urbanization in China is advancing at a rapid pace, with about 12 million people moving to cities each year from agricultural regions. As a result, Chinese cities are facing a variety of problems such as urban population growth, air pollution, and chronic traffic congestion, and finding solutions to such problems has become an urgent issue. Though the problems that Japanese cities face are not as serious as those in China, the Great East Japan Earthquake that struck on March 11, 2011, has prompted reviews of electric power supplies and energy plans, and interest in smart cities that intelligently utilize electric power and energy has been growing.

This paper presents the case of Fujisawa Sustainable Smart Town (Fujisawa

SST) that Panasonic, a major electronics manufacturer, is constructing at the former site of one of their factories in Fujisawa City, Kanagawa Prefecture, Japan, in order to verify the process of co-creation among firms of different industries.

4-1. Overview of Fujisawa SST

Fujisawa SST is a project that Panasonic is undertaking to construct an advanced town for about 1,000 households, or 3,000 residents, on approximately 19 hectares of land formerly occupied by one of the company's factories in Fujisawa City, Kanagawa Prefecture. At a total cost of approximately JPY 60 billion, the project started in 2011 and is scheduled for completion in 2018. The factory that was originally built on this site in 1961 was used to manufacture black and white televisions, refrigerators, fans and other electrical appliances, and after it closed in 2007, Panasonic was engaged in discussions with the local government of Fujisawa City about what to do with the site. A decision was then made to construct Fujisawa SST, and the rough details of this project are described next.

First, photovoltaic systems and storage cells would be standard equipment for all residences, facilities, public zones and other areas of the town. In addition, in the public spaces there would be a battery charging infrastructure for electric cars and plug-in hybrid cars, as well as eco-cycle packages such as power-assisted bicycles and solar parking lots. Also planned are mobility share services using electric cars, security services with optimum control for lights, sensors, and surveillance cameras, and healthcare services that provide equipment for elderly residents to live comfortably.

As a community platform supporting this structure, there will be portals and terminals with applications for conveniently using the various services. There will also be a Smart Energy Gateway (SEG, a central device for managing networked electrical appliances within the home) that residents can operate from the living room enabling them to monitor energy, receive notifications about time sales at commercial facilities, or management their appointments. With this structure, Fujisawa SST aims to reduce overall carbon-dioxide emissions by 70% and water use for daily life by 30%, compared with 1990.

4-2. Five value creations at Fujisawa SST
  4-2-1. Energy
The first of the five values that Fujisawa SST is aiming to create is energy.

As mentioned above, the Great East Japanese Earthquake that occurred on March 11, 2011, and the Fukushima nuclear power plant accident that followed have raised concern for the problem of energy to a level that has never before been higher. The problem of how to secure electric power at times of disaster is extremely important in Japan where natural disasters are a frequent occurrence. Given this situation in Japanese society, Fujisawa SST has placed the creation of new value in the field of energy at the top of its list of objectives.

Specifically, the new value that is created concerns self-sufficiency in such areas as using renewable sources of energy and as much as possible generating on their own the energy they need. To this end, all residences will be standard equipped with photovoltaic systems and storage cells and include a Home Energy Management System (HEMS) so that electric power is used intelligently. In Japan, the electric power market was liberalized from April 2016, and consumers can now choose an electric power company. While it is expected that regional monopolies of the major electric power companies will gradually deteriorate, Fujisawa SST is ahead of the times in its efforts to aggressively promote self-sufficiency in electric power.

4-2-2. Security

The second value creation at Fujisawa SST is security. With people, things, money, and information converging in cities, there are also many crimes and one of the most important values for cities is to ensure that life is safe. In recent times especially, the international situation is becoming unstable and atrocious crimes such as indiscriminant terrorism targeting places where many people gather have been occurring with greater frequency, underlining people's growing needs for safety and security in their daily lives.

To provide safety and security for residents, Fujisawa SST has created the Virtual Gated Town utilizing state-of-the-art technologies. In American cities, especially in areas where many of the affluent live, a gate has been set up at the entrance to enhance security by strictly controlling the coming and going of vehicles and pedestrians. This setup, however, turns the town into something like a fortress and some people say it gives residents unnecessary psychological stress. Fujisawa SST therefore will not have a gate at the entrance but instead have about 50 "guardian cameras" and lights effectively placed mainly at the entrance, public buildings, near shadows in the parks, and at the intersections of the main streets.

4-2-3. Mobility

One of the various problems that cities face concerns transportation. The problems of chronic traffic congestion, air pollution, and traffic accidents caused by growing numbers of vehicles are issues that cities around the world face. Developing countries in particular, where motorization has been undergoing rapid growth in recent years, have not been able to keep up with the need to construct urban infrastructure and it is becoming a serious social problem.

To solve the problem of urban traffic, Fujisawa SST adopted a new system known as Total Mobility Service. The details include (a) a sharing service utilizing electric cars, electric motorcycles, and power-assisted bicycles, (b) a car rental delivery service, and (c) a Battery Station where rechargeable batteries can be rented. With the Mobility Concierge service, for instance, a resident can consider distance, travel time, and timeframe, and can then receive advice about whether to go somewhere by shared car, rented car, or not to use a car but go by electric motorcycle. When using an electric motorcycle or power-assisted bicycle, a resident can freely change batteries at a Battery Station located in the town and use that battery. This way, a resident does not need to recharge the battery after returning home or worry about the remaining battery charge when commuting to and from work or going shopping.

4-2-4. Healthcare

Declining birth rates and aging populations is a trend common to all developed countries, and in Japan this trend is moving faster than in other developed countries. Japan has many natural disasters, and the evacuation and rescue of elderly people whenever a disaster occurs attracts the concern of society as a whole. While the problem of aging is particularly severe in agricultural regions where population is declining, this problem of course exists in cities as well. In cities where human relationships are not strong, there is a serious problem of solitary deaths among elderly people living alone.

To address this problem, Fujisawa SST will provide new services in the field of healthcare under the keyword "Tsunagari" (connection). Specifically, in one corner of the town there will be a cluster of facilities known as "Well SITE" that will comprise a home for elderly requiring special care, service-equipped residences for the elderly, various types of clinics, a daycare center, an educational facility, and other amenities. All of them will be seamlessly connected so that optimal services can be provided for each individual resident. For example, a resident who returns home after being released from the hospital will be able to receive appropriate home care services through the connection between medical and home care services. To that end, Fujisawa SST is building a system known as the Comprehensive Regional Care System. This system will be used to manage all information concerning a resident's health and medical treatments, and when needed, this information can be accessed to provide appropriate services for the resident.

4-2-5. Community

One of the major problems of cities is the absence of community. "Community" refers to the space in which people are connected to each other or to the town. Fujisawa SST aims to build a community where people are linked to each other and to the town. Specifically, this means setting up a variety of spaces such as a book corner that can be used by people of all ages, a parent and child science classroom, a general consultation space, and other kinds of spaces where people can interact with one another. With the smart city concept, there is a tendency to focus only on the hard aspect, i. e., building an infrastructure that utilizes ICT, but the soft aspect of building a community must not be neglected. No matter how wonderful the infrastructure may be, the city cannot become an attractive place to live if residents cannot mentally feel "at home" there. Fujisawa SST is thus working on creating new value for the soft aspects as well.

4-3. Value co-creation by firms in different industries

Fujisawa SST is a project that aims to build a new smart city at the former site of a Panasonic factory, and it is essentially Panasonic's project. Panasonic's intentions and strategies are strongly reflected throughout the entire process from the formation of the original plan to its implementation. It is not possible, however, for Panasonic to carry out this project entirely by itself. Eight companies are participating in the project as partners, and these companies come from a wide variety of industries. Through a process of co-creation with these other firms, Panasonic is attempting to create value for Fujisawa SST that it could not create on its own. The roles of the eight partner firms are shown in Table 1.

At Fujisawa SST, the five values described above – Energy, Security, Mobility, Healthcare, and Community – are being co-created by Panasonic and partner firms by combining each other's specific knowledge and expertise. Panasonic and Tokyo Gas, for instance, are providing the elemental technolo-

Figure 3: Value Creation in Fujisawa SST

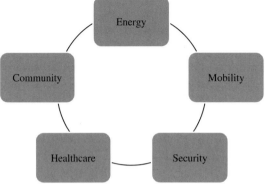

Created by the author

Table 1: Roles in Fujisawa SST

Accenture	· Smart town conceptualization, service model planning and promotion · Smart town platform support in light of global trends
Orix	· Service planning for increased overall town value, and comfortable, ecological, safe and secure lifestyles
Nihon Sekkei	· Space design and optimal planning for deploying new energy devices etc
Sumitomo Trust and Banking	· Smart town evaluation index design (environment and real estate value) · Product planning for environmentally friendly housing loans designed for Fujisawa SST
Tokyo Gas	· Installing the latest "Ene-farm" home fuel cell equipment · Proposals for comfortable and ecological living using Ene-farm
PanaHome	· Basic land readjustment project arrangements · Residential land and housing sales
Mitsui Fudosan	· Basic land readjustment project arrangements · Residential land and housing sales
Mitsui & Co	· City block, infrastructure and real estate development also applicable for global expansion · Energy management services that take into account global smart city trends

Source: Created from Materials on Fujisawa SST.

gies of the Home Energy Management System (HEMS), the Building Energy Management System (BEMS), and the Community Energy Management System (CEMS); Nihon Sekkei, a specialist in the field of urban planning, and Orix, a firm with a wealth of experience in the field of car sharing, are providing their knowledge when building a self-reliant energy management system that will enable the town overall to use energy efficiently and manage it intelligently. The town is being designed with tree-lined streets and garden paths so that refreshing breezes from the sea will easily pass through, and town design guidelines require a minimum space of 1.6 meters between houses to allow sunlight to enter. This town design is being produced jointly by urban planner Nihon Sekkei; Accenture, a firm with expertise on cases overseas; PanaHome, a builder of residential homes; and Mitsui Fudosan of the real estate industry, who all combine each other's knowledge in the process.

In 2014, on the occasion of the opening of the town, Fujisawa SST welcomed new partner companies which accelerated the value co-creation process. One of them is So-Two, Inc., which is in charge of a commercial facility known as Shonan T-SITE, a space they created where anyone can come and spend quality time with a book, magazine, or coffee, and the company aims to transmit the unique Fujisawa SST lifestyle to the world. The keyword for this effort is "power of persuasion". Shonan T-SITE does not simply change products on sale at the stores to keep up with changes in customer needs, an endeavor that has been conducted by conventional large-scale commercial facilities, but looks ahead of the times before the changes in customer needs occur, proposes new lifestyles, and then selects for the stores only items based on those lifestyles. So-Two is thus at the center of continuous efforts to think about new lifestyles together with stores inside the facility, and they develop new products.

The key to success in the co-creation of value by companies from different industries at Fujisawa SST has been the formation of a Ba. An organization called the Town Creation Council was formed at Fujisawa SST to produce town concepts, overall goals and guidelines, and all partner companies as well as Panasonic are members of the Council. At this Ba, the knowledge and expertise of the companies came together, resonated, and were combined to create new value. For the Ba to function effectively and achieve co-creation, however, it was important for the Ba to be given autonomy. If various restraints and power relationships hampered the words and actions of members participating in the Ba, it would be difficult for co-creation to occur. Thus, in the case of Fujisawa SST, since this is a project completely led by Panasonic, it would be interesting to look into the degree of autonomy that was given to the Town Creation Council.

According to the investigative interviews[1] conducted by the author, the relationship between Panasonic and the partner companies on the Town Creation Council is approximately as follows. First of all, the role of the leader who controls the Town Creation Council – the Ba – is assumed by Panasonic. It is clear that the various approaches concerning value creation for Fujisawa SST are planned and guided by Panasonic. This does not mean, however, that other partner companies have no authority at all and that they simply follow Panasonic's plan. In fact, Panasonic incorporates the knowledge and expertise of partner companies and desires co-creation. Although Panasonic assumes the role of leader in controlling the Ba at the Town Creation Council, partner companies also actively impart their own knowledge and expertise. The approach of So-Two mentioned above is a case in point. In other words, the Town Creation Council Ba is equipped with a certain amount of autonomy. This is an important point when analyzing value co-creation at Fujisawa SST. If Panasonic exercised total leadership and other partner companies simply acted according to the plan that Panasonic laid out in advance, any value that was then produced would only have embodied an "intended value" and it would be difficult to call it co-creation. It would be a collaboration akin to the mass game model described earlier. Fujisawa SST does not aim for a mass game type of collaboration but for a soccer match type of co-creation, or "unintended value". Even though Panasonic is the leader of the project, Panasonic also established a framework in which the spontaneity of members and autonomy are respected and valued. This means that Panasonic as the leader does not create value for Fujisawa SST on its own but aims to co-create it with partner companies.

The decision-making process at the Town Creation Council involves Panasonic making the overall plan and basic outline and having the knowledge and expertise of partner companies concerning individual areas reflected in the plan. Each partner company has its own area of expertise, and Panasonic plays its role as the leader of the Ba to link their knowledge to value creation.

---

1) The author conducted an interview investigation about Fujisawa SST at the Panasonic Tokyo Shiodome Building on April 2, 2014.

5. Conclusion

Finally, this paper will present some implications obtained from this discussion and some issues for future consideration. The message of this paper has been that the construction of a smart city represented a "Ba of co-creativity" among firms from different industries and that the creation of new value through value co-creation becomes a source of competitive advantage for the firms. In other words, whether it be the Positioning View or the Resource-based View, the common ground underlying these viewpoints is that existing theories of competitive advantage all focus on how companies can come out ahead in the competition with other companies. The viewpoint of this paper, however, has not been to basically see other companies as competitors but that value creation through co-creation with other companies brings competitive advantage to one's own company. It is probably safe to say that this represents a new paradigm with respect to competitive advantage.

Through Fujisawa SST as a case study, this paper aimed to verify its hypothesis that "co-creation builds competitive advantage". Though Fujisawa SST is a project still in progress and the work of verifying this hypothesis is not yet complete, a number of important implications can be identified. One of them is the role of the leader at a Ba. In the co-creation of value among companies, the role of the Ba leader who controls and manages the Ba is extremely important. If companies attempt to engage in co-creation without the presence of a clear Ba leader, it is possible that conflicts of interest will impede progress. Since Panasonic was the clear Ba leader in the case of Fujisawa SST, co-creation among member companies was able to proceed.

The fusion of "analysis" and "synthesis" can also be mentioned. In other words, it is necessary for the Ba leader to take the initiative for carefully aligning and combining the portion where top-down approaches are used and the portion where bottom-up approaches are emphasized for the sake of eliciting emergence from other members and establishing links with value creation. At Fujisawa SST, Panasonic exercises leadership and uses a top-down approach to proceed with the project, while at the Town Creation Council, autonomy is given to this Ba with the aim to incorporate the knowledge of partner companies. In other words, though Panasonic determines the overall framework, it follows a policy of non-intervention wherever possible so that partner companies can exercise their own expertise in individual areas.

As for future issues, whether co-creation between companies is successful or not depends on how open each company is to the other companies concerning their own knowledge, know-how and technologies. While debates on co-creation often are linked to debates on open innovation, in a nutshell, open innovation concerns the problem of what should be open or closed and to what extent. It of course takes a good judge of technology and know-how to suitably make such decisions: if it is open, it will be necessary to accurately project such matters as the possibilities of value co-creation and the assessments of any value that is created. The fruits of co-creation cannot be expected when companies are afraid that their technologies and know-how will be leaked to other companies and have a passive attitude toward open innovation. Having said that, however, it is not necessary for everything to be made open. In other words, there are human resources in all companies who are well-versed in both technology and strategy, and when relationships of mutual trust have been established through the Ba, it is possible that co-creation will bear fruit.

References

Barney, J. (1986), "Strategic Factor Markets: Expectations, Luck, and Business Strategy", *Management Science,* Vol. 32, No. 10, pp. 1231−1241.
Barney, J. (1991), "Firm Resources and Sustained Competitive Advantage", *Journal of Management,* Vol. 17, No. 1, pp. 99−120.
Chesbrough, H. (2003), "The Era of Open Innovation", *Sloan Management Review,* Vol. 44, No. 3, pp. 35−41.
Chesbrough, H. (2003), "Open Innovation: How Companies Actually Do it", *Harvard Business Review,* Vol. 81, No. 7, pp. 12−14.
Chesbrough, H. (2006), *Open Business Models: How to thrive in the New Innovation Landscape,* Harvard Business School Press: Boston, MA.
Christensen, C. M. (1997), *The Innovator's Dilemma: When New Technologies Cause Great Firms to Fail,* Harvard Business School Press: Boston, MA.
Mintzberg, H. (1973), "Strategy-making in Three Models", *California Management Review,* Vol. 16, No. 2, pp. 44−53.
Mintzberg, H. (1978), "Patterns in Strategy Formulation", *Management Science,* Vol. 24, No. 9, pp. 934−948.
Mintzberg, H. (1990), "The Design School: Reconsidering the Basic Premises of Strategic Management", *Strategic Management Journal,* Vol. 11, pp. 171−195.
Porter, M. (1980), *Competitive Strategy,* Free Press: New York.
Porter. M. (1985), *Competitive Advantage: Creating and Sustaining Superior Performance,* Free Press: New York.
Prahalad, C. K. and Ramaswamy, V. (2003), "The New Frontier of Experience Innovation", *Sloan Management Review,* Vol. 44, No. 4, pp. 12−18.
Prahalad, C. K. and Ramaswamy, V. (2004), "Co-creation Experience: The Next Practice in Value Creation", *Journal of Interactive Marketing,* Vol. 18, No. 3, pp. 5−14.
Rumelt, R. P. (1984), "Towards Strategic Theory of the Firm", in Lamb, R. (ed.), *Competitive*

Strategic Management, Prentice-Hall: Englewood Cliffs, NJ, pp. 556-570.

Rumelt, R. P. (1991), "How Much Does Industry Matter?, *Strategic Management Journal*, Vol. 12, No. 3, pp. 167-186.

Ueda, K. (ed.) (2004), *What is Co-Creation?,* Baifukan: Tokyo.

Vargo, S. L. and Lusch, R. F. (2004), "Evolving to a New Dominant Logic for Marketing", *Journal of Marketing*, Vol. 68, pp. 1-17.

Wernerfelt, B. (1984), "A Resource-based View of the Firm", *Strategic Management Journal*, Vol. 5, pp. 171-180.

Wernerfelt, B. (1995), "A Resource-based View of the Firm. Ten Years After", *Strategic Management Journal*, Vol. 16, pp. 171-174.

IV.

Ecological Modernization of Business Management: The Innovation of Environmental Management for Changing into Sustainable Society

Masatoshi YAMADA

1. Introduction

The global ecological crisis, which includes pollution and contamination, climate change, waste, resource depletion, the extinction of wildlife species and biodiversity crisis, has been a world-wide concern since the United Nations' Rio Declaration on Environment and Development in 1992. Countries recognized the necessity to change into a sustainable society, or a recycling-oriented and low-carbon society in order to solve the ecological crisis. There is much discussion on how to facilitate this transformation. Deep ecologists argue that we can achieve sustainability by radically changing from the current economic system of mass production-consumption-disposal. In contrast, shallow ecologists allege that we can make society more sustainable and solve the ecological crisis by partially modifying the existing economic system (Fukai, 2006). In reality, the various environmental measures that have been introduced and practiced by businesses and societies have not radically changing the system of mass production-consumption-disposal.

Sustainability as a concept, focuses on inter- and intra-generational ethics. Therefore, it may be difficult for single generation to judge the appropriateness of environmental measures in terms of constructing a sustainable society. That is particularly why the current generation must seek sustainability in business and society so as to enable a future generation to regard "conventional" measures as appropriate. The ecological crisis has shown insufficient signs of improvement for 25 years – since the Rio Declaration – at least.

How can we establish a sustainable society and solve the ecological crisis?

To answer the above question, this paper aims to understand the features of existing environmental management and discuss the direction of business management in this area. The following sections provide seven typologies of environmental management, the concept of *gradual innovation* as a form of environmental management innovation, and the relationship among the concepts of sustainability, corporate social responsibility (CSR), business ethics, and creating shred value (CSV). In addition, we refer to previous studies on sustainable management, innovation, and ecological modernization. The latter section of this paper reviews the group-wide environmental management programs of one particular modern company, the Ricoh Company Ltd. (hereafter referred to as Ricoh) as a case study.

2. Environmental management and ecological modernization

2-1. The concept of sustainability and the origin

The modern environmental protection movement is determined to achieve sustainability globally. Sustainability means to combine economic, social, and ecological rationalities propounded by the United Nations (UN) and International Union for Conservation of Nature and Natural Resources (IUCN). Sustainable development is a political concept that includes both generational and intergenerational ethics. The concept originated in the Declaration of the United Nations Conference on the Human Environment (1972). Principle 1 of the Declaration says:

> Man has the fundamental right to freedom, equality and adequate conditions of life, in an environment of a quality that permits a life of dignity and well-being, and he bears a solemn responsibility to protect and improve the environment for present and future generations.[1]

The IUCN states in their World Conservation Strategy (1980) that development is "the modification of the biosphere and the application of human, financial, living, and non-living resources to satisfy human needs and improve the quality of human life". It continues to say "For development to be sustainable, it must take account of social and ecological factors, as well

---

1) United nations Environmental Programme homepage, http://www.unep.org/Documents. Multilingual/Default.asp?DocumentID=97&ArticleID=1503&l=en (last access, Decmeber 31, 2016).

as economic ones; of the living and non-living resource base; and of the long-term as well as the short-term advantages and disadvantages of alternative actions".

In the context of these discussions on a new style of development until 1980, the report *Our Common Futures*, also known as the Brundtlrand Report, was presented by the World Commission on Environment and Development (WCED) in 1987. The report describes that one of the main causes of poverty in developing countries is environmental problems such as pollution and contamination, and that we have "the ability to make development sustainable to ensure that it meets the need of the present without compromising the ability of future generations to meet their own needs".

In fact, immediately after the United Nations Conference on Environment and Development (UNCED) in 1992, the Rio Declaration on Environment and Development and Agenda 21, the action plan of the Declaration, were announced. Almost at the same time, other international political and economic guidelines for environmental conservation and sustainable development were established, such as the United Nations Framework Convention on Climate Change (1992), Convention on Biological Diversity (1992), and the Forest Principle (1992). Rules for environmental protection were formulated in various countries and regions, represented by the Japanese government's Basic Environment Law (1993), and the Basic Law for Establishing a Recycling-based Society (2000). Thus, humanity had begun to share the challenges of solving the ecological crisis through sustainable development in order to build a sustainable society.

2-2. Diversity and the developmental process of environmental management

A corporation is a socio-economical organization that changes its management practices and methods in response to business environment consisting of the market, society, and nature. Today, corporate survival depends on both profitability and ecology because stakeholders of a corporation recognize the common challenge to establish a sustainable society and solve the ecological crisis. Environmental management is business management and is essential for adapting to this change of business environment.

Even when the common term "environmental management" is used, we can distinguish several variations of the term based on the different measures and management concepts employed against the ecological crisis. According to previous studies that focused on the chronological features of environmental management by Japanese firm, there are six phases of environmental management in firms over time: (1) *Ignoring*, or giving priority to only economic objectives as seen in the 1950s, (2) *Compliance*, intended to meet regulatory standards on aspects like pollution control as seen in the 1960s, (3) *Technological measures* for economic and ecological reasons in the 1970s, (4) *Social communication* in the form of corporate philanthropy and sponsorship in the 1980s, (5) *Environmentalism* as part of economic profit in the 1990s, and (6) the *Sustainable* phase which puts ecological objectives in the corporate mission. This has been seen as a main strategic issues in the 2000s (Suzuki, 2005, pp. 1−13). Similarly, another scholar describes the Japanese environmental management modes as (1) *compliance* − intended to meet regulatory standards as seen in the 1960s and 1970s; (2) *pollution control* − treat toxic substances in the 1960s and 1970s; (3) *Pollution Prevention* − reducing discharge of toxic substances and waste from 1980s; (4) *competitive strategic environmental measures* − a sources of competitive advantages in the 1990s; and (5) *sustainable* practices to contribute to society in the 2000s (Horiuchi, 2006, pp. 69−108).

A study on American environmental management since 1990s presents the following types: (1) *rejection* (of environmental management) which regards all management resources as measures for gaining profit; (2) *non-responsiveness*, when companies are only interested in profit and ignore the ecological impact, (3) *compliance*, or taking measures reactively to environmental regulations and social needs; (4) *efficiency*, recognizing competitive advantages with proactive environmental measures, (5) *Strategic proactivity*, or pursuing sustainability as a main strategic issue; and (6) *the sustaining corporation*, one that sees not only self-profit of corporation but also business function in society (Benn, Dunphy, and Griffiths, 2010).

Of the previous studies on environmental management described above, those that focus on Japanese corporations are characterized by attempting to clarify the chronological features of Japanese environmental management and the overall developmental process. On the other hand, the study on American corporation is characterized by stressing the diversity of environmental management that can exist the same period, and showing that the environmental management practice depends on decision making by the individual corporations.

Referring to the typologies of environmental management presented by these previous studies, we can say that there are six versions of environmental management for the present: *Ignoring, complying, controlling pollution, preventing pollution*, *strategic*, and *sustainable*. Except for "ignoring" and "sustainable", the other four versions of environmental management are similar in terms of taking environmental measures as a part of self-interest. Profit made when attempting to solve or improve social issues is called *enlightened self-interest*. The common feature among "complying", "controlling pollution", "preventing pollution", and "strategic" environmental management is not just to gain profit but to pursue enlightened self-interest.

Engaging in sustainable environmental management not only means to make light of profit but also to necessarily not propose self-interest through environmental measures because it is based on sustainability and this attempts to combine economic, social, and ecological rationalities. Even if profitability and environmental measures are related to each other, they are not in relation to the ends and means, and are in parallel structure as that of business goals. Leading companies all over the world have proactively established sustainable environmental management which combines profitability and ecology by implementing the concept of sustainability into business mission.

Here, for deeper understanding sustainable environmental management, we should focus on the concepts of sustainability, corporate social responsibility (CSR), business ethics, creating shared value (CSV), and ecological modernization for business management.

As mentioned above, sustainability is a concept for development that includes generational and intergenerational ethics. Therefore, the sustainability movement means taking ethical action. To achieve generational and intergenerational ethics, businesses must merge their economic and ecological rationalities.

Business management must share common beliefs with society. Ethics are norms for determining good and evil, and can differ among different situations, times, contexts, individuals, religious beliefs, families, social role models, and media etc. (Post, Lawrence, and Weber, 2002). Because the ecological crisis is a common and global-wide problem, environmental management to establish a sustainable society is a significant part of practicing business ethics.

CSV means to create shared value for the business and its stakeholders (Porter, Kramer, 2011). CSV is a socio-ecological function that a business demonstrates through practicing environmental management when business management requires sharing common sense with society; and ecological crisis is one of the common global-wide problems.

The concept of CSR is important for company to show CSV function. Because CSR emerges from the interaction between business and stakeholders (Post, Lawrence, and Weber, 2002). CSR management enables a company to recognize the ethical circumstances that are required to establish sustainability. Consequently, establishing sustainable environmental management means to demonstrate CSR management and ethical behavior from the perspective of CSV.

Next, ecological modernization is the social theory on building sustainability. There are "weak" and "strong" versions of ecological modernization depending on the approach to the ecological crisis (Fukai 2006; Gibbs, 1998). The essence of weak ecological modernization is the idea that we can achieve sustainability by partially modifying the existing socio-economical structure of mass production and mass consumption rather than by making radical changes. Weak ecological modernists believe in the significance of greening the economy, technocratic policy-making, technological solutions such as eco-products, and corporatism.

In contrast, the essence of strong ecological modernization is the advocacy of critical rethinking by tracing mass production and mass consumption to its structure. Strong ecological modernists insist that it is necessary to shift into reflective development process which radically changes the relationship between humanity and ecology by demanding innovative institution reform as well as eco-friendly products and policies.

Historically, leading companies in the world have practiced environmental management by adding sustainability as a management principle without radically changing the existing socio-economical structure of mass production and mass consumption. Therefore, the current environmental management is *weak sustainable environmental management* based on the process of weak ecological modernization. Because of the lack of improvement in the ecological crisis, there is possibility that strong ecological modernization will be required to establish a sustainable society. In this case, business management will have to transform into *stronger sustainable environmental management* in order to help bring about a radical change in the structure of the production and consumption. Accordingly, there are two kinds of sustainable ecological management based on weak sustainability and strength. So, to be accurate, as shown by Table 1, there are seven versions of environmental management: "Ignoring", "complying", "controlling pollution", "preventing pollution", "strategic", and "weak sustainable" and "strong sustainable".

Weak sustainable environmental management is the business management

Table 1: Seven Typologies of Environmental Management

Typology of Environmental management	The Response to The Ecological Crisis	Management Principle
Ignoring	• Being interested in gaining profit and other economic objectives • No measurements for ecology	Profitability • Pursuing economical rationality
Complying	• Taking measures reactively to meet regulatory standards on ecological crisis	Enlightened Self-interest • Pursuing profit made with contributing to solve or improve social issues
Controlling pollution	• Treating the toxic substances after exhausting them	
Preventing pollution	• Not treating but proactively reducing waste	
Strategic	• Putting measurements for ecological crisis in the main strategic plan in order to gain economical profit and competitive advantages	
Weak sustainable	• Creating self-profit while contributing to build sustainable society through measures for ecological objectives • Modifying and greening mass production and mass consumption system	Weak Sustainability • Economic, social, and ecological rationalities are not in relation of ends-and-means but in parallel structure as business goals. • Partially modifying the existing mass production and mass consumption system
Strong sustainable	• Creating self-profit while contributing to building a sustainable society through measures for ecological objectives • Restructuring and changing socio-ecological system radically	Strong Sustainability • Economic, social, and ecological rationalities are not in relation of ends-and-means but in parallel structure as business goals Changing radically the existing mass production and mass consumption system

which attempts to achieve sustainability by modifying the existing system of mass production-consumption-disposal. This type of environmental management approaches the ecological crisis with increasing eco-efficiency by taking measures such as developing eco-products and services, building and improving environmental management system – i. e., conforming to ISO14001 – and implementing green procurement etc. Further this is one of the driving forces of weak ecological modernization. Sustainable society established as the consequence of weak sustainable environmental management and weak ecological modernization is the new modern society which can build in the process of modernization.

Strong sustainable environmental management is the business management which intends to radically change the economic structure of mass production-consumption-disposal with improving eco-efficiency and eco-effectiveness by reforming the management system and industrial institutions. Strong sustainable environmental management is the requirement of strong ecological modernization. Sustainable society based on strong sustainable environmental management and strong ecological modernization is the postmodern capitalist society.

Modernization of capitalist society since the Industrial Revolution is seen in the process of transforming production from handicrafts and cottage industries to manufactured products in factory-based industries with a global division of labor.

We can assess sustainability and the strength of ecological modernization by observing whether sustainable environmental management creates or will create industry with revolutionary ecological harmony.

3. Gradual innovation: the feature of environmental management innovation

In the preceding section, we discussed seven typologies of environmental management. According to previous researches, especially in the case of Japanese companies, the development process of environmental management means to shift from one typology to another. This development is called *eco-innovation* (for example, Kinbara, Kaneko, Fujii, and Kawahara 2011) or *environmental management innovation* (for example, Kokubu, Iwata, 2010). However, the transformation process of environmental management is not necessarily clarified; so we do not always understand the features of an innovation. We can examine the direction and development of environmental management by understanding eco-innovation or environmental management innovation. Here, we review environmental management innovation, referring to previous studies on innovation and the concept of gradualism which is discussed in political economics.

3-1. Radical innovation separated from incremental innovation

It is commonly accepted that innovation means creating new value by changing product, service, and process including in production system, procurement method, sales method, and industrial organization. There are two kinds of innovation, namely radical innovation, which means discontinuous change, creating revolutionary and epoch-making outputs, and incremental innovation, which means continuous improvement to renew or upgrade conventional product, service, and process. Radical innovation and incremental innovation are dealt with as separate phenomena in popular theories. For example, the Abernathy-Utterback Model (A-U model), describes the kinds of innovation that occur frequently in each phase of the industry lifecycle (Utterback 1994). Many radical product innovations are made in fluid phase before a dominant design has been specified. Many of radical process innovations occur in the transitional phase when a product design is solidified and product innovations shift from radical into incremental. And in the specific phase after the design of product and process is complete, both product-level and process-level incremental innovations are managed. As represented by the A-U model, it is said that radical innovation and incremental innovation are different; radical changes cannot be realized through incremental improvements.

3-2. Continuity lurking in radical innovation

Study on innovator's dilemma presents the incrementalism perspective of innovation (Christensen 1997). According to the study, a company which managing sustaining innovation which means keeping to improve the existing technology often underestimates or neglects the significance of new technology that is developed and refined in the niche markets. When a firm penetrates the main market with the new technology and is supported by many customers, the new technology is disruptive for the existing dominant technology in the main market. The entrant can occur disruptive innovation against the dominant company in the main market when the new technology replaces the existing technology.

Disruptive innovation is a discontinuous change for a company managing sustaining innovation; however, the innovation is a continuous change and sustaining innovation for the entrant that has developed and refined the "disruptive" technology in the niche market. Therefore, an innovation can be both disruptive and sustaining, depending on the company's position. In other words, an innovation is radical or incremental depending on the participant.

However discontinuous a change may be, there is always an incremental process somewhere. This relevance between disruptive and sustaining innovations or radical and incremental innovations is useful for understanding eco-innovation or environmental management innovation which means the process of transformation of environmental management.

3-3. Environmental management innovation as gradual innovation

ISO14001 is an environmental management standard accepted among companies all over the world. As of 2014, according to the most recent data, 324,148 bodies have adopted ISO14001, including companies, NGO/NPOs, educational institutions like universities, governmental organizations, and local public bodies. Under ISO 14001, organizations are obligated to practice continuous improvement through a Plan-Do-Check-Action (PDCA) cycle. The objective is to realize the heretofore unthinkable greening of business management on a long term basis. This shows that modern environmental management aims to transform into radically different stage by stepping up increasingly through incremental innovation. This transformation process is the feature of environmental management innovation and cannot be understood from the typical outlook on radical innovation. Therefore, we need a new idea in order to examine the development process of environmental management.

The political concept of *gradualism* provides us a very useful perspective for examining the development process of environmental management. Gradualism is propelling reform incrementally while sequencing the necessary policies for radical innovation (Lindblom, and Woodhouse 1993, 林, 蔡, 李 1995, Mehran, Nordman, and Laurens 1996; and Hayes 2006). Gradualism directly drives incremental innovation; it is defined the process-oriented innovation with the intention to create radical innovation by an accumulation effect of the continuous improvements. In political economics, gradualism is exemplified by economic policies in developing country and countries in transition, such as retightening of environmental laws like the regulation of motor vehicles exhaust, or the vision for low-carbon society in Japan. Gradualism is an alternative strategy to "the development by radicalism" approach and "big-bang approach" which implement a comprehensive and simultaneous policy package recommended by the International Monetary Fund (IMF) and World Bank. In this paper, we regard gradualism as process-oriented and gradual innovation, which can be distinguished from radical and incremental innovations, but incorporates radical and incremental innovations as demon-

Figure 1: Gradual innovation of environmental management

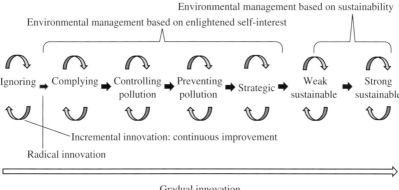

* ↻ shows the accumulation of incremental innovation such as continuous improvements in the phase.
* ➡ shows the radical innovation which evolves environmental management for the corporation.

strated in Figure 1.

Figure 1 is the conceptual diagram of the gradual innovation of the development process of environmental management. A corporation practices continuous improvement in a PDCA cycle in each phase of environmental management such as *Complying, Controlling pollution* etc. Continuous improvement practice enables a corporation to accumulate technology and know-how for solving the eco-crisis and discovering breakthroughs. If an organization has the intention, it can evolve its environmental management to the next higher phase by using accumulated technology and know-how. Through repetition, the corporation can practice higher levels of environmental management. In fact, many Japanese corporations have developed environmental management programs gradually moving from the *Ignoring* to *Strategic* stages in this manner. Today corporations are required to develop sustainable environmental management to help solve the eco-crisis although there is still an argument whether a weak sustainable or strong sustainable environmental management program is best.

4. Environmental management in Ricoh Group[2]

Ricoh Company, Ltd., established in 1936, is well known for environmen-

---
2) Unless specially noted, the description in this section is from Ricoh homepage, http://www.ricoh.co.jp/ (last access, December 31, 2016).

tal management practices. The group's companies share the following mission statement: "contributing to improve the quality life of people and construct a sustainable society by creating and supplying new available values continuously". Ricoh's environmental management has been lauded both by market and society. For example, since 2004, Ricoh has been on the FTSE4Good Index Series, which measures the performance of companies demonstrating strong environmental, social, and governance (ESG) practices. It is also ranked on the Dow Jones Sustainability Indices, which assess CSR management from the perspectives of economy, environment, and society and has been rated Prime B+ on the Oekom Corporate Rating, which selects excellent companies in terms of sustainability performance.

At the end of fiscal 2015, the Ricoh group recorded gross sales 2,209 billion yen, with 109,361 employees, and operations in about 200 countries or regions. The company's business domain and the products is divided into three areas: (1) the imaging and solution field which supplies imaging equipment such as multi-functional printers (MFPs) copiers, and related consumables, support service, and software, (2) the industry field which makes and sells products for business such as thermal media, semiconductors, and electric equipment units, and (3) other fields such as digital cameras, omnidirectional cameras, and watches. Imaging and Solutions is the core business for Ricoh Group, and accounts for 89.3 % of the total annual sales of the group. Ricoh divides this core business into three categories, including office imaging, production printing, and network system solution. Office imaging is the most competitive business, and accounts for 64.8% in total annual sales of the Ricoh group. Competitiveness is based on positive promotion of group-wide environmental management of the Ricoh Group.

4-1. Environmental management as corporate strategy and CSR

Ricoh and the group companies practice environmental management as part of their strategy and CSR. They manage environmental measures with their original strategic management by objectives (MBO), which adds environmental measures to the four perspectives of balanced scorecard,[3] (finan-

---

3) Performance evaluation system developed by Robert S. Kaplan and David P. Norton in 1992. The characteristics of this system are establishing financial and non-financial goals, evaluation indexes, targets, specific programs based on vision and strategy. Recently, this performance evaluation system is discussed as a strategic management system. See Kaplan, Robert S. and Norton, David P. (1996) *The Balanced Scorecard: Translating Strategy into Action*, Harvard Business Review Press, and Kaplan, Robert S. and Norton, David P. (2008) *The Execution Premium: Linking Strategy to*

cial, customer, internal business process, and learning and growth).

Ricoh Group's basic strategies are (1) creating customer values, (2) streamlining management, and (3) creating and focusing on eco-solution business. The customer values referred to mean supplying user-friendly products and services enabling environmental preservation, and helping to customer create knowledge.

One of Ricoh Group's strategic issues is to develop, produce, and sell eco-friendly products and services and to supply solutions for environmental preservation through increasing customer value. The main line of their business is multifunctional printers and copiers for industrial use. They must help their customers increase productivity and gain competitive advantage to survive in the copier market. Actually, the aim of the printer and copier business is to contribute to the increase in the productivity of the customer.

Ricoh Group wants to contribute to constructing a sustainable society and increasing corporate value. To do so, they distinguish three CSR domains: (1) basic social responsibility, such as compliance, (2) contribution to solving social issues through business (or CSV, creating shared value), and (3) proactive social actions through awareness of their obligations, such as corporate philanthropy. They call the second domain CSV. Solving social issues includes improvement of the social and industrial infrastructure and quality of life, respect for human rights, development of the next generation as member of a sustainable society, protection for the sustainability of ecology, and promotion of social and business activity against outstanding issues. Corporate growth at the Ricoh Group is realized by new market development, acquisition of innovative marketing methods, human resource development, enhancing employee loyalty, and increasing the bland value.

The Ricoh Group made a CSR charter in 2003. The charter consists of four priority areas as follows: (1) faithful business operations – supplying products and services which meet customer needs, ensuring open competition and fair trade, prohibiting insider trading and antisocial behavior, managing corporate secrets, protection and properly using assets and intellectual property (2) harmony with and respect for the environment, (3) respect for basic human rights, and (4) harmony with society by making social contributions and communicating with stakeholders such as customers, stockholders, employees, business accounts, and local communities.

From the above, the Ricoh Group tries to increase customer value, to

---

Operations for Competitive Advantage, Harvard Business Review Press.

streamline its business, and reinforce profitability through strategic environmental management based on the original CSR.

4-2. Road map for environmental management at Ricoh Group

According to the Ricoh group, there are three types of corporate environmental practices, namely environmental response, environmental conservation, and environmental management. First, environmental response means to take defensive and passive behaviors in absorbing regulation, competitor's action, customer needs, and then following the trends in administrative circumstances. Second, environmental conservation means to choose behaviors based on a sense of mission as a corporate citizen, and to take independent and proactive measurs such as an energy saving, 3R, pollution and contamination prevention, and reforming the ways of thinking of the employees about the ecological crisis and business. And third, environmental management is business management that combines environmental conservation and profitability. Environmental conservation means implementing actions that promote quality, cost, and delivery (QCD), such as part count reduction and improved working processes, improved rates of yield and operation, and the development of clean technology.

Focusing on third type of corporate environmental practices, Ricoh group draws a road map to sustainable environmental management. The map shows that Ricoh establishes sustainable environmental management by gradually developing their environmental management. There are three phases in the process of development of sustainable environmental management. Phase 1 is creating corporate culture and system of full-participation. In this phase, to create the culture of participation by all employees in environmental management, Ricoh group implemented zero emission and acquired ISO14001 certification on factories and offices.

Phase 2 constitutes of the creation of successful business cases and systems balance gaining profits and protecting the environment. To establish efficient and effective environmental management system (EMS), the Ricoh group uses a strategic MBO with a balanced scorecard to construct a business model based on an ecological perspective in each department. Ricoh develops eco-products and practices green marketing, and supports suppliers to construct EMS to promote green procurement.

When attaining Phase 3, sustainable environmental management is established. At this phase, the Ricoh group creates environmental business systems by integrating profitability and ecology. By implementing thorough environmental measures in phase 1 and 2, they set a goal of economic effects, developed indicators of evaluation for environmental management, and deploy a sustainable vision.

The Ricoh Group set environmental principles with basic policies and agendas in 1992 and revised them in 2008. The 2008 version says: "Environmental preservation is our mission, and we grasp that environmental preservation and administrative behavior are coaxial, and engage in the preservation, on our own initiative". The 2008 version of the agenda is shown in the Table 2.

Table 2: Agendas for Environmental Management at Ricoh Group

- Setting higher goals: Gaining value by complying with legal restrictions and anticipating societal expectations

- Developing clean technology: Creating customer value, and developing and spreading ecofriendly technology in society.

- Activity by all: continuously improving preventive measure against pollution and contamination and improving ways to utilize energy and resources.

- Product lifecycle: reducing the impact on the environment in the whole of business process.

- Aware improvement through active learning

- Contributing for society: contributing a sustainable society by participating in and/or supporting environmental protection movement.

- Communication: cooperating with stakeholders and obtaining social trust.

Source: Ricoh homepage, http://www.ricoh.co.jp (last access, December 31, 2016).

4-3. Transition of organization for environmental management at Ricoh

Ricoh organizes environmental managing committee and the environmental measurement committees in order to develop gradually sustainable management. The environmental managing committee began as the Environmental Measure Promotion Office in 1976, aiming at pollution control by managing chemical substances in products and in the factory. In response to the shift in focus from pollution problems to an overall ecological crisis, Ricoh reorganized the Environmental Measure Promotion Office into Environmental Office in 1990. Ricoh, in order to take measures against the ecological crisis, organized six committees as shown in Table 3. The Environmental Office set environmental management policies in 1992 as mentioned above, completed the "Comet Circle" concept (see below for further details) in 1994, and acquired ISO14001 in 1995. The Environmental Office was reorganized into the Social Environmental Office in 1998 to promote environmental management and implement strategic MBO. Moreover, Ricoh renewed the Social Environmental Office as the Society and Environmental Division in 2001. Today, Ricoh practices environmental management and measures against the ecological crisis under the Society and Environmental Division and six committees as shown in Table 3.

Table 3: Six Environmental Committees at Ricoh: Purposes and Achievements

Fluorinated Gasses Control Measures Committee:
・Abolished specified chlorofluorocarbon in 1993

Product Design Committee:
・Planning and promoting the design for the environment (DfE)
・Set the project team for framing recyclable design policy in 1992
・Framed the recyclable design policy in 1993
・Set the project team for energy-saving products in1997

Clean Technology Committee:
・Planning and promoting new business for environmental conservation
・Investigating the technology for environmental conservation

Ecological Mark Committee:
・Promoting acquisition of the label for environmental protective products
・Acquired The Blue Angle
・Enhancing measuring equipment

Recycling Committee:
・Collection and disposal of used product and promotion of recycling
・Developing the recycling system and roots

Environmental Improvement Committee:
・Reducing the impact on environment from plant and office
・Promoting reducing waste, energy saving, and management of chemical substance

Source: Tani, Tatsuo (2012), p. 136.

4-4. Environmental management system and planning

Ricoh manages to combine environmental preservation and profitability as part of its corporate strategy and CSR, and tries to achieve sustainability through gradual development of environmental management under the initiatives of environmental managing committee and the six committees. Ricoh sets goals of environmental management with the backcasting method and ISO14001. The backcasting method and ISO14001 allows Ricoh to plan the necessary behaviors and measures in the short-term based on long- and medium-term objectives and vision.

The Ricoh group devised the Ecological vision 2050 to restore global

Table 4: Long- and medium-term objectives of Ricoh Group's environmental management by domain

Domain: Saving energy and prevention of global warming for climate change
• Objective by 2050: To reduce the input of new resources by 87.5% from 2007 levels and complete to conclude reduction and substitution non-renewable resources such as crude oil, copper, and chromium etc.
• Objective by 2020: To reduce the input of new resources and by 25% from 2007 levels.

Domain: Saving resources and recycling for recycling-based society
• Objective by 2050: To reduce total CO_2 emissions by 87.5% from 2007 levels.
• Objective by 2020: To reduce total CO_2 emissions by 30% from 2007 levels.

Domain: Prevention of pollution and contamination through development of eco-friendly products and business process
• Objective by 2020: To achieve minimizing the environmental risk from chemical substances on life cycle by 2020 based on the Strategic Approach to International Chemicals Management (SAICM)

Domain: Biodiversity conservation for improvement of regenerative capacity of nature
• Objective: Constructing sustainable framework for managing forest

Source: Ricoh homepage, http://www.ricoh.co.jp (last access, December 31, 2016).

ecological balance, namely, planet-people-profit (3P) balance. They establish long-term objectives for the reduction of environmental impact until 2050 based on this vision. Next, they set medium-term objectives for the reduction of environmental impact until 2020 followed by a three-year environmental action plan.

Ricoh operates a plan-do-check-action (PDCA) cycle in reference to ISO14001 to fortify group-wide sustainable EMS. In the process of group-wide planning, they look to the Ecological vision 2050 and environmental principles of the basic policies and agendas. The group-wide process is equivalent to divisional and company-wide PDCA cycles. Each division and group company also utilize ISO 14001 to plan and practice a three-year environmental action plan and continuously improve upon their existing EMS.

Through divisional and company-wide EMS, the Ricoh group can develop and operate organizational procedures, environmental education, and clean technology in their own businesses. The Ricoh group confirms achievement of the environment action plan with various eco-balance indicators and environmental accounting, and review the EMS.

The Ricoh group defines four domains of environmental actions, and sets objectives of each domain with the backcasting method. Table 4 shows the four domains and the objectives. We will discuss concrete measures of products and process for these domains.

4-5. Saving energy and prevention of global warming of products and process

The Ricoh group has adopted measures against energy over-consumption and climate change through such measures as developing eco-products, pursuing flexibility of production, and improving logistical efficiency. One of Ricoh's main products, the multi-functional printer (MFP) and copier, operates only 5% of the time in *use* phase, and remains in *standby* for 95% of the time, reducing power consumption in both the operation and stand-by states. Ricoh developed a power saving mode that puts the machine automatically in sleep mode to reduce energy consumption in a stand-by state. However, Ricoh realized that if it takes a long time to restart from a sleep state, the mode would hardly be used, so the company developed a lower temperature fixable toner[4] and efficient heat conducting parts that shorten the time required to start up Ricoh calls Quick-Start-Up (QSU) technology and it enables the MFP and copier to reduce power consumption down by 22%.

The development of QSU technology lead to the evolution of a strategic eco-product the *imagio* in 2001. The *Imagio* Neo 350 / 450 is the first generation of Ricoh's eco-products in the middle or low speed monochrome copier range. This copier series is equipped with heaters that control the lowering of thermal capacity and dispersion of printing density by down-sheet metal gauging of fixing roller. This copier improves thermal conductivity utilizing a sponge pressure roller. By developing this product, Ricoh has succeeded in being the first company in the world to provide a middle or low speed monochrome copier that reduces start-up time by 10 seconds when returning from a power saving mode to a normal mode.

The second generation of Ricoh's strategic eco-product, the *imagio* Neo 752 / 602ec series is a high-speed monochrome copier introduced in 2003. This copier series, by using energy charged in electrical storage device capacitors during power saving mode, can suppresses the temperature drop of the fixing roller. Though this product, Ricoh also succeeded in providing a high speed monochrome copier that reduces start-up time by 10 seconds when returning to a normal mode from a power saving mode.

In 2008, Ricoh began selling the *Imagio* MP C5000 / C4000 series color

---

[4] Standard toner was fixed at 120℃ to 180℃ until Ricoh was successfully developed a lower temperature fixable toner. The printer has improved picture quality at a 30℃ lower fixation temperature.

copier, its third generation eco-product. This copier series improves heat transfer efficiency significantly with a fixing device that uses a new Induction Heating (IH) technology. Ricoh succeeded in reducing start-up time in a color copier by 9.9 seconds when returning from a power saving mode to a normal mode.

The fourth generation of Ricoh's strategic eco-product, the *imagio* MP C5002 / C4002 / C3302 / C2802 series, is new color copier, which it has supplied since 2012. This copier series improves heat transfer efficiency by drastically lowering the thermal capacity of the fixing roller, and with a halogen heater system that directly heats the fixing roller. The QSU technology evolved from heater-roller system. The start-up time when returning from a power saving mode to a normal mode was significantly improved by 9.1 seconds in 2012, and is now less than 5 seconds. The development of QSC technology, on the whole, has contributed to an upgrade in environmental performance and efficiency, and has created customer value.

Ricoh has forgone a conveyor line and gradually shifted to a layout-free cart production system since 1999. Office automation equipment reached a peak in market growth in 1985. At that time, Ricoh produced similar devices in large quantities with a conveyor line. With the diversification of customer needs and the emergence of the compound copier machine, Ricoh gradually shifted to various kinds of small quantity production to cope with the change in the business environment. This gradual shift of production method and implementation of a cart production system in 1999 enabled the company to change the layout of line corresponding to volume, and to make reductions in several areas: power consumption (by 99%), the number of stock in process, lead-time, maintenance time , and space needed for each assembly area (by 70% to 80%). Today, Ricoh operates flexible and energy-saving production system using carts.

The Ricoh group has also reduced energy use and CO_2 emissions in logistics. Ricoh had procured by transporting the necessary parts and materials by several trucks from each supplier. On occasions of small transaction volumes, loading efficiency was lower. To solve this inefficiency, Ricoh group uses the "Milk Run" method. This method allows for picking up parts distribution with fewer trucks. As a result, logistics has improved loading efficiency from 30% to 60%, shortened total distance traveled, and reduced annual CO_2 of 310 tons – corresponding to about 30% of total annual emission.

4-6. Saving resources and recycling for recycling-based society

The Ricoh Group strives to restore ecological balance by combining planet, people, profit (3P balance). According to Ricoh, the three activities of manufacturing, consumption, and recycling have a disruptive impact on the environment because we have a low awareness of society and economy in ecology. The Ricoh Group propels its socio-economic business endeavors based on the concept of society-and-economy in ecology to contribute to the conservation of ecology and saving of resources, and approaches sustainable management which corrects the three activities of manufacturing, consumption, and recycling within the allowable range of ecosystem.

Ricoh has developed long-lifecycle products that reduce ink consumptions. The older type cartridge injected extra ink as it was pumped by the micro motor. To save excess consumption of ink, Ricoh developed a new type of cartridge with a built-in tubing pump to reduce ink usage. More efficient usage of ink also means a long duration of product lifetime for the customer by reducing waste.

Ricoh has developed both long-lifecycle eco-products with design for recycling (DfE) and a resource circulation system called "Comet Circle". In order to improve the efficiency of the recycling process and recycling rate, since 1994, Ricoh has developed and implemented compatible labels on their MFP and copiers that enable MFP and copiers to be recycled without quality degradation of the recycled-products, save the peeling process of labels, to reduce the peeled label waste and its disposal. The Ricoh group has set original internal standards for recycled-copier business in terms of recycling rate and utilizing reused parts. Since 1997, Ricoh has recycled and remanufactured copiers, which have over 80% reused parts and can be recycled again. over 95%. Since Ricoh sold the first recycled-copier in 1997, they has expanded the range of the re-built products.

Ricoh applies eco-labels on their products according to the codes of ISO14020 to ISO14024. There are three types of eco labels that Ricoh uses: Type I is authenticated as eco-friendly by the third party. Type II is a self-declared eco label by the corporation according to the Ricoh group's internal standards on reuse rate of parts. Type III shows lifecycle assessment (LCA) data that allow the customer to judge whether the product is eco-friendly or not.

The Ricoh group established their original recycling system, the "Comet Circle", to reduce the effects on the environment in the total life cycle of products. Products such as MFP and copiers are used by customers after being fabricated through a series of procurement-manufacturing-sales processes. In the "use" phase, maintenance service ensures longevity as much as possible. Products disposed of by the user are sent to a recycle service. If a disposed product can be reusable as a recycled-product, it will be sold again to another customer by a distributor after going through a product-recycling center. If it is not reusable as a recycling-product, it will be sent to the recycling center to be disassembled, and the parts will be separated into reusable and non-reusable parts of new MFP or copiers. Parts that are reusable are sent to the manufacturer of finished goods after going through a parts recycling center. Non-reusable parts are shredded to be made into new raw material or sent to material recycling firms, petrochemical plants or smelters, or recovered as thermal energy. Only when materials cannot be reused, recycled, or used to recover energy, will they go to final disposal companies.

Through the "Comet Circle", Ricoh Group aims at pushing the 3R – reduce, reuse, recycle – toward establishing a sustainable society. The Basic Law for Establishing the Recycling-based Society was established in 2000 in Japan. Acts aims at recycling various kinds of products have also existed since the 1990s. Ricoh has anticipated the tightening of regulations when they developed "Comet Circle" and DfE in the 1990s, and has monetized the recycling process since 2006.

4−7. Prevention of pollution and contamination through development of eco-friendly products and business process

Restrictions against Chemicals were declared by the EU – European Union – in 2007. One of the restrictions is the RoHS – Restriction of Hazardous Substances – Directive. The RoHS Directive is an EU regulation to restrict the launch of products with six regulated pollutants: lead, hexavalent chromium, cadmium, mercury, compounds of these pollutants, polybrominated biphenyl, and polybrominated diphenylether. Another regulation, the REACH – Registration, Evaluation, Authorization and Restriction of Chemicals – requires products exported into the EU to be registered and with the disclosure of information on toxic chemicals.

Ricoh has managed chemical substances with environmental impact, which can be used for products since 1993. The Ricoh Group has prepared for the tightening of regulations by focusing and managing chemicals in addition to the regulated pollutants. The Ricoh Group has positioned the EU area as one of its main markets; so, with the RoHS Directive and REACH as triggers, Ricoh started with green procurement in 2006 by establishing and operating its CMS – Chemical Substance Management System – with suppliers to monitor and manage chemical substance that have an environmental impact. Since 2006, the Ricoh Group companies also operate the MSC – Management System for Chemical – so that all members of the group manage and understand the restrictions of prohibited or controled substances.

Ricoh is one of the promotors of Joint Article Management Promotion-Consortium (JAMP). The Consortium, founded in 2006, has the objective to establish and penetrate mechanisms to facilitate disclosure or transfer of information on chemicals in products across the supply chain.[5] As of 2016, the consortium has 439 members. Ricoh has already constructed a mechanism for tracing and managing chemicals contained in products and parts by utilizing the JAMP server, which stores information on chemicals and its sharable among manufacturer, parts makers, material suppliers, and chemical makers. Today, Ricoh supports and certifies the group members and suppliers to establish and refine CMS and EMS with its own guidelines for transacting with Ricoh under its standards of green procurement.

In the pursuit of risk aversion and international competitiveness, Ricoh has been proactive in managing chemicals prior to the current regulations. Consequently, Ricoh's management behavior has led to group-wide readiness for the enactment of the REACH and RoHS Directive.

4-8. Environmental measures as social activity

Since 1999, Ricoh has initiated a project for conservation of forest ecosystem in collaboration with NGOs and local communities in Ghana, Malaysia, the Philippines, Brazil, Russia, and China among others.[6] With the objective to construct a sustainable framework for managing forests that combines conservation of the local forest ecosystem and a self-sustaining life for local residents, Ricoh is driving the plans, management, and practice of reforesting through education of volunteer environmental leaders, investigations on ecosystems, and tree planting campaigns.

There are 5 stages in this project: preparation, start-up, cooperation, self-support, and goal. The preparation stage sets a roadmap and plans a partnership with a cooperation organization. Ricoh joins in making the vision, and provides funds for the project and collaborative planning in this stage. In the start-up stage, workshops for residents are held to educate them and the local

---

5) JAMP homepage, http://www.jamp-info.com/ (last access, December 31, 2016).
6) Ministry of the Environment homepage, http://www.env.go.jp/nature/shinrin/fpp/partnership/partnership_case/ricoh.html (last access, December 31, 2016).

ecology is investigated. Ricoh inspects in the field, has discussions with the residents, and provides education tools. The native residents begin to join in the activities for managing the forest in the cooperation stage. Collaboration with stakeholders other than the local residents is also started at this stage through a management plan and workshops. Ricoh continuously inspects in the field, creates dialogue, and participates in workshops at this stage. The self-supporting stage comes when forestry management methods are established as follows; (1) regenerative and sustainable forest management by the local residents such as agroforestry, fair-trade, and eco-tourism, and (2) conservative and sustainable agriculture and forestry management through thorough legal protection such as trusts, setting wildlife preservation area, and eco-tourism. At the goal stage, a sustainable framework for managing the forest is established and operated by an initiative of the local residents in order to ensure conservation of the local forest ecosystem and biodiversity. Ricoh exists the activities when the project reaches the self-supporting and goal stages.

5. Management issues or challenges for changing into sustainable society

The preceding section reviewed the group-wide environmental management by Ricoh Co., Ltd. for the purpose of understanding the features and direction of its existing environmental management. The environmental management of Ricoh shows that environmental management is a strategic and corporate social responsibility issue. The Ricoh Group practices various measures against ecological crisis on a product-level and a process-level in order to (1) save energy and prevent global warming, (2) save resources and recycle them, (3) prevent pollution and contamination, and (4) promote biodiversity. The measures of (1) saving energy and prevention of global warming and (2) saving resources and recycling are practices of the basic strategy and CSR for creating shared value of at the Ricoh Group. In contrast, the measures of (3) preventing pollution and contamination is part of risk aversion, and (4) biodiversity conservation is a volunteer activity at the present time. Table 5 shows the relationship between the basic strategies and CSR and Ricoh Group's environmental measures.

Ricoh Group attempts to manage the gradual refinement of environmental management with methods like backcasting and continuous improvement by PDCA cycle in order to combine profitability and environmental measures.

Table 5: Relationship between the basic strategies and CSR and Ricoh Group's environmental measures

Strategy	Environmental measurements
Creating customer values	• Developing and improving QSU technology and lower temperature fixable toner; product-level measures for saving energy and prevention of global warming • Product development and improvement to reduce ink usage; product-level measures for saving resources
Streamlining management	• Implementation and improvement of cart production system; process-level measures for saving energy and prevention of global warming • Optimization of logistics by milk run method; process-level measures for saving energy and prevention of global warming • Optimization of recycling process with DfE; product-level and process-level measures for saving resources and recycling
Creating and focusing on eco-solution business	• Creating recycling business via Comet Circle; process-level measures for saving resources and recycling
CSR	Environmental measurements
Risk aversion	• Managing chemical substances; product-level and process-level measures for prevention of pollution and contamination • Implementing and promoting green procurement; process-level measures for prevention of pollution and contamination • Establishing and refining group-wide sharing information system; process-level measures for prevention of pollution and contamination
Contribution to social activity	• Joining the project for conservation of forest ecosystem in collaboration with NGOs and local communities; biodiversity conservation as volunteer activity

This environmental management has a certain generality, taking into account of diffusion of ISO14001 all over the world.

The existing studies on business administration, as mentioned in this paper, discriminate between radical innovation and incremental innovation, and say radical innovation can't be caused by incremental innovation and the accumulation effect of it. With this commonly accepted view of innovation, we can't explain the development process of environmental management; the management practice by corporation such as Ricoh to colligate radical innovation and incremental.

Gradual innovation, asserted in this paper, is the new concept of innovation that can explain the development process of environmental management such as seen in the Ricoh Group. The feature of gradual innovation is to accumulate many improvement activities and develop them over time. In other words, the target of gradual innovation is to cause strategically radical innovation by accumulation effect of incremental innovation.

A corporation proactively practicing environmental management pursues incremental, radical, and gradual innovations simultaneously on product-level and process-level. Table 6 shows the relationship between the types of innovation and environmental measures at Ricoh Group.

Table 6: Relationship between the types of innovation and environmental measures at Ricoh Group

Type of innovation	Environmental measures
Incremental	· Development of QSU technology · Reduction of ink consumption of MFP and copiers · Implement of logistics with milk run method · Development of DfE
Radical	· Establishment of recycling process (Comet Circle) · Management system and sharing information system on chemicals
Gradual	· Implement of cart production system · Monetization of recycling business · Joining in the project for conservation of forest ecosystem

The environmental measures track incremental innovations that will create heterogeneous and brand new business and value through an accumulation effect. The measures will be regarded as radical innovation caused by incremental or gradual innovation as of the time. In fact, Ricoh's recycling business which was started in 1994 has been monetized since 2006. The forest ecosystem conservation project that Ricoh has joined will gradually establish a framework of sustainable forest management.

New environmental measures may be required depending on ecological crisis. For example, Ricoh Group's recycling process and management system for chemicals is a de novo business since 1990s. These practices can be called radical innovation under environmental management.

Corporations such as Ricoh attempt to upgrade its environmental management through various environmental measures. The revolution in the style of environmental management can be regarded as a radical innovation in the sense of the shift into a different stage, as already shown Figure 1. In examining the development of environmental management over the longer timespan, we can say the development process is the succession of the emergence of radical change from incremental modification. When we examine this development process of environmental management represented by Ricoh Group, the concept of gradual innovation is effective.

References

Journal, books and articles

■ English

Benn, Suzanne, Dexter, Dunphy, and Andrew, Griffiths (2014), *Organizational Change for Corporate Sustainability, 3rd edition,* Routledge: Oxon.

Christensen, Clayton M. (1997), *The Innovator's Dilemma: When New Technologies Cause Great Firms to Fail,* Harvard Business School Press: The USA.

David, Gibbs (1998), "Ecological Modernisation: A Basis for Regional Development?", (Seventh International Conference of The Greening of Industry Network *Partnership And Leadership: Building Alliances for a Sustainable Future),* Rome, 15-18 November.

Kaplan, Robert S. and Norton, David P. (1996), *The Balanced Scorecard: Translating Strategy into Action,* Harvard Business Review Press: Boston.

────── (2008), *The Execution Premium: Linking Strategy to Operations for Competitive Advantage,* Harvard Business Review Press: Boston.

Lindblom, Charles E. and Woodhouse, Edward J. (1993), *The Policy-making Process* (third editon), Prentice Hall: New Jersey.

Mehran, H., Quintyn, M., Nordman, T., and Laurens, B. (1996), *Monetary and Exchange System Reforms in China: An Experiment in Gradualism,* Occasional paper 141, International Monetary Fund, Washington DC, September.

Michael T. Hayes (2006), *Incrementalism and Public Policy,* University Press of America: New York.

Post, James E., Lawrence, Anne T., and Weber, James (2002), *Business And Society: Corporate Strategy, Public Policy, Ethics* (Tenth edition), Irwin: The McGraw-Hill.

Porter, Michael E, and Kramer Marck R. (2011), "Creating Shared Value", *Harvard Business Review,* January, pp. 2-17.

The International Union for Conservation of Nature and Natural Resources, The United Nations Environmental Programme, and The World Wildlife Fund (1980), *World Conservation Strategy: Living Resource Conservation for Sustainable Development,* The International Union for Conservation of Nature and Natural Resources.

Utterback, James M. (1994), *Mastering of The Dynamics of Innovation,* Harvard Business School Press: Boston.

World Commission on Employment and World Commission on Environment and Development (1987), *Our Common Future: The World Commission on Environment And Development.* Oxford University Press: New York.

■ Japanese

Horiuchi, Ikuzou (2006), "Senryakuteki kankyou keiei", in Horiuchi, Ikuzou and Mukai, Thuneo *Jissen Kankyou Keiei Ron (Practicing Theory of Environmental Management),* Tokyo Keizai

Publication.

Kokubu, Katuhiko and Hiyoki, Iwata (2010), "Kankyou Keiei Inobeishon no Bunseki Shikaku (Analytical Perspectives of Environmental Management Innovation)", in Ueda, Kazuhiro and Kokubu, Katsuhiko (eds.), *Kankyou Keiei Inobeishon no Riron to Jissen (Theory And Practice for Innovation of Environmental Management)*, Chuo Keizai-sha: Tokyo.

Suzuki, Kouki (2005), "Kankyou Keiei no Shiteki kousatsu", in Takahashi, Yoshiaki and Suzuki, Kouki *Kankyou Mondai no Keieigaku (Business Administration against Ecological Crisis)*, Minerva Shobou: Kyoto.

Yamada, Masatoshi (2012), "Kankyou Keiei no Dankaiteki Inobeishon (Gradual Innovation in Environmental Management)", in Hayashi, Masaki (ed.), *Gendai Kigyou no Shakaisei (Sociality of Modern Corporation)*, Chuo University Press: Tokyo.

Fukai, Shigeko (2006), *Jizokukanou na sekairon (Theories on A Sustainable World)*, Nakanishiya Publication: Kyoto.

Kinbara, Tatsuo Kaneko, Shinji, Fujii, Hidemichi and Kawahara, Hiromitu (2011), *Kankyou keiei no Nichibei Hikaku (Environmental Management)*, Chuo Keizai-sha: Tokyo.

Tani, Tatsuo (2012), *Kankyou Keiei Nyumon (Handbook for Practice of Environmental Management)*, Shuwa System: Tokyo.

■ Chinese

林毅夫，蔡昉，李周 (1995)，中國的奇蹟：發展戰略與經濟改革，中文大學出版社．

Websites

Joint Article Management Promotion-Consortium homepage, http://www.jamp-info.com/ (last access December 31, 2016).

Ministry of the Environment homepage, http://www.env.go.jp/ (last access December 31, 2016).

Ricoh homepage, http://www.ricoh.co.jp/ (last access December 31, 2016).

United nations Environmental Programme homepage, http://www.unep.org/ (last access December 31, 2016).

V. How Japanese Paper Manufacturers Resolving Social Desire: Evaluating a Japanese Paper Manufacturer's Waste Paper Usage Condition

Youngjin SON

1. Introduction

In the 2000s, the 'sustainability' became an important topic in the practical aspects of the economics, the business administration, and the business management. However, the meaning of the sustainability varies by principal agent. In the aspect of a country, the question is if a welfare state, which persistently requires an increase in the tax revenue in the course of the expansion of the public social security system, can sustain. We are living in the era where the environmental and social issues have become as important as the sale. Under this environment, companies are mandated to manage sustainably. On the other hand, to sustain a life has become a serious problem to some individuals and families because the polarization of income has been exacerbated.

The creating shared value (CSV)[1] has emerged as a strategy to maintain the sustainability from the standpoint of a company and a society. The CSV is a policy and an operating action to improve the competitiveness of a company as well as develop economic and social values. It caused a global sensation in the business, the media, and the academic world of business administration. Moreover, many Japanese companies have paid attention to the CSV.

However, there are criticisms that the concept of the CSV is ambiguous, the strategy of creating the CVS is not clear, and it is not easy to distinguish

---
1) Porter, M. E. and Kramer, M. R. (2011), "Creating Shared Value", *Harvard Business Review*, 89 (1/2), pp. 67–70.

the CSV from the CSR.[2] Muhammad Yunus stated, "The CSV directed the vector of a company from the profit-oriented to the people-and planet-oriented... (omission) ... However, a company in the capitalism must have the highest priority on the profit. Consequently, a company can pursue the social benefit only within the possible extent.... (omission) ... I believe that the CSV will end up a slight expansion of CSR concept".[3] Echoing his argument, the core criticism on the CSV is that when the social value and the economic value conflict, it is inevitable of a company to make a decision favoring the economic value. In addition, a company will invest in a social issue, which is relatively easy to resolove.[4]

In other words, it can be said that the CSV. underestimates a tough decision of a company regarding the trade-off between economics and sociality, which a company frequently encounter in real business, remains in simple and wishful thinking, and does not provide a solid strategy how to modify the business behavior pattern.[5]

As reviewed, the CSV holds possibilities to cause various issues due to its exclusive property, which is included in its concept. Nonetheless, the CSV has been deployed at a very fast speed and studies on the CSV reproduced success stories of the CSV expansively.

However, it is required to examine how the CSV is unfolded with focusing on what kind of issue. In particular, it is essential to review in-depth what kind of a social value the CSV tries to make a company deliver. This study tried to examine the problem of a company to neglect the fundamental change of a business behavior, which the CSV truly aimed for, and consider the CSV as a simple small business activity. This study attempted to confirm this issue by reviewing the case of the raw material supply chain between a paper manufacturer and a waste paper recycler.

---

2) Palazzo, A. G., Spence, L. J. and Matten, D. (2014), "Contesting the value of "Creating Shared Value"", *California Management Review*, 56 (2), pp. 134–135.
3) Yunus, M. (2015), "What is Social Business? – Sosyarubijinesu toiu mouhitotuno sentakushi", *DIAMOND Harvard Business Review*, Jan, p. 85.
4) Pirson, M. (2012), "Social entrepreneurs as the paragons of shared value creation? A critical perspective", *Social Enterprise Journal*, 8 (1), pp. 25–26.
5) Okuda, M. (2015), CSV: The New Competitive Advantage (CSV wa kigyouno kyousouyuuini naruka), *DIAMOND Harvard Business Review*, Jan, p. 50.

2. Theoretical background

2-1. The concept of the CSV and the analytical method of this study

The CSV concept first appeared in 2006 and it caught attention due to two major reasons. (1) It is possible to ensure the sustainability of a company only when the conventional limit of the capitalism, which only emphasizes the competition and the profitability, is overcome.[6] (2) There is an increased need for a strategic CSR, which can lead a substantial management achievement in addition to charity activities focusing on simple social contributions. The CSV start from the belief that the success of a company and the prosperity of the surrounding communities (or the prosperity of a society) are closely related and interdependent. Consequently, it emphasizes that a business activity should create a social value and pursue an economic profit at the same time rather than a company contributes a society with the remaining profit after creating a profit.[7]

Porter and Kramer proposed three strategies to create the CSV. The first was 'the re-recognition of the product and the market'. This pays attention to the bottom of the pyramid or the low-income bracket. Porter and Kramer emphasized that a company can discover a new market by continuously searching 'the social needs' and obtain (an opportunity to have) a differentiated competitiveness.[8] The second strategy was to redefine the productivity of the value chain by finding a solution for the increased operating cost of a company. It means to improve the productivity of a company by revolutionizing the value chain.[9] The second strategy was dealt in many studies by improving the labor condition and the welfare of employees. The last strategy was to develop a local cluster, which made the above two strategies possible. It indicated that the local economy should be developed to increase the productivity and the competitiveness of a company. A company should find a weakness of the region and try to reduce or remove the obstacles preventing the growth of a company. The CSV would be maximized when these efforts were properly made.[10]

Starting from the study of Porter and Kramer, various studies were conducted with using the CSV as a keyword. In this academic trend, Dembek et

---

6) Porter, M. E. and Kramer, M. R. (2011), *op. cit.*, p. 67.
7) *Ibid.*
8) *Ibid.*, p. 68.
9) *Ibid.*, pp. 69-70.
10) *Ibid.* pp. 72-74.

al. analyzed studies listing the CSV as a keyword by referring academic databases of various fields.[11] Dembek et al. analyzed 392 papers and specified how the CSV was used in each study. Moreover, they selected 73 papers, which mainly focused on the CSV.[12] In addition, they extracted 30 papers, which defined the CSV, and analyzed how each paper defined the CSV.[13]

As shown in Table 1, Dembek et al. divided these 30 papers, which defined the CSV, into 2 groups. The group 1 (13 papers among 30 papers) used the definition of Porter and Kramer without modifying it. They defined the CSV as the profit creation through maximizing the social and economic values. The group 2 (17 papers among 30 papers) defined the CSV in various ways depending on viewpoints of various stakeholders. In other words, they defined the CSV with emphasizing the fact that various stakeholders generated diverse values. These studies defined the CSV with stressing various value creations (e. g., organizational value, social value, environmental value, and regional value) because it emphasized various stakeholders surrounding an organization in addition to stockholders.[14] These studies are different from the studies in the group 1 in the aspect of emphasizing the creation of various values instead of maximizing the total value through producing two values. Although these two definitions are different in a strict sense, both definitions are based on the study of Porter and Kramer.

The importance of Dembek et al.'s study was to clearly show that 13 papers among 30 papers defined the CSV directly adopted the Porter and Kramer's definition, the majority of other studies also presumed that the CSV conducted at lease of one three strategies (i. e., re-recognition, value chain, and cluster development), and studies assumed that there was a positive relationship between the social profit and the organizational profit.[15] In other words, the majority of studies defined the CSV with excluding the potentially strained relationship between the social profit and the organizational profit.

---

11) This study is based on Business Source Complete, Econlit, Emerald Journals, Jstore, Proquest, and Central Web of Science databases.
12) Among 73 papers, only 30 papers provided the definition of the CSV. It indicated that majority of studies used the CSV as a common word rather than a theoretical concept. See, Dembek, K., Singh P., and Bhakoo, V. (2015), "Literature review of shared value: a theoretical concept or a management buzzword?", *Journal of Business Ethics*, 01 February, pp. 2-3, for the details about this aspect.
13) *Ibid.*, p. 2.
14) *Ibid.*, p. 6.
15) *Ibid.*, pp. 6-11.

Table 1: The summary of CSV definitions in previous studies

Studies	Definition of shared value
Group 1 Chatterjee (2012), Crane et al. (2013), Follman (2012), Hamann (2012), Hancock et al. (2011), Hartmann et al. (2011), Juscius and Jonikas (2013), Kapoor and Goyal (2013), Porter and Kramer (2011), Schmitt and Renken (2012), Sojamo and Larson (2012), Spitzeck et al. (2013), Spitzeck and Chapman (2012)	Policies and operating practices that enhance the competitiveness of a company while simultaneously advancing the economic and social conditions in the communities in which it operates
Group 2 Aakhus and Bzdak (2012), Porter and Kramer (2006)	A meaningful benefit for society that is also valuable to the business
Athanasopoulou and Selsky (2012), Brown and Knudsen (2012), Cao and Pederzoli (2013), Kendrick et al. (2013)	Creation of economic value "in a way that also creates value for society by addressing its needs and challenges"
Driver, M. (2012), "An interview with Michael Porter: Social entrepreneurship and the transformation of capitalism", *Academy of Management Learning and Education*, 11 (3), pp. 421–431.	The ability to create both economic value and ... social or societal benefit simultaneously
Dubois, C. L. and Dubois, D. A. (2012), "Expanding the vision of industrial-organizational psychology contributions to environmental sustainability", *Industrial and Organizational Psychology*, 5 (4), pp. 480–483.	Creating organizational value while simultaneously adding value to society and to the environment
Fearne, A., Garcia Martinez, M. and Dent, B. (2012), "Dimensions of sustainable value chains: Implications for value chain analysis", *Supply Chain Management: An International Journal*, 17 (6), pp. 575–581.	Value that is mutually beneficial to both the value chain and society
Maltz, E. and Schein, S. (2012), "Cultivating shared value initiatives: A three Cs approach", *Journal of Corporate Citizenship*, 47 (Autumn), pp. 55–74.	A global commercial organization's initiative to simultaneously create value for shareholders and the communities in which the firm operates, beyond the efforts required by law
Maltz, E., Thompson, F. and Jones Ringold, D. (2011), "Assessing and maximizing corporate social initiatives: A strategic view of corporate social responsibility", *Journal of Public Affairs*, 11 (4), pp. 344–352.	Consider the shared value of multiple stakeholders instead of focusing solely on firm value
Pavlovich, K. and Corner, P. D. (2014), "Conscious enterprise emergence: Shared value creation through expanded conscious awareness", *Journal of Business Ethics*, 121 (3), pp. 341–351.	Putting social and community needs before profit
Pirson, M. (2012), "Social entrepreneurs as the paragons of shared value creation? A critical perspective", *Social Enterprise Journal*, 8 (1), pp. 31–48.	Balance of social and financial value creation
G.K.H. (2009), "Harmonious society and Chinese CSR: Is there really a link?", *Journal of Business Ethics*, 89 (1), pp. 1–22.	Choices that benefit both society and corporations that arise out of the "mutual dependence of corporations and society"
Shrivastava, P. and Kennelly, J. J. (2013), "Sustainability and place based enterprise", *Organization & Environment*, 26 (1), pp. 83–101.	The simultaneous creation of economic value for the firm and social and environmental value for the places in which they do business
Verboven, H. (2011), "Communicating CSR and business identity in the chemical industry through mission slogans", *Business Communication Quarterly*, 74 (4), pp. 415–431.	Creation of value not only for shareholders but for all stakeholders
Arjalie's, D. L., Goubet, C, and Ponssard, J.P. (2011), "Approches straté giques des emissions CO_2", *Revue Francaise de Gestion*, 215, pp. 123–146.	Shared value (i. e. concerning at the same time economic and social progress) [own translation]

Source: Dembek, K., Singh, P. and Bhakoo, V. (2015), "Literature review of shared value: a theoretical concept or a management buzzword?", *Journal of Business Ethics*, 01 February, p. 6.

Note: Papers of the group 1 and group 2 listed in Table 1 are as follows.

Group 1 Chatterjee, B. (2012), "Business and communities—redefining boundaries.", *NHRD Network Journal*, 5 (1), pp. 55–60. Crane, A., Matten, D., Palazzo, G., and Spence, L. J. (2013), "Contesting the value of the shared value concept", *California Management Review*, 56 (2), pp. 130–153. Follman, J. (2012), "BoP at ten: Evolution and a new lens", *South Asian Journal of Global Business Research*, 1 (2), pp. 293–310. Hamann, R. (2012), "The business of development: Revisiting strategies for a sustainable future", *Environment: Science and Policy for Sustainable Development*, 54 (2), pp. 18–29. Hancock, C., Kingo, L. and Raynaud, O. (2011), "The private sector, international development and NCDs", *Globalization and Health*, 7 (23), pp. 1–11. Hartmann, L., Werhane, P., and Lane Clark, K. (2011), "Development, poverty and business ethics", *Universia Business Review*, 30 (Segundo Trimestre), pp. 96–108. Juscius, V., and Jonikas, D. (2013), "Integration of CSR into value creation chain: Conceptual framework", *Engineering Economics*, 24 (1), pp. 63–70. Kapoor, A. and Goyal, S. (2013), "Inclusive healthcare at base of the pyramid (BoP) in India", *International Journal of Trade and Global Markets*, 6 (1), pp. 22–39. Porter, M. E., and Kramer, M. R. (2011), "Creating shared value", *Harvard Business Review*, 89 (1/2), pp. Schmitt, J., and Renken, U. (2012), "How to earn money by doing good! Shared value in the apparel industry", *Journal of Corporate Citizenship*, 45 (Spring), pp. 79–103. Sojamo, S., and Larson, E. A. (2012), "Investigating food and agribusiness corporations as global water security, management and governance agents: The case of Nestle", *Bunge and Cargill. Water Alternatives*, 5 (3), pp. 619–635. Spitzeck, H., Boechat, C., and França Leão, S. (2013), "Sustainability as a driver for innovation: Towards a model of corporate social entrepreneurship at Odebrecht in Brazil", *Corporate Governance*, 13 (5), pp. 613–625. Spitzeck, H., and Chapman, S. (2012), "Creating shared value as a differentiation strategy—the example of BASF in Brazil", *Corporate Governance*, 12 (4), pp. 499–513.

Group 2 Aakhus, M. and Bzdak, M. (2012), "Revisiting the role of "Shared Value" in the business–society relationship", *Business and Professional Ethics Journal*, 31 (2), pp. 231–246. Porter, M. E., and Kramer, M. R. (2006), "Strategy and society: The link between competitive advantage and corporate social responsibility", *Harvard Business Review*, 84 (12), pp. 78–92. Athanasopoulou, A. and Selsky, J. W. (2012), "The social context of corporate social responsibility: Enriching research with multiple perspectives and multiple levels", *Business and Society*, 1–43. doi:10.1177/0007650312449260. Brown, D., and Knudsen, J. S. (2012), "No shortcuts: Achieving shared value means changing your business culture", doi:10.2139/ssrn. 2179926. Cao, L., and Pederzoli, D. (2013), "International retailers' strategic responses to institutional environment of emerging market retailers' strategic responses: Multiple case studies in China", *International Journal of Retail & Distribution Management*, 41 (4), pp. 289–310. Kendrick, A., Fullerton, J. A. and Kim, Y. J. (2013), "Social responsibility in advertising: A marketing communications student perspective", *Journal of Marketing Education*, 35 (2), pp. 141–154.

2-2. Critical review and alternative for the development and studies of the CSV

Since Porter and Kramer published 'Creating Shared Value' in 2011, it had been used in the google for 1,843 times until Mar 2015. This clearly indicates that the appearance of the CSV concept has influenced the global community considerably.

Crane et al. analyzed 250 papers cited Porter and Kramer and reported that the majority of studies (89%) were favorable to the study, approximately 9% were neutral to it, and only 2% showed a critical standpoint.[16] Moreover, various success cases were reported in many papers but 49% of these cases were already used in the Porter and Kramer's work.[17] This suggested that the majority of the CSV's concept, case, and achievement were not apart from the Porter and Kramer. It is noteworthy that no CSV studies are apart from the arguments of Porter and Kramer, although it was said that CSV studies had two main streams in the preceding paragraph, section.

This section summarizes the critics on the concept and the flow of the CSV in previous studies in more detail.

There is a critic that the CSV concept is not unique or innovative.[18] Burke and Logsdon also emphasized that the social contribution of a company should be conducted to maximize the profit of a company in the study on the strategic CSR, which had been applied.[19] Moreover, Freeman, Wicks, and Parmer criticized that the socioeconomic value creation for various stakeholders was similar with the conventional stakeholder theory.[20]

However, regarding the viewpoint of this study, this section will discuss problems occurring while applying the CSV in reality rather than the attributes of the concept.

The main problem of applying the CSV to run a company is that a company expands the CSV without specifying what kind of social values a company wants to create and how to create them. In other words, one may criticize that the logic of maximizing the profit by binding an economic value with a combinable social value is too shortsighted.

---

16) Crane, A., Palazzo, G., Spence, L. J. and Matten, D. (2014), "Contesting the value of "Creating Shared Value"", *California Management Review*, 56 (2), p. 133.
17) Dembek, K., Singh, P. and Bhakoo, V. (2015), *op. cit.*, p. 15.
18) Crane, A., Palazzo, G., Spence, L. J. and Matten, D. (2014), *op. cit.*, pp. 134-136.
19) Burke, L. and J. M. Logsdon (1996), "How corporate social responsibility pays off", *Long Range Planning*, Vol. 29, No. 4, p. 496.
20) Freeman, R. E., A. C. Wicks and Parmar, B. (2013), "Stakeholder theory and the corporate objective revisited", *Organization Sciences*, Vol. 15, No. 3, p. 366.

Table 2: Social achievements and beneficiaries suggested in Dembek et al. (2015)

Company	Outcome	Beneficiary
Amazon	Reduced service cost	Customers
Basf Grameen	Improvement in employment, local companies, and health	Local residents and small to medium enterprises
BASF, Andre Maggi Group, and Fundacao Espaco Eco in Brazil	Improved social environment	Unclear
Becton-Dickinson	Health and medical treatment & the health of employment	Employee
BracNET	Internet and technology assessment	Local residents, teachers, and students
Chetna, Zameen, Oxfam, Trade Craft, ACF, SSM, Arvind, Prathiba, BioRE	Improvement in income, environment, health, and education	Tenant farmers and local residents
Cisco Systems	Supply of good jobs	The young
Coca-Cola	Improvement in employment prospect	The young
Daewoo	Economic benefit in Libya region	Local residents
Doosan Heavy Industry	Better access to water	Local residents
Dow Chemical	Increased income and the development of environment-friendly products	Farmers and customers
Fabindia	Improved life quality	Local residents
Ferrero	Employment, acquiring new technology, and improved service quality	Unclear
GE and Embrace	Better health	Local residents
Google, Apple, Kindle	Reduced environmental issues	Region
Grameen, Adidas	Employment, the development of local companies, and skill acquisition	Local residents and local companies
Grameen, Danone	Improved nutrition, employment, and the development of local companies	Small to medium enterprise and region
Grameen, Intel	Employment and an access to new services and products	Unclear
Grameen Phone	Response to the income and the poverty	Rural area
Grameen Veolia	Development of local companies, employment, and skill acquisition	Unclear
H&M	Improved human rights of child issue	Children
Heineken	Improved AIDS problems	Employees and their families
HP	Improved HIV diagnosis	Children
Ikea	Employment, new technology acquisition, and the development of local companies	Unclear
Ikea	Improved human rights of child issue	Children
Intel	Improved educational achievement	Children
Mahindra Group	Tractor production and education	Women and the rural area

Mahindra Navistar Automotive Ltd.	Employment	Early retiree
Marks & Specer	Improved environmental issues	Environment
Marriott	Employment	The long-term unemployed
Nestle	Improved health and medical treatment, better education, and increased income	Farmers
Nestle	Employment, the development of local enterprises, and skill acquisition	Unclear
Nestle	Improved nutritional supply	Local residents
Nestle	Improved local soil quality and reduced environmental pollution due to agricultural activities	Farmers
NIKE	Labor condition	Unclear
Novartis	The sense of belonging and income	The disabled
Odebrecht	Employment and income, and environmental issues	Local residents
Odebrecht	Employment, income, illiteracy, and technology improvement	Unclear
Olam International	Reduced CO_2 emission and employment	African region
P&G	Accessibility to services and products	Unclear
Santam	Reduced the risk of flood and fire	Farming and fishing communities
SKF group	Reduced cost	Customers
Sysco	Maintaining local companies	Small enterprises
Thomson Reuter	Increased income	Farmers
Toyota	Improved environmental problem	Unclear
Unilever	Decreased disease and increased income	Women in poverty
Urbi	Improved residential issues	Unclear
Vodafone & Safaricom	Increased employment and income	Unclear
Walmart	Reduced medical cost and improved health	Unclear
Walmart	Improved environmental issues	Unclear
Waste Concern	Increased agricultural production and improved environmental problems and health issues	Unclear
We're	Improved environmental problems and increased local income	Local residents
Whole foods	Environment-friendly management	Unclear
Woolworths	Increased rural household income and improved environmental problems	Farmers
Yara	Employment	Unclear

Source: Reorganized based on the tables in Dembek, K., Singh, P. and Bhakoo, V. (2015), "Literature review of shared value: a theoretical concept or a management buzzword?", *Journal of Business Ethics*, 01 February, pp. 17-34.

For example, it is impossible to say that a company creates a social value while it produces products giving a negative effect on the public interest in the social dimension. Similarly, it is ironical of a company to create a social value through CSV while the company does so resolve the structural problem of the company (e. g., low-wage, unstable hiring, and labor rights violations).[21] Therefore, a company is required identifying a subject and a problem of a social value, which the company wishes to create, and evaluating if it is deployed harmoniously within its social value.

Regarding these problems, Dembek et al. analyzed 73 papers, which used the CSV as a keyword, with using social and organizational criterion (i. e., the social achievement, the social cost, the organizational achievement, and the organizational cost). They proposed three frames (i. e., mean, outcome, and beneficiary) to evaluate the CSV. Dembek et al. could not analyze the mean frame due to the lack of data.[22]

The cases of social achievements listed in Dembek et al. were summarized (Table 2). The beneficiary section was additionally organized and supplemented. The social achievement of the CSV can appear in very diverse forms (Table 2). They can be organized into several categories (e. g., the increased income of farmers or a region, the improvement in health issues, the improvement of environmental problems, the increased employment, the development of local companies, the improved labor condition, the access to information technology, and the achievement of educational goals).

If the social achievement of a company is specified and the means of CSV is invented, the cost-benefit analysis will be possible. Consequently, it would be possible to analyze the achievement (relatively) accurately. Moreover, the achievement should be analyzed from the viewpoint of the desire. To analyze this systematically, a company should operate after understanding what kind of a desire exists in a society, how it is being solved, and if the desire is resolved in the society. Lastly, there are various beneficiaries of the CSV including companies, specific communities or groups, or the environment. If these diverse beneficiaries are specified, the social achievement can be embodied.

---

21) Crane, A., Palazzo, G. L. and Spence, D. Matten (2014), *op. cit.*, p. 141.
22) Unless one is an insider of a company, it is very hard to identify the means of the CSV (e. g., the social cost and the organizational cost). It was reported that only 3 papers among 73 described the mean. Dembek, K., Singh, P. and Bhakoo, V. (2015), "Literature review of shared value: a theoretical concept or a management buzzword?", *Journal of Business Ethics*, 01 February, p. 14.

When a social value and an economic value conflict in running a company, the importance of the social value inevitably decreases. It is the most fundamental limitation in the CSV application. Many researchers already have pointed it out. Pirson criticized that the CSV strategy was unrealistic because the structural imbalance between two opposing objectives always favored the commercial objective, a biased decision[23]. In the aspect of the CSV, Spence and Rinaldi also indicated,. The economic drivers are more deeply embedded (in our case study) company than environmental and social drivers, and these consistently win out. Embedding sustainability in decision-making is bound, in the current paradigm of business, to mean translating sustainability imperatives into economic ones.[24] The core of criticism was that the win-win situation expected by Porter and Kramer was hard to be achieved and, consequently, the CSV neglected the potential tension between a social value and an economic value. When these two values conflict, a company may invest in an easy-to-solve social issue to minimize the conflict. It can be a problem.

We have reviewed the potential problems and criticisms on the limitations of the CSV in the process of the CSV application. They can be summarized as ① it is required to clearly define and extend what the CSV means and the concept of the CSV and ② the social value, which the CSV tries to deliver, should be evaluated objectively. In other words, a cost-benefit of a company should be analyzed and the social achievement should be realized through specifying the beneficiaries reflecting a diversity, identifying the social outcome of a company, and creating the means of the CSV. If it is possible to extend the concept of the CSV by responding to these two criticisms, it will be able to maximize the social outcome in corporate management when a social value and an economic value crash.

This study aimed to review the social contribution activities of Japanese paper manufacturers. In particular, this study focused on the contents related to social value creation within a cluster. Specifically, this study tried to point out the problems and limitations by observing the relationship between paper manufacturers and waste paper recyclers and evaluate the conflict between the social desire of processing the released paper of waste gypsum board and the economic desire of paper manufacturers to purchase inexpensive water paper raw material.

---

23) Pirson, M. (2012), *op. cit.*, p. 43.
24) Spence, L.and Rinaldi, L. (2012), *op. cit.*, p. 31.

3. Introduction to Japanese paper manufacturers

Paper products are used in our daily lives and they are essential for our living such as newspapers, magazines, wrapping paper, and tissue. These paper products can be generally classified into printing paper, packaging paper, and sanitary paper.

Japanese paper manufacturers became mature in the 1990s and there are relatively many paper manufacturers in Japan. Among them, the competition between sanitary paper manufacturers is severe. The packaging paper market is represented by stencil paper production, which is used for producing cardboard. The market has relatively stable demand and the aggregation of cardboard manufacturers has been completed largely. This is an oligopoly market.

The stencil paper for cardboard and the printing paper are typical equipment industries, which require a substantial capital investment. They are ruled by the economies of scale. On the other hands, the paper production for industrial materials and general consumer papers requires less capital investment but it needs continuous research and development to develop new products.

It is hard to say that paper industry is a high value-added industry, except a portion of paper used as industrial materials. It varies by the market condition, but it has a low-profit rate over net sales and the profit rate decreases when the price of raw material and fuel rise.

Moreover, depending on the product types, a paper manufacturer needs to have different equipment scale, specifications, and stock cycle. However, considering important production equipment (e. g., the pulp production facility and tissue machine), overall investment cycle is relatively long.

Although the cost structure and the equipment and stock investment cycles vary by business and product type, the printing paper and the packaging paper require a certain size of investment to install manufacturing facilities. Therefore, they have high fixed cost (e. g., depreciation and repair expenditure) and low flexibility in the aspect of the cost structure. Main raw materials (e. g., woodchip) and fuel (e. g., heavy oil and coal) are mainly imported so they are easily influenced by global market condition and currency exchange rates. Therefore, paper manufacturers try to prepare for fuel price dynamics by using the sludge, discharged during pulp production, or biomass as fuel. This fuel problem will be reviewed as a part of the environmental management of paper manufacturers later. Moreover, a manufacturer can decrease manufacturing equipment investment if it carries the deinked pulp equipment compared to manufacturers without it. In other words, a manufacturer can reduce the raw material cost by using waste paper. The usage of waste paper will be discussed later as well.

Factories for industrial materials and general consumer papers requires less equipment investment cost compared to the printing paper and the packaging paper. Therefore, the pressure of fixed cost is relatively small. However, industrial materials need a certain level of research and development cost to increase fixed cost. General consumer papers have higher marketing cost (e. g., sales promotion and advertisement).

3-1. Size and growth of the market

According to the Japan Paper Association, the global paper and cardboard production was 400 million ton in 2013, which is 0.8% increase year-on-year. According to major regional statistics, the importance of the Asian market is getting higher because various paper markets are growing rapidly in the Asia on the behalf of fast economic development. On the other hand, the market share of North America, Europe, and Japan decreases gradually, while they have led the world paper and pulp industries.

The paper and cardboard consumption per capital of Japan in 2013 was 214.6kg. It is the world top level. Paper consumption per capital tends to be large in developed countries compared to developing countries. The mean paper consumption per capital of the world is 56.5kg.[25]

Japan is the third largest paper producer in the world following China and the United States. Although the production volume of Japan became smaller than that of China recently, Japan has been the second-largest producer since the 1970s until the 2000s. The paper production of Japan increased until the 2000s mainly because domestic paper demand increased. As the lifestyle of Japanese changes since the 1960s owing to high economic growth, the paper became essential for a living. Moreover, the demand of the paper as printing and information paper increased in proportion to the economic growth.

The paper industry of Japan has grown with the growth of Japanese economy. However, the paper production decreased drastically in 2009 right immediately after the Lehman shock due to population decline caused by a decrease in a birth rate and paperless due to internet service supply (Figure 1). The production volume is not recovered with maintaining the production

---

25) Seirengyoukai homepage, www.jpa.gr.jp/states/global-view/index.html (last access, Nov. 22, 2015).

Figure 1: The paper and cardboard production dynamics (excluding pulp)

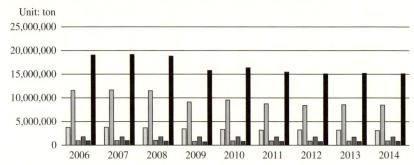

Source: Ministry of Economy, Trade and Industry homepage, http://www.meti.go.jp/statistics/tyo/seidou/result/ichiran/08_seidou.html#menu9 (last access, Nov. 22, 2015).

level of 2009. The current paper production, excluding pulp and paper processed goods, is estimated as approximately 1.5 million tons.[26]

3-2. Business structure and competition status

According to Japan Paper Association, the overall size of paper companies is 4,737.4 billion Yen based on the company sales and the overall ordinary profit of the business is estimated as 179.2 billion Yen based on the 2015 fiscal year. It is about 2.4% of the total Japanese manufacturing industry and it is the 17th position among 24 industries. However, the production of paper products is in its decreasing trend since 2009. The industry growth rate of the past five years shows negative growth of -0.01% (see Table 3).

The table shows that all manufacturers are facing a tough competition although each paper manufacturers reveals distinctive performance. The competition status of each field will be reviewed in detail in following sections.

In the industry of the printing paper, led by Oji Paper and Nippon Paper, the two largest companies, many companies including small-scale manufacturers compete with each other. Since it is a mature industry, there is a low probability of having a new competitor. However, the number of competitors

---

26) When the production trend of paper and cardboard, the main goods of Japan, is evaluated, the year-on-year production increased until 1991 and maintained around 20 million tons until the 2008 Lehman shock (refer Figure 1). However, it decreased to 1.6 million tons after 2009 due to world economic downturn. The negative growth continued until 2014 to produce only 1.5 million tons. It is hard to expect that the production will be recovered much.

Table 3: Paper product sales by company (2015)

(Unit : 100 million Yen)

Name of a Company	Product Type	Rank	Sales
Oji Holdings Corporation	Containerboard、Paperboard、household paper、Functional Speciality Paper、Newsprint、Printing and Writing Paper	1	13,325
Nippon Paper Group	Containerboard、Paperboard、household paper、Functional Speciality Paper、Newsprint、Printing and Writing Paper	2	10,812
Rengo	Containerboard、Paperboard、kraft paper	3	5,231
Daio Paper Corporation	Containerboard、Paperboard、Household paper、Functional Speciality Paper、Newsprint、Printing and Writing Paper	4	4,300
Hokuetsu Kishu Paper Group	Printing and Writing Paper、Paperboard、Functional Speciality Paper	5	2,238
Mitsubishi Paper Mills Limited	Paperboard、Functional Speciality Paper, Household paper	6	2,074
Lintec	Printing and Writing Paper、Functional Speciality Paper	7	2,032
Tomoku Co., Ltd.	Containerboard、craft paper	8	1,503
Chuetsu Pulp & Paper	Paperboard、household paper、Functional Speciality Paper、Newsprint、Printing and Writing Paper	9	997

Source: It was made by the author on the base of 'Annual Paper and Cardboard Statistics'. Paper Association homepage, www.jpa.gr.jp/states/global-view/index.html (last access, Nov. 22, 2015).

is still large. However, the top three companies in the paper production for newspaper occupy more than 80% of the market. It can be said that high rankers are aggregated. It is due to the capital relationship between the Japanese newspaper media and the paper for newspaper production as well as the closed trading relationship, which has been firmly established.

On the other hand, in the general printing paper industry, there has been higher inports of coated paper and copying paper from China and Indonesia since 2009 owing to the strong Yen. Consequently, the competition in the Japanese domestic market is getting severe. This shows that the continuity and stability of printing paper industry are vulnerable.

The top three companies occupy 65% of the box packaging paper market, especially the stencil paper of corrugated cardboard. The corrugated cardboard box requires the sheet maker and the box maker. The sheet maker processes stencil paper to make corrugated cardboard and the box maker reforms the sheet into a box form. The stencil paper manufacturers are systematizing corrugated cardboard and box makers to influence the market formation of the industry. For example, the profitability focusing management technique of stencil paper manufacturers has penetrated into the small- to medium-size corrugated cardboard makers. According to the statistics of Japan Paper Association, the import rate of cardboard is approximately 3% and the import of stencil paper for corrugated cardboard is approximately 1%. Domestic products still have high market share. Consequently, the top two domestic manufacturers of stencil paper for corrugated cardboard occupy approximately 50% of the market and the top three manufacturers occupy approximately 70% of the market.

It is very hard to differentiate the quality of stencil paper for corrugated cardboard. The continuity and stability of stencil paper for corrugated cardboard are also low. However, the stencil paper manufacturers are systematizing the cardboard industry so they could secure the stable sales. Consequently, the continuity of customers is relatively high from stencil paper to corrugated cardboard sheet and it decreased toward the final consumers.

On the other hand, the industrial paper market is small and requires technical investment to limit the number of players at the point of the overall paper industry. Since products have distinct characteristics and functions suitable for consumer companies, it is very hard for a consumer to change a product. Therefore, it is a market showing the continuity of consumers. However, this field definitely has high competition because advanced technological development increases market share.

Contrarily, the general consumer paper market has a low technical entrance barrier. Particularly, many small- to medium-size companies use waste paper as a raw material for sanitary paper. Moreover, it is very hard to clearly differentiate the function of sanitary paper so it is very easy to have a price competition. Therefore, it is hard to expect consumer continuity. However, it shows a minimum fluctuation in market share, just like the industrial paper market. It is because there is substantial cost in sales promotion and new products introduction. As a result, the market competition is severe. As the import of cheap goods increases since the late 2000s, competition in the Japanese market is increasingly intensified.

The size of the paper industry, the market growth potential, and the business structure have been reviewed. The important factors are: ① Four paper industries have different supply structures and the profitability is influenced by the raw material of products, market situation, and the currency dynamics. Four paper industries are the printing paper including paper for the newspaper, cardboard including the stencil paper for corrugated cardboard, industrial paper, and general consumer paper; ② The paper industry requires the merit of scale, so the fixed cost can be a factor of reducing profit. Consequently, improvement in production capacity is always an important management goal. To ensure the stable operation rate by acquiring a market proportional to its production capacity is the only way to increase its competitiveness. Particularly, the mass production effects as an equipment industry are very important in the printing paper and the packaging paper industries; ③ In the packaging paper including the stencil paper for corrugated cardboard, the cost of waste paper is responsible for the majority of the product cost. Therefore, the stability of raw material supply is important.

4. How Japanese paper manufacturers resolving social desire: Focusing on environmental issues

4-1. The conventional image of Japanese paper manufacturers

The conventional images of the Japanese paper industry are 'pollution production industry', 'deforestation industry', and 'garbage production industry'. In short, it had a poor image. These images largely rely on. The bottom sludge problem at the Tagonoura harbor.[27] Occurred in the 1970s and the dioxin problem in October 1990.[28] The bottom sludge problem at the Tagonoura harbor indicates the bottom sludge pollution at the Tagonoura harbor to deteriorate the harbor function and cause serious odor. The dioxin problem is a water pollution problem nearby a pulp factory in the process of bleaching pulp. Although Japanese Environmental Agency announced that that quality of seafood and water near a pulp factory is not different from that near a normal area and the water quality does not harm people's health, the paper industry has improved pulp cleaning process after this social incident. For example, it introduced the oxygen bleaching instead of the conventional

---

27) *Mainichi Shinbun*, Aug. 9, 1970.
28) Ministry of the Environment homepage, https://www.env.go.jp/recycle/circul/venous_industry/ja/history.pdf (last access, Nov. 22, 2015).

chlorine bleach.

These responses and efforts of the paper industry should be highly evaluated by the public and the Japanese paper industry gives an effort in environmental issues and energy issues including air pollution, water pollution, odor, and waste.

Japan imports most of major resources and it recently enacted. act on facilitating the beneficial use of resources",[29] which 'aims to contribute to the healthy development of the national economy by acquiring useful resources, inhibiting the used goods and byproduct production, and enforcing all necessary measures to stimulate the use of recycled resources and recycled parts because resources are heavily used, used products and byproducts are massively produced, the majority of them are discarded, and the majority of recycled resources and recycled parts are not used to be discarded'.

The pulp industry uses a large amount of energy and water. Moreover, it creates pulp from wood chips and the pulp is the main raw material of paper. These factors would make it most relevant to the objectives of the law mentioned above, which are 'facilitating the effective use of resources' and 'waste production inhibition and environment conservation'.

People believe that paper is made out of living wood and, consequently, it has a bad image of destroying forests. However, the paper industry of Japan mainly (>60%) uses waste paper, considered as a recycled resource, as main raw material. Japan is one of major waste paper utilization countries and it tries to make the paper industry as a resource circulation type industry.

Furthermore, the paper industry, known as an energy-guzzling industry, has reduced 30% of its energy usage. It has contributed to CO_2 reduction through energy conservation.

If we consider the paper industry mainly using waste paper as a raw material in the aspect of 'the social desire' in addition to 'the economic desire', the inhibition of waste production and the environmental conservation are important keywords in the aspects of the CSV. Moreover, the paper industry, known as an energy-guzzling industry, is directly related to the social desire of resolving an environmental problem. The next section will review how the paper industry connected an economic desire with social desires such as resource saving, environmental conservation, and recycle.

---

29) Shigen no yukona riyouno sokusinni kansuru houritsu (act on facilitating the beneficial use of resources) (1991), 18, Sousoku (general rules).

4-2. Plan to have a low carbon society by the Japanese paper industry

The resource saving through recycling and the environmental conservation are two keywords best describing the Japanese paper industry. Japan Paper Association[30] declared 'the voluntary action plans for the environment'[31] in the 1997 and strengthened the goals for eight times. It actively responds to global climate change and resource environmental problems. The basic policies of 'the voluntary action plans for the environment' are ① to try the best to resolve the global climate change issue including the international responses, ② to protect the environment and establish a circulation society using resources efficiently, and ③ to aim for newly establishing an environmental management system. Japanese paper manufacturers conducted the voluntary plan until 2011 and enacted new 'environmental action plan'[32] from 2012 (Table 4). They have tried to harmonize the environment and economic activities and found a sustainable society.

Let's summarize the management efforts of Japanese paper manufacturers. In other words, the fossil fuel usage and the efforts to reduce CO_2 emission will be summaries in detail with using the investigation results of the Japan Paper Association.

The goals of low carbon society action plan, which has been voluntarily conducted, are ① to Reduce 1.39 million tons of CO_2 emission originated from fossil fule (compared to 2005) until 2020 and ② to increase the size of domestic and foreign forestation, a CO_2 sink, by 425 thousand ha (total 700 thousand ha) compared to the formation size in 1990 until 2020 (Table 4).

The achievements in 2014 among the goals of low carbon society action plan are summarized in Table 5. The actual CO_2 emission was 18.05 million tons per year in 2014, which is 27.6% (24.94 thousand tons per year →18.05 thousand tons per year) decrease compared to the emission of 2005.

The progress of the low carbon society action plan between 1990 and 2014

---

30) The Japan Paper Association is a paper industry business association and made by Japanes paper companies and related companies after 'the paper product control company', which controlled the production and distribution of paper and pulp during the World War II, was dissolved. Currently, it consists of 33 Japanese paper manufacturers (regular members).
31) Nihon seisi rengoukai (Japan Paper Association) (2008), Kankyouni kansuru jisyukoudou keikaku (the voluntary action plans for the environment), May 20.
32) Nihon seisi rengoukai (The Japan Paper Association) (2012), *Kankyou koudou keikaku: Environmental Action Plan,* May 20.

Table 4: Environmental Policies and Action Plans of the Environmental Action Plan

Environmental Policies	Action Plan
1. Realizing a low carbon society	Pursue 'low carbon society action plan (phase 1 and phase 2)' to realize a sustainable society. ・Reduce 1.39 million tons of CO_2 emission originated from fossil fuel (compared to 2005) until 2020 (phase 1). Reduce 2.86 million tons of CO_2 emission originated from fossil fuel (compared to 2005) until 2030 (phase 2). ・Increase the size of domestic and foreign forestation, a CO_2 sink, by 425 thousand ha (total 700 thousand ha) compared to the formation size in 1990 until 2020 (phase 1). Increase the size of domestic and foreign forestation, a CO_2 sink, by 525 thousand ha (total 800 thousand ha) compared to the formation size in 1990 until 2030 (phase 1).
2. Realizing a society coexisting with nature	・Conduct illegal deforestation measures such as not using illegally harvested and imported wood. ・Actively use domestic wood included thinned trees. ・Try to have a sustainable forest management by actively acquiring forest certifications.
3. Realizing a circulation type society	・Increase the waste paper usage rate to 64% until 2015. ・Aim to reduce the final industrial waste to 350 thousand tons until 2015.
4. Responding to environmental risks	Prepare, conduct and inspect an environmental management plan to improve environmental problems from raw material supply to the recycling process. ・Try to reduce the environmental load. ・Try to reduce environmental risks caused by using chemicals for producing paper and cardboard products.
5. Reliable environmental management	Run a business with considering the coexistence with the environment as a core value of management. Respond to resource and environmental issues of the paper industry at the international viewpoint. Actively complete our duties. ・Aim to establish an environmental management. ・Contribute internationally.

Source: Japan Paper Association homepage, www.jpa.gr.jp/env/plan/brief/ (Last access, November 15, 2015).

is shown as follows. The demand for paper and cardboard demand has decreased since the 2008 Lehman shock. The paper and pulp production in 2014 was 23.11 thousand tons, which is 1.6% reduction year-on-year. Fossil energy usage was decreased by approximately 3.4%, which was larger than the paper and pulp production reduction, because each paper manufacturer conducted energy saving measures, fuel conversion measure, efficient equip-

Table 5: The low carbon society action plan and 2014 achievements

	Production (paper and pulp) (10 thousand tons / yr)	CO_2		Fossil Fuel	
		Emission quantity (10 thousand tons / yr)	Basic unit (t-CO_2/t)	Consumption (PJ/ yr)	Basic unit (GJ/t)
2005 result (standard)	2,744	2,494	0.909	345	12.6
2013 result	2,347	1,874	0.799	244	10.4
2014 result	2,311	1,805	0.781	236	10.2
Low carbon society action plan (2020)					
BAU (no plan)	Estimated production 2,472	2,244	0.909	← Basic unit 2005 standard ← Original unit if the goals are achieved.	
Goal		2,105	0.852		
Target reduction quantity		139			

Source: Nihon seisi rengoukai (Japan Paper Association) (2015), *Teitansou syakai jikkoukeikaku-Ondanka taisaku: Low Carbon Society Action Plan-climate change measures*, September 24, p. 4.

ment operation through production re-evaluation, and high-efficiency gas turbine operation. Consequently, the basic unit index of fossil energy decreased by 1.2pt from 69.6 in 2013 to 68.4 in 2014 with using 1990 as a standard. CO_2 emission decreased by 690 thousand tons (18.05 million tons in 2014). However, the basic unit of CO_2 emission was exacerbated in 2011 and 2012 compared to that in 2010 (76.8) because of the stoppage of nuclear power plant. However, it decreased by 1.6pt year-on-year again in 2014.

When 2013 and 2014 are compared, the basic unit of total energy slighted increased along with the reduction in paper production. However, the basic unit of fossil energy continuously decreased because the basic unit of renewable energies also increased. Moreover, the composition ratio of fossil energy decreased from 58.3 to 47.3% (11pt), while the ratio of renewable energy increased from 37.54 to 43.5% (6.1pt) in 2005 and 2014, respectively. Heavy oil, fossil energy, substantially decreased by 14.9pt and it showed a continuous decreasing trend.

These numbers agreed with the policies included in the environment action plan of Japan Paper Association. In other words, Japanese paper manufacturers had tried to run a company with emphasizing the coexistence with the environment. It is a case of achieving a social desire (i. e., environmental

Table 6: The investment trend for the countermeasures of environmental problem
(100 million Yen)

Year	2000	2001	2002	2003	2004	2005	2006	2007	2008	2009	2010	2011	2012	2013	2014	Total
Fuel conversion	0	0	67	78	184	177	350	286	447	155	3	37	20	7	0	1,811
Energy saving	230	169	82	103	249	84	92	314	73	64	68	49	31	56	130	1,796
Total	231	169	148	181	433	261	441	601	520	219	72	86	52	63	130	3,607

Source: *Ibid.*, p. 7.

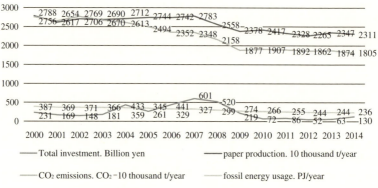

Figure 2: paper production, CO_2 emission, fossil energy usage

Source: Author added investment trend on a figure at, *Ibid.*, p. 4.

conservation) through a company management.

For this low carbon society action plan, Japanese paper manufacturers have made following investment activities. Table 6 shows the investment trend of each company. Moreover, Figure 2 shows the paper production, CO_2 emission, fossil energy usage, and investment trend for creating countermeasures for environmental problems. It implies that energy saving investment is within 1~2% of the fossil energy usage reduction, which was a feature of the overall paper industry. Moreover, a lot of investment was made between 2002~2009 for switching fuel. The fossil energy reduction showed more than 5% effect at max through an investment for switching fuel and saving energy.

As shown, Japanese paper manufacturers satisfy the economic desire of companies by investing in technological development and acquiring energy efficiency based on the voluntary action plan. Moreover, they meet the social desire of improving environmental problems.

5. Waste paper as a raw material

5-1. The concept and usage of waste paper

Waste paper, a raw material, is delivered to paper manufacturers through various distribution channels in Japan (Figure 3). Professional recovery companies collect waste paper from where waste paper is produced and the collected waste paper is sent to waste paper compression field, which supplies waste paper to paper manufacturers as a raw material. Sometimes, a waste paper compression company collects waste paper directly. The collected waste paper, through various routes, is classified in the waste paper compression field and pressed by a waste paper baler into 1 ton unit mass. Afterward, it is transferred to paper manufacturers. Important tasks of a company running a waste paper compression field are to organize waste papers into a unit quantity as select only suitable waste paper to maintain high quality.[33]

Generally, more than 25 types of waste paper are used for paper production. It goes through a recycling process to be turned into various types of recycled stencil paper (e. g., paper for newspaper and stencil paper for corrugated cardboard). According to the definition of Japanese waste paper recycling promotion center, waste paper generally means 'something collected to be used as paper raw material'. In Japanese law, 'the promotion of effective utilization of resources (enacted on Oct. 25, 1991) defined it as. The whole or

Figure 3: Supply and distribution of paper raw material

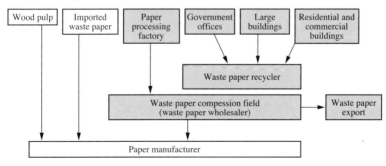

---

33) Zaidan houjin kosisaisei sokusin center (Paper recycling promotion center) (2015), *Japanese Paper recycling,* Zaidan houjin kosisaisei sokusin center, Aug. p. 3.

a portion of it is paper such as paper, paper products, and books. It is useful paper among once used paper, collected without being used, and discarded paper. It should be usable as a raw material of paper (including imported papers after collection) or have a potential to be used as a raw material of paper. However, it excludes paper produced during the paper manufacturing process at a paper manufacturer factory or a place of business.[34]

Waste paper can effectively substitute wood pulp in producing paper products. In other words, waste paper can be defined as a product. In Japan, 27,363 thousand tons of paper products were produced in 2010 and 62.5% of their raw material was waste paper (pulp 37.4%).[35] As shown, the waste paper used for producing paper (e. g., paper for the newspaper) and cardboard is an important resource. The paper and pulp industry, the main user of this waste paper, is one of the energy-guzzling industries, as stated. Technology development is essential for using waste paper as a raw material.

It is clear that recycling of waste paper is to represent social desires such as resource saving and waste reduction as well as to acquire raw material for paper production. In other words, it plays an important role to form a circulation type economic society.

5-2. Waste paper recovery in Japan

According to the statistics of Japan Paper Association, 63.9% of paper and cardboard was made out of waste papers in 2014. The waste paper recovery rate was 80.8% in 2014, which is 0.4 pt increase year-on-year.

Japan does not have a big land area and has a very good waste paper recovery system. Therefore, it has high waste paper recovery rate, which is one of the best in the world.

The waste paper recovery of Japan abruptly increased after 2000 owing to the group recovery at schools or condominiums and administrative recovery (Figure 4). The recovery rate was 79.70% in 2010. The recovery rate reached 80.4%. In particular, the waste paper was heavily used in cardboard and newspaper productions. In 2013, the waste paper utilization rate for paper and cardboard was 63.9% in 2013.[36] The consumption of waste paper increased from 7,857 thousand tons in 1980 to 17,091 thousand tons in 2014,

---

34) Zaidan houjin kosisaisei sokusin center (Paper recycling promotion center) (2011), *Koshi handbook 2010*, Zaidan houjin kosisaisei sokusin center, p. 1.
35) *Ibid.*, p. 29.
36) Zaidan houjin kosisaisei sokusin center (Paper recycling promotion center) (2011), *op. cit.*, p. 6.

Figure 4: Waste paper recovery and waste paper utilization rate of Japan

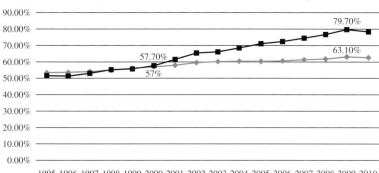

Source: Zaidan houjin kosisaisei sokusin center (Paper recycling promotion center) (2011). *Koshi handbook 2010*, Zaidan houjin kosisaisei sokusin center, p. 47.

which was 2.2 times increase. The waste paper utilization rate continuously increased since the 1980s; 41.5, 51.5, 56.1, 60.2, and 60.3% in 1980, 1990, 1999, 2003, 2005, 2009, and 2014, respectively.[37]

Higher recycle rate of waste paper is deeply related to the environmental issue, as discussed previously. Waste paper consumption is also important in the economic aspect because paper manufacturers can use a cheap raw material.

At a glance, the waste paper consumption of Japanese paper manufacturers looks like a case of increasing social contribution as well as improving economic profit. However, this study aimed to clearly evaluate the reason for an abrupt increase in the waste paper recovery rate and the waste paper utilization rate in the late 1990s.

The waste paper recovery rate abruptly increased in the 2000s (Figure 4). It was highly related to the economic development of China. China made a substantial economic growth in the 1990s. Consequently, it has considerably more paper consumption to found numerous paper manufacturers. Many Chinese paper manufacturers, particularly manufacturers producing stencil paper for corrugated cardboard, had to import waste paper from the US and Japan because China did not have waste paper recovery system (Figure 5). Waste paper price in Japan skyrocketed because waste paper export soared. Consequently, waste paper recovery companies increased the quantity of

---

37) *Ibid.*, p. 8.

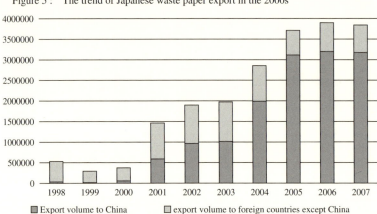

Figure 5 : The trend of Japanese waste paper export in the 2000s

Source: Trade Statistics of Japan (Minister of Finance) homepage, http://www.e-stat.go.jp/SG1/estat/OtherList.do?bid=000001008800&cycode=1 (last access, Nov. 15, 2015).

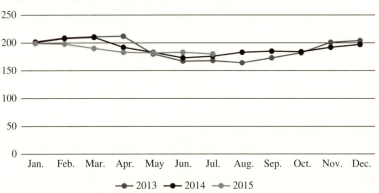

Figure 6: Eexport price trend of Japanese waste paper (Mixed Paper)

Source: Nippon Materio Co., Ltd. (Internal document).

waste paper collection owing to the proper market price of waste paper. Furthermore, more companies entered into the waste paper recovery market. As a result, the waste paper recovery rate increased and the trend has persisted.

Figure 6, 7, and 8 show the export price trend of Japanese waste paper. It well shows that the export price of waste paper varies by the market condition. The mean export price of mixed paper, old newspaper, and corrugated cardboard were approximately 17, 20, and 17 Yen per kg, respectively, which are

Figure 7: Eexport price trend of Japanese waste paper (Old NewsPaper)

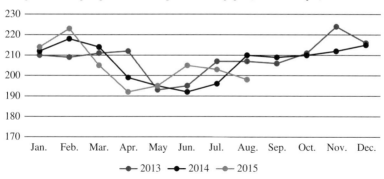

Source: Nippon Materio Co., Ltd. (Internal document).

Figure 8: Eexport price trend of Japanese waste paper (Old corrugated cardboard)

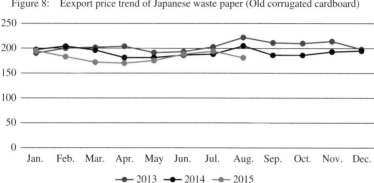

Source: Nippon Materio Co., Ltd. (Internal document).

substantially higher than domestic prices.

Previously, Japanese paper manufacturers granted some waste paper compression companies to directly supply waste paper and fixed waste paper price in return. In other words, the Japanese waste paper market was controlled by paper manufacturers, not by the market. It was because paper manufacturers could abuse the weakness of waste paper compression companies, which was waste paper compression companies could not have stock due to the excessive volume of waste paper.

As the competition structure and the characteristics of market competition were reviewed, the cost of raw material is significant to paper manufacturers. Therefore, reduction in the raw material cost is directly connected to the competitiveness of a company. Due to this reason, paper manufacturers reduced the burden of raw material cost by controlling the waste paper market. This can be explained as the economic desire of companies. Many manufacturers indicated in their CSR reports that they satisfy the economic desire of companies and the social desire at the same time by increasing waste paper usage. This interpretation is far apart from their statements.[38]

This interpretation of this study results was specifically shown in the re-use case of the released paper of waste gypsum board in the next section.

6. Case study: The strategy of paper manufacturer regarding the recycling of waste gypsum board

6-1. Recycling of waste gypsum board

Table 7 estimated the quantity of waste gypsum board discharge by region. Currently, total 1,091 thousand tons per year of waste gypsum board are discharged in Japan, where 295 and 796 thousand tons per year are produced at the new construction sites and demolition construction sites, respectively.

In general, various gypsum boards are used in Japanese buildings for the purpose of soundproof and fire prevention. Gypsum board is widely used as a construction material and it is made of recycled materials. However, waste gypsum boards are discarded without being recycled. Especially, waste gypsum boards generated from demolished buildings are mostly discarded without being recycled because there were not enough related regulations and technologies. Discharging waste gypsum board can cause environmental pollution (e. g., hydrogen sulfide emission). Therefore, it is mandatory to dispose it at a managed final waste treatment facility. Regulations also specify that waste containing waste gypsum board cannot be treated at a managed final waste treatment facility. It causes a social problem of shortening the capacity of industrial waste treatment facilities. Therefore, recycling of gesso and released paper from waste gypsum board can be considered as a desperate social demand in Japan.

Generally, waste gypsum board, produced during building demolition, can be processed after being discharged separately. Gesso can be used as a raw

---

38) For example, Nippon Paper Group (2016), *CSR Report 2015*, Nippon Paper Group, p. 31., contains Green Action Plan, which was about ① responding to global climate change, ② saving and promoting forest resources, and ③ using resources in circulation. In particular, it delivers a message that companies satisfy the social desire and the economic profit through promoting the usage of waste paper.

Figure 9: The flowchart of waste gypsum board recycle

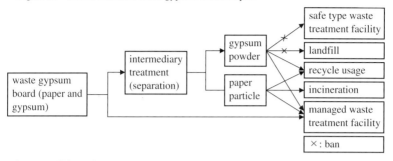

Source: Ministry of Land, Infrastructure, Transport and tourism homepage, http://www.mlit.go.jp/sogoseisaku/region/recycle/recyclehou/manual/sekkou.htm (last access, Nov. 1, 2015).

Figure 10: Issues in recycling waste gypsum board

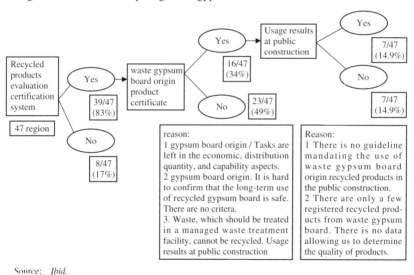

Source: Ibid.

material of gypsum board and released paper on gypsum board can be recycled for paper production.

Currently, waste gypsum board is one of the major building waste following concrete, asphalt, soil for construction, and wood for construction in the aspect of discharge quantity. It is expected that the quantity of waste will soar in the near future. Waste gypsum board leftover from new construction sites is rapidly recycled by gypsum manufacturers because the wide-area certifi-

Table 7: Estimated quantity of waste gypsum board discharge by region in Japan

Region	New Building			Building Demolition			Total
	Area of New Building (m²)	Area ratio of new building by region (%)	Discharge quantity of new building (10 thousand t)	Area of demolished building (m²)	Area ratio of demolished building by region (%)	Dischage quantity at demolition site (10 thousand t)	Yearly discharge quantity (10 thousand t)
Hokkaido	5,792,923	3.9%	1.1	1,305,477	5.8%	4.6	5.7
Aomori	1,302,112	0.9%	0.3	331,804	1.5%	1.2	1.4
Iwate	1,406,635	0.9%	0.3	234,567	1.0%	0.8	1.1
Miyagi	2,750,171	1.8%	0.5	378,737	1.7%	1.3	1.9
Akita	1,176,693	0.8%	0.2	262,499	1.2%	0.9	1.2
Yamagata	1,181,172	0.8%	0.2	360,073	1.6%	1.3	1.5
Fukushima	2,101,173	1.4%	0.4	485,101	2.1%	1.7	2.1
Ibaraki	3,977,658	2.7%	0.8	477,046	2.1%	1.7	2.5
Tochigi	2,708,385	1.8%	0.5	377,314	1.7%	1.3	1.9
Gumma	2,674,333	1.8%	0.5	334,681	1.5%	1.2	1.7
Saitama	8,587,189	5.8%	1.7	851,601	3.8%	3.0	4.7
Chiba	7,423,909	5.0%	1.5	851,810	3.8%	3.0	4.5
Tokyo	15,647,734	10.5%	3.1	2,436,141	10.8%	8.6	11.7
Kanagawa	9,923,780	6.7%	2.0	1,355,870	6.0%	4.8	6.7
Niigata	2,859,357	1.9%	0.6	682,847	3.0%	2.4	3.0
Toyama	1,408,868	0.9%	0.3	219,153	1.0%	0.8	1.1
Ishikawa	1,506,859	1.0%	0.3	167,140	0.7%	0.6	0.9
Fukui	967,449	0.6%	0.2	151,112	0.7%	0.5	0.7
Yamanashi	984,988	0.7%	0.2	171,142	0.8%	0.6	0.8
Nagano	2,436,600	1.6%	0.5	450,178	2.0%	1.6	2.1
Gifu	2,538,511	1.7%	0.5	381,122	1.7%	1.3	1.8
Shizuoka	5,320,538	3.6%	1.1	686,066	3.0%	2.4	3.5
Aichi	10,409,600	7.0%	2.1	1,699,964	7.5%	6.0	8.0

Mie	2,626,252	1.8%	0.5	316,321	1.4%	1.1	1.6
Shiga	2,162,663	1.5%	0.4	380,063	1.7%	1.3	1.8
Kyoto	2,493,191	1.7%	0.5	292,680	1.3%	1.0	1.5
Osaka	9,647,326	6.5%	1.9	1,060,934	4.7%	3.7	5.6
Hyogo	6,319,071	4.2%	1.3	919,961	4.1%	3.2	4.5
Nara	1,259,351	0.8%	0.2	183,624	0.8%	0.6	0.9
Wakayama	1,001,065	0.7%	0.2	153,844	0.7%	0.5	0.7
Tottori	527,784	0.4%	0.1	136,844	0.6%	0.5	0.6
Shimane	723,633	0.5%	0.1	286,796	1.3%	1.0	1.2
Okayama	2,025,318	1.4%	0.4	326,378	1.4%	1.1	1.6
Hiroshima	2,991,210	2.0%	0.6	412,545	1.8%	1.5	2.0
Yamaguchi	1,451,210	1.0%	0.3	355,298	1.6%	1.3	1.5
Tokushima	809,357	0.5%	0.2	105,062	0.5%	0.4	0.5
Kagawa	1,219,811	0.8%	0.2	179,809	0.8%	0.6	0.9
Ehime	1,561,674	1.0%	0.3	213,983	0.9%	0.8	1.1
Kochi	614,820	0.4%	0.1	79,579	0.4%	0.3	0.4
Fukuoka	5,856,597	3.9%	1.2	493,190	2.2%	1.7	2.9
Saga	1,039,192	0.7%	0.2	121,204	0.5%	0.4	0.6
Nagasaki	1,137,365	0.8%	0.2	164,779	0.7%	0.6	0.8
Kumamoto	1,944,251	1.3%	0.4	597,347	2.6%	2.1	2.5
Oita	1,416,635	1.0%	0.3	438,579	1.9%	1.5	1.8
Miyazaki	1,243,084	0.8%	0.2	310,521	1.4%	1.1	1.3
Kagoshima	1,745,926	1.2%	0.3	163,070	0.7%	0.6	0.9
Okinawa	1,940,054	1.3%	0.4	268,396	1.2%	0.9	1.3
Total	148,843,434	100.0%	29.5	22,612,249	100.0%	79.6	109.1

Source: Ministry of the Environment homepage, https://www.env.go.jp/recycle/report/h25-06.pdf (last access, Nov. 1, 2015).

cate system is established. However, waste gypsum board produced from old building is rarely recycled.

Figure 10 summarizes the issues of waste gypsum board recycle in Japan. The gypsum powder recycle flow can be explained as follows.

Gypsum board manufacturers collect and recycle gypsum board leftover produced at new construction sites through product evaluation certificate system of each local government. Eighty-three percentage of all Japanese local governments use this system to recycle gypsum board leftover. On the other hand, waste gypsum board produced from building demolition sites has become a serious issue. Waste gypsum board produced from building demolish has various foreign substances on it, so it has technical difficulties in recycling gesso. Moreover, the wide-area certificate system makes a gypsum board manufacturer treat only its products, while products from various companies are mixed at a demolition site. Therefore, these companies do not purchase waste from building demolition sites.

The recycling treatment status of gypsum powder from waste gypsum board was reviewed. The recycling of released paper from waste gypsum board also has the same issue. Although it is not much, released paper from waste gypsum board is used to produce paper. Generally, released paper from the waste gypsum board produced at demolition site is not recycled because it contains a lot of foreign substances.

There are many problems associated with recycling waste gypsum board. However,

waste gypsum board treatment companies and industrial waste treatment companies seek ways to recycle waste gypsum board to minimize environmental pollution issues. Particularly, the efforts of intermediate industrial waste treatment companies to differentiate released paper have many implications. Industrial waste treatment companies of each region make substantial technology investment on the recycle of waste gypsum board, which is deeply related to environmental problems. Moreover, if release paper is used for producing paper, it will bring considerable economic effects and the recycle of waste gypsum board will be activated.

The next section will review the case of C company, an intermediate waste treatment company, located in Yokohama city, Japan, to infer the strategical thoughts of paper manufacturers on released paper from waste gypsum board.

6-2. The case of C company's A factory, an intermediate waste treatment company, located in Yokohama city[39]

The C company's A factory, an intermediate waste gypsum board treatment company, located in Yokohama city has approximately 2.44 acres stock yard and 825 m^2 factory building. The intermediate treatment facility of the factory acquired permission on February 6, 2008, from Yokohama city. In 2008, C company installed waste gypsum board separation facility at A factory and acquired technology to utilize released paper from waste gypsum board to produce paper. This separation facility was developed by the C company and the C company holds the patent on it. Processed piece of released paper is compressed in a press and pressed released paper bale is used by Japanese paper manufacturer O Paper and D Paper. It is mostly commercialized as liner cardboard, which is used for producing corrugated cardboard.

The factory takes waste gypsum board collected by the company as well as primarily treated released paper separated from waste gypsum board by other companies12. The price of primarily treated released paper separated from waste gypsum board by other companies is between 15 and 20 Yen per kg. The factory can process 166 tons per day at max when the factory is operated 24 hours. The company treats one thousand tons of waste gypsum board per month. Generally, the treatment cost of primarily treated released paper from waste gypsum board is 30 and 30 Yen per kg for incineration and landfill, respectively. The C company charges 15 Yen per kg to primarily treated released paper from waste gypsum board. Therefore, the request from other companies is in its increasing trend.

To sell released paper separated from waste gypsum board, it must ① maintain the size of released paper to conserve enough pulp fiber and ② remove gypsum powder attached to released paper as much as possible.

Previously, paper companies hesitated to purchase released paper as a paper raw material because it was not possible to remove gypsum powder from pieces of released paper to a satisfactory level and eliminate plastic wallpaper from released paper. However, the A factory of the C company crushes waste gypsum board as a primary treatment to produce pieces of paper without foreign substances on gypsum board or gypsum powder. According to the company, released paper of the company contains equal or less than 18% of gypsum powder in 2015 so it is readily useful for paper production. The company reported 30% attachment rate in 2013 and its gypsum powder sepa-

---

[39] The C company at Yokohama city was visited three times between 2013 and 2015. Interview was made on the condition of not revealing the names of paper manufacturers and

ration has improved almost twice for 2 years. Moreover, the size of released paper is around 10cm, which is good enough to extract pulp fiber.

According to the C company, Japanese paper manufacturers started to use waste gypsum board origin released paper to produce paper because intermediate treatment companies made technological development and separation of gypsum powder and foreign substances became possible in most parts. It means that there was advancement in technology to treat hard or banned materials for using waste paper and additional facility investment. In other words, it symbolizes that the barrier of banned or hard-to-treat elements, which were inevitably contained in paper although they were the trace amount, is somewhat broken. However, the following statement of the company had implications.

The company said that Japanese paper manufacturers were not willing to use released paper from waste gypsum board. They were hesitant because it was hard to define released paper mixed with gypsum powder as normal waste paper, although gypsum separation and impurity removal technologies are quite advanced. Moreover, they were not willing to pay a normal unit price to purchase released paper from waste gypsum board. Consequently, the recycled released paper after separation is mostly used as refuse paper & plastic fuel.

Table 8 shows the sales unit of C company's recycled material. The range of unit price was wide. Gypsum powder supplied as a raw material of gypsum board was economically feasible the most. The released paper used for a paper material was 3 Yen per kg, which was the price on the door. When

---

C company when the field investigation results are used for academic purpose. It was because the relationship with Japanese paper manufacturers was not smooth yet. The C company has not secured enough economic feasibility compared to the equipment installation cost. It was said that the increase in waste paper sales price to paper manufacturers is the only way to acquire the economic feasibility.

Table 8. The purpose and unit of the C company's recycled products

Purpose	Unit price (Yen/Kg)
Gypsum board raw material	0.1~15
Soil solidifying material	0.1~14
Cement raw material	0.2~5
Fertilizer	0.7~3.5
Paper raw material	1~3

transportation price was excluded, it was 0-1 Yen per kg.

According to the C company, the unit price only reflected the position of paper manufacturers. The disposal fee for released paper from waste gypsum board burdened paper manufacturers. Therefore, paper manufacturers believed that 1 Yen per kg for converting waste into valued goods was a reasonable price to intermediate treatment companies. Moreover, they believed that intermediate treatment companies could take the equipment installation back by selling gypsum board raw material.

When considering the limitation in the cost of separating gypsum powder from released paper, it was urgent to stabilize the market price and make paper companies accept the value of products. According to the intermediate treatment companies, there was not enough return for an investment and it was hard to maintain a business economically. It was not the sole view of the C company and it was told that it is the general consensus of the intermediate treatment companies.

The detailed hearing investigation was described with using the C company as an example of advanced gypsum board recycle treatment. The C company had a technology to recycle gypsum powder acquired from waste gypsum board and improved the utilization rate of recycled gypsum powder. Moreover, it was selling recyclable released paper as a product by acquiring new treatment technology acknowledged by paper manufacturers, while released paper from waste gypsum board used to be buried or incinerated. Furthermore, it formed multiple sales markets to establish a recycled released paper market.

However, it was hard to find active efforts of paper manufacturers to utilize waste gypsum board as a resource, although efforts were made to improve the added value of recycled products (i. e., released paper from waste gypsum board) and a company network was made to secure stable sales. In other words, paper manufacturers had to prioritize the profit of companies in reality and they only could pursue social benefit within a limited range.

There could be various reasons why it was hard to secure marketability of it as a paper raw material. However, it was required to create a healthy raw material market led by paper manufacturers. The creation of a raw material market will be a way to resolve a social issue called waste gypsum board recycle.

7. Conclusions – derived points

Figure 11 schematizes the CSV management of Oji, a household paper manufacturer. The company started 'nepia 1000 toilet project' to revolve toilet and water issues of developing countries. The project donates a portion of sales of target products (e. g., Oji's tissue and toilet paper) to UNICEF and supports 'activities related to water and sanitary'. The objectives of the support are to resolve outdoor toilet usage of the poverty in East Timor and eradicate diseases related to it. The importance of the project is that a company and consumers share a social issue. In other words, it wins the sympathy of consumers to improve the sales of target products.[40] The last goal of this project is to secure the profitability by winning the sympathy and support of consumers.

As Porter and Kramer stated, this project is based on the recognition that the success and social prosperity are closely related and inter-dependent. This could be an example showing that a business activity can create a social value and economic profit at the same time.[41] However, as this study showed, Japanese paper companies prioritized company profit, although they managed companies with emphasizing people and planet within the territory of regulations and the social pressure. In other words, they pursued the social benefit within a possible range.

This study evaluated what kinds of desires a society wanted to resolve through the fuel supply chain of Japanese paper manufacturers and what are the fundamental desires of companies based on their economic feasibility.

Analysis results showed that companies tried to improve social outcome and economic outcome through administrative activities on the line of legal regulations or emphasized the environmental issue resolution as a voluntary social activity. These results indicated that the social contribution of Japanese paper manufacturers concurred with previous studies and they were unfolded with focusing on environmental issues.

However, this case showed that the social desire on released paper from waste gypsum board was ignored because the existing structural problem (e. g., the necessity of low-cost raw material supply) was not resolved while the productivity was emphasized in paper production. It was because the supply of raw material affected the profitability of paper manufacturers the most.

---

40) Masatoshi, Tamamura (2014), *Social Impact-Kachi kyousou (CSV)ga kigyou business hatarakikatawo kaeru,* Sangakusya, pp. 109 – 113.
41) Porter, M. E. and Kramer, M. R. (2011), *op. cit.*, p. 67.

Figure 11: Providing product service to resolve social tasks of paper manufacturer

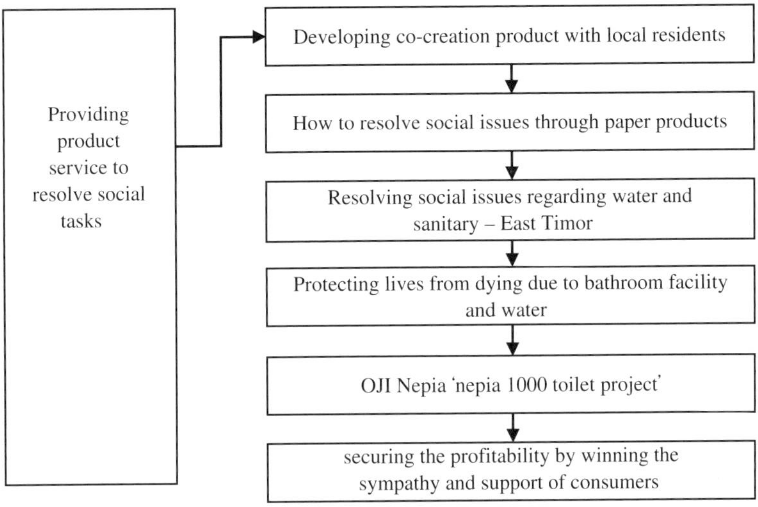

```
┌─────────────┐    ┌─────────────────────────────────────────────────┐
│             │───▶│   Developing co-creation product with local residents │
│             │    └─────────────────────────────────────────────────┘
│  Providing  │                           │
│   product   │    ┌─────────────────────────────────────────────────┐
│  service to │───▶│  How to resolve social issues through paper products │
│ resolve social │    └─────────────────────────────────────────────────┘
│    tasks    │                           │
│             │    ┌─────────────────────────────────────────────────┐
│             │    │  Resolving social issues regarding water and    │
│             │    │              sanitary – East Timor              │
│             │    └─────────────────────────────────────────────────┘
                                          │
                   ┌─────────────────────────────────────────────────┐
                   │ Protecting lives from dying due to bathroom facility │
                   │                   and water                     │
                   └─────────────────────────────────────────────────┘
                                          │
                   ┌─────────────────────────────────────────────────┐
                   │       OJI Nepia 'nepia 1000 toilet project'     │
                   └─────────────────────────────────────────────────┘
                                          │
                   ┌─────────────────────────────────────────────────┐
                   │     securing the profitability by winning the   │
                   │        sympathy and support of consumers        │
                   └─────────────────────────────────────────────────┘
```

Source: Author creates it by summarizing, Masatoshi, Tamamura (2014), *Social Impact-Kachi kyousou (CSV) ga kigyou business hatarakikatawo kaeru*, Sangakusya, pp. 108–133.

As it was confirmed in the case study, the main question was how to join the flow of the CSV without disturbing the core social value. The first answer is to accept the fact that the CSV cannot be a basic tool to create social benefit and economic benefit at the same time. In other words, a company cannot resolve all social problems through the CSV, although it is possible to resolve social problems with gaining economic profit to some degree. As shown in the example, a company may solve some problems (e. g., issues in a poor region) through the CSV. However, it cannot eliminate the poverty issue itself. Therefore, it would be required to clearly define social issues, which can be improved through the CSV. Companies also can maximize the impact on social and economic outcomes by materializing social issues to be solved through the CSV. As shown in the analysis results, main social outcomes are to improve environmental problems and enlighten poverty regions. It is necessary to materialize the property of these areas.

The second is how to understand the social and economic outcome. In other words, we must have an in-depth discussion on tension and conflicts occurring in the process of conducting two values at the same time. Social and economic outcomes on supply chain were proposed in previous foreign CSV case studies. However, the results of this study ignored the social desire within a supply chain and company activities were made based on the linear economic outcome of paper manufacturers. It will be required actively monitoring the outcome of the CSV and not emphasizing the CSV with ignoring fundamental issues.

References

Burke, L. and Logsdon, J. M.(1996), "How corporate social responsibility pays off", *Long Range Planning*, Vol. 29, No. 4, pp. 495−502.

Crane, A., G. Palazzo, L. and Spence, D. Matten (2014), "Contesting the Value of the Shared Value Concept", *California Management Review*, Vol. 56, No. 2.

Dembek, K., Singh, P. and Bhakoo, V. (2015), "Literature review of shared value: a theoretical concept or a management buzzword?", *Journal of Business Ethics*, 01 February, pp. 1−37.

Freeman, R. E., Wicks, A. C. and Parmar, B. (2013), "Stakeholder theory and the corporate objective revisited", *Organization Sciences*, Vol. 15, No. 3, pp. 364−369.

Pirson, M. (2012), "Social entrepreneurs as the paragons of shared value creation? A critical perspective", *Social Enterprise Journal*, Vol. 8, No. 1, pp. 31−48.

Porter, M. E. and Kramer, M. R. (2006), "Strategy and society: the link between competitive advantage and corporate social responsibility", *Havard Business Review*, December, pp. 78−92.

Porter, M. E. and Kramer, M. R. (2011), "Creating shared value: how to reinvent capitalism", *Harvard Business Review*, Jan-Feb, pp. 62−77.

Porter, M. E., Hills, G., Pfitzer, M., Patscheke, S. and Hawkins, E. (2012), *Measuring shared value: How to unlock value by linking social and business results,* in Conference Report available at FSG homepage, www.fsg.org/publications/measuring-shared-value (last access, Nov. 3, 2015).

Prahald, C. K. (2005), *The Fortune at the Bottom of the Pyramid*. Wharton School Publishing.

Rocchi, M. and Ferrero, I. (2014), "Systematic shared value in Finance: expanding Porter's approach". *Universidad de Navarra Working Paper*, 07/14.

VI.
Employment Management Reform and the Japanese Production System: The Experience of Japanese Manufacturers During the "Lost Decade"

Kota SHIMAUCHI

1. Introduction

The boom in the Japanese economy that lasted from 2002 to 2007 was called the "Beyond the Izanagi Boom". During this period, the performance of the Japanese manufacturing industry was brisk. However, the prosperity has been characterized as "polarized prosperity", as the improvement in corporate performance was associated with an increase in the use of non-regular employees, and the wage and living standard gaps between regular and non-regular employees were also expanded.

In the early 1990s, Japanese companies faced a long recession after the burst of Japan's economic bubble and the intensification of global competition, and looked to employment management reform to promote business recovery. The employment portfolio management (EPM) system that the Japan Federation of Employers' Associations (Nikkeiren, currently Nippon Keidanren) proposed in 1995 then had an impact on the employment management reform among many Japanese companies.

Nikkeiren argued that the introduction of a new human resource management system was required for companies to respond to the changes in the business environment, and it proposed the concept that regular employees with long-term, open ended employment contracts and non-regular employees with fixed-term employment contracts should be flexibly combined as necessary. This proposal was intended to force Japanese employment practices, which focused on long-term employment for regular employees and internal human resources development, to change significantly.

The easing of the Worker Dispatch Law occurred in the late 1990s.[1] The economy also experienced an upturn in the early 2000s. Japanese manufacturers achieved the expansion of production volume by significantly increasing numbers of non-regular employees. Employment management based on EPM involving the flexible combination of multiple employee types (regular employees, directly employed temporary workers, and indirectly employed dispatched workers) became widespread among Japanese companies from the 1990s through the 2000s. In 2005, ten years after Nikkeiren proposed EPM, according to the *"labor force survey"* of the Health, Labor, and Welfare Ministry, the percentage of non-regular employees reached 32.6 percent.

However, amid the recession caused by the Lehman Brothers bankruptcy that occurred in the fall of 2008, Japanese companies ended the employment of non-regular employees in large numbers, corresponding with significant decreases in production volume. The number of terminated non-regular workers reached approximately 240,000 between October, 2008 and September, 2009.[2]

As described above, the employment management featuring the flexible combination of increasing numbers of non-regular employees and decreasing numbers of regular employees has become the typical management style of today's Japanese manufacturers. Why did this management style become popular? Has this management style improved or harmed Japanese companies' competitiveness? The answers to these questions are key issues for researchers engaged in analyzing corporate competitiveness.

In this chapter, based on the above problem consciousness, we will clarify the effects of employment management reform among Japanese manufacturers on their production systems and skill formation practices which are major sources of competitiveness, focusing on the period from the 1990s to the 2000s (the so-called "lost decade").

In its conclusion, this chapter shows that employment management reform during this period was focused on cutting personnel costs as well as maxi-

---

1) The easing of the Worker Dispatch Law regulations has been promoted. This law was enacted in 1985. At that time, worker dispatch was permitted for thirteen types of services (positive list system). When the law was amended in 1999, worker dispatch was permitted for all services except for six specific prohibited services, including manufacturing operations. In the Worker Dispatch Law amended in 2003, the dispatch for manufacturing industry was also permitted. EPM, which was legally supported, prevailed rapidly.

2) According to the Health, Labour and Welfare Ministry's survey (*Hiseiki roudousya no yatoidome tou no jyokyo ni tsuite*) on July 21, 2009.

mizing workforce flexibility, and resulted in the widespread use of non-regular employees and in a reduction of domestic consumer demand, which is essential to business success. Moreover, this chapter shows that the reform caused damage to the skill formation practice as the infrastructure supporting production system which is major source of Japanese strength.

These conclusions suggest that a management style pursuing cost reduction and employment adjustment depending on the use of non-regular employees is an unsustainable solution.

In Section 2, we consider the features of EPM introduced by many Japanese companies. Then, in Section 3, we illustrate the features of the Japanese production systems and skill formation practices which are the sources of Japanese manufacturers' competitiveness. Finally, in Section 4, in order to clarify the effects of employment management reform on the Japanese production system and skill formation practice, we analyze the case of Toyota.

2. Features of employment management reform

2-1. Employment portfolio management - Nikkeiren's proposal

Nikkeiren's report must be studied to understand the background and content of employment management reform in Japanese companies. The report is titled "*Shinjidai no Nihonteki Keiei (A New Era of Japanese Business Management)*". In this report, Nikkeiren proposed a new human resource management system to respond to the changes in the management environment after the 1990s (slower economic growth, falling birthrate and aging population, conversion of industrial structure, and globalization).

Here, we identify the philosophy and practice of the new approach.[3] In this report, Nikkeiren pointed out that conventional Japanese management, based on the philosophies of being "human-centered" and adopting a "long-term view", achieved stable employment, ability development, motivation maintenance and improvement, and positive labor relations, and argued that this philosophy should be firmly maintained in the future.

However, at the same time, this report pointed out that companies should reform their human resource management in response to the changes in the management environment, and proposed new employment management methods allowing them to flexibly respond to the changes in the industrial structure, labor market, and laborers' attitudes. These features constituted

---

3) Nikkeiren shin nihonteki keiei kenkyu project (ed.) (1995), pp. 22–34.

employment portfolio management.

According to the explanation of Nikkeiren, by combining the stable, long-term employment type and the fluid, fixed-term employment type, EPM allows companies not only to secure the number of employees needed with the skills and abilities required, but also to prepare a variety of options meeting workers' personal needs for their working life and their personal life.

EPM reorganizes employees into three groups as shown in Figure 1 and Table 1, and encourages companies to manage the combination flexibly as necessary. The classification is as follows. Group A is characterized by long-term services and stable employment based on open-ended contracts, and Groups B and C are characterized by short-term services and frequent movements between companies based on fixed-term contracts.

Nikkeiren argued that the long-term employment relationships, which were the norm for regular employees, should be limited to managerial career track, core technical occupations henceforth, and that specialist occupations (e. g., planning, sales, R&D, etc.) and regular service employees (clerical, technical, and sales positions) should be replaced by fixed-term non-regular employees. Focusing on employment types, it is clear that Nikkeiren's EPM proposal was intended to decrease the use of regular employees and increase

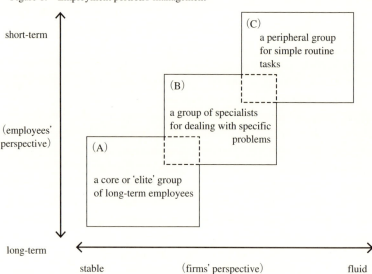

Figure 1: Employment portfolio management

Source: Nikkeiren shin nihonteki keiei kenkyu project. (ed.) (1995), p. 32, chart 7.

Table 1: Features of three employment groups

	Type of employment	Employees eligible	Wages	Bonuses	Basis for Promotion / advancement
Core group of long-term employees (A)	Open-ended employment contract	Managerial career track, Core-technical Occupations	Monthly salary or yearly remuneration package; ability-based wages; wage increment	Specified rate and sliding scale for performance	Promotion to managerial ranks; pay increase based on job performance qualifications
Specialists (B)	Fixed-term employment contract	Specialist occupations (planning, sales, R&D, etc.)	Yearly remuneration package; performance results	Sharing of company performance results	Evaluation of performance
Flexible workforce (C)	Fixed-term employment contract	Clerical, technical, sales positions	Hourly wages; Job-based wages; no wage increment	Specified rate	Switch to higher ranking position

Source: Nikkeiren shin nihonteki keiei kenkyu project. (ed.) (1995), p. 32, chart 8, and Arjan B. Keizer (2009), p. 54, table4. 7.

the use of non-regular employees.

2-2. Purposes of EPM introduction

Why do Japanese companies increasingly hire non-regular employees? The first reason is flexibility. Non-regular employment is based on fixed-term employment contracts, so flexible employment adjustment in response to environmental changes is enabled by increasing non-regular employees. The second reason is labor cost cutting. The use of non-regular employees allows the companies to change their labor cost from a fixed cost to a variable cost. From the above, it can be said that the purpose of introducing EPM is to increase the labor force that can be flexibly used at low cost.

According to the Ministry of Health, Welfare and Labor *"General Survey on Diversified Types of Employment"* (2004), there are 3 reasons why Japanese companies utilize non-regular employees in 2003. The first is "wage saving" (51.7 percent); the second is "responding to business conditions on a daily or weekly basis" (28.0 percent) and the third is "adjusting the employment level according to economic fluctuations" (26.6 percent).[4] Also, according to JIL-PT (2006), the first reason is "for labor cost cut" (80.3 percent).

As described above, many companies increased their use of non-regular employees for the benefits of cutting personnel costs and flexible employment adjustment. As a result, according to the *"Labor Force Survey"* by the Ministry of Internal Affairs and Communications, the numbers of regular and non-regular employees and the ratio of non-regular employees have been changing, as shown in Table 2. For fifteen years since the end of the 1990s, while regular employees' numbers decreased by four million, the number of non-regular employees increased by seven million. Many companies replaced regular employees with non-regular employees, and, as a result, one out of three Japanese workers has become a non-regular employee.[5]

Table 2: Transition table of employment types in Japan

	Number of regular employees (10,000)	Number of non-regular employees (10,000)	Ratio of non-regular employees (%)
1995	3,779	1,001	20.9
2000	3,630	1,273	26.0
2005	3,374	1,633	32.6
2010	3,355	1,756	34.3

Source: Ministry on Internal Affairs and Communications, *"Special Labour Force Survey"* (1995) (2000).
Ministry on Internal Affairs and Communications, *"Labour Force Survey (Detailed Tabulation)"* (2005) (2010).

---

4) According to the Ministry of Health, Welfare and Labor *"General Survey on Diversified Types of Employment"* (2014), Japanese companies utilize non-regular employees in order to save costs (38.6%) and respond to the press and stack of business of a day or a week (28.0%) in 2014.

5) According to the Ministry on Internal Affairs and Communications *"Special Labour Force Survey"* (1995) (2000), and the Ministry on Internal Affairs and Communications *"Labour Force Survey (Detailed Tabulation)"* (2005) (2010).

2-3. Effects of EPM on workers

Japanese society is called an "unequal community", and we have focused on the negative aspects of non-regular employees in recent years. Non-regular employment, however, also has positive aspects. Workers can use their professional knowledge and skills in different companies and also can work during flexible office hours suitable for their lifestyles. They can work without being bound by a specific company and work time. Non-regular employment is expected to contribute to the promotion of work-life balance and creation of various methods of work.[6]

On the other hand, it is a fact that treatment disparities also exist between non-regular and regular employees. Non regular employees (1) are exposed to employment end risks due to fixed-term contracts; (2) receive relatively lower pay; (3) are not covered by pay raises based on promotion/advancement; (3) have fewer chances for career development because many of them handle routinized work; and (4) have limited rights and social benefits as workers. In other words, non-regular employees are not protected by safety nets.

In addition, it is also a fact that many non-regular employees do not choose their employment type voluntarily. As there are no companies where they can work as regular employees, many are "unwilling workers" who choose to work as non-regular employees reluctantly.

According to the Health, Labour and Welfare Ministry's *"Basic Statistical Survey on Wage Structures"* (2005), the fixed monthly salary is 348,000 yen for male regular employees versus 221,000 yen for male non-regular employees. A similar pay disparity is present for female employees, with regular employees earning 239,000 yen versus 168,000 yen for non-regular employees. The non-regular employees clearly receive lower wages. Also, according to the Health, Labour and Welfare Ministry's *"Basic Survey on Ability Development"* (2006), the training opportunities that the companies provided non-regular employees with (both planned on-the-job training and off-the-job training) remain half of the opportunities provided for regular employees. In this way, in Japan, unstable workers with low wages are increasing, and many of them have no hope of acquiring enough skills to escape from poverty. They are becoming the "working poor".[7]

---

6) Kumazawa (2007), pp. 111-116.
7) Working poor refers to people who are working but who remain in conditions of poverty. They are the working class who are forced into an impoverished lifestyle, although they are working. If a worker whose annual income is less than 2 million yen is defined as a

It seems that the increase in non-regular employees has some effects on the economy of consumption as well. When the lives of workers from 1995 to 2005 are checked according to the Internal Affairs and Communications Ministry's "*Survey Report on the Family Income and Expenditure*" (each year), household net income, disposable income, and consumption expenditure have been falling (see Table3).

Also, according to the Ministry of Internal Affairs and Communications' survey "*National Field Survey of Family Income and Expenditure*" (1994 and 2004), the household net income (with two persons or more) decreased from 536,000 yen to 502,000 yen, and the consumption expenditure decreased from 344,000 yen to 320,000 yen for the ten years from 1994 to 2004. Of the net incomes, the income from employment significantly decreased from 400,000 yen to 357,000 yen. The employment management reform is negatively affecting the living of workers.

What do these facts mean? The employment management reform among

Table 3: Increase of non-regular employees and economy of consumption

	Family income and expenditure (monthly average)						Number and ratio of employees		
	Household net income (JPY)	Ratio (1995 =100) (%)	Disposable income (JPY)	Ratio (1995 =100) (%)	Consumption expenditure (JPY)	Ratio (1995 =100) (%)	Regular (10,000)	Non-regular (10,000)	Ratio (non-regular) (%)
1995	570,817	100	482,174	100	349,663	100	3,779	1,001	21
1996	579,461	102	488,537	101	351,755	101	3,800	1,043	22
1997	595,214	104	497,036	103	357,636	102	3,812	1,152	23
1998	588,916	103	495,887	103	353,552	101	3,794	1,173	24
1999	574,676	101	483,910	100	346,177	99	3,688	1,225	25
2000	560,954	98	472,823	98	340,977	98	3,630	1,273	26
2001	551,160	97	464,723	96	335,042	96	3,640	1,360	27
2002	538,277	94	452,501	94	330,651	95	3,489	1,451	29
2003	524,542	92	440,461	91	325,823	93	3,444	1,504	30
2004	530,028	93	444,966	92	330,836	95	3,410	1,564	31
2005	522,629	92	439,672	91	328,649	94	3,374	1,633	33

Source: Ministry of Internal Affairs and Communications "*Survey report on the family income and expenditure*" (1995–2005), "*Special Labour Force Survey*" (1994–2004), and "*Labour Force Survey (Detailed Tabulation)*" (2005).

working poor, there were 550,000 people in this group as of 2005.

Japanese companies had been chipping away at the quality of life (for example, stable employment and compensation) by increasing the proportion of non-regular employees rapidly. In other words, Japanese companies reduced the consumer demand essential to their own success by means of their own reform.

3. Competitiveness, production system and skill formation practice in Japan

In order to clarify the effects of the employment management reform among Japanese companies on competitiveness, the production system and skill formation practices that are major sources of Japanese manufacturers' competitiveness needs to be analyzed. Here, we focus on the automobile industry that has been leading the Japanese economy.

3-1. Toyota production system and competitiveness

Japanese major automotive and consumer electronics manufacturers were highly competitive in the world market from the 1980s to the 1990s. These companies achieved both price competitiveness (low cost, high productivity) and nonprice competitiveness (high quality, product diversity), that had been traditionally considered to be traded off against each other, at a high level. Many studies point out that the source of the competitiveness is the production system.[8] In what follows, the features of Toyota production system (TPS) which is representative of Japanese companies' production system are studied.[9]

The core element of TPS is just-in-time (JIT) production. JIT is the production management system that produces "what is necessary, when necessary, only at the necessary volume". This management method is called the pull-system. Given that Toyota adopts a reverse method of "the following process withdrawing the parts from the preceding process" instead of "the

---

8) This chapter focused on the production system and the skill formation practice as the sources of Japanese companies' competitiveness (resulting in low cost, high quality, short lead time, product diversity). To understand the processes of generating the competitiveness more correctly, it is necessary to study various factors such as R&D systems, supplier systems, and labor-management relation systems.

9) In this chapter, in order to understand the features of TPS, Sugimori, Kusunoki, Cho, and Uchikawa (1977), Ohno (1988), Womack, Jones and Roos (1990), Suzuki (1994), Liker, Fruin and Adler ed. (1999), Fujimoto (1999), and Monden (2001) are used as reference.

preceding process supplying the parts to the following process" (Sugimori, Kusunoki, Cho, and Uchikawa, 1977), the parts plant (or parts supplier) produces the amount of parts used at the final assembly plant closest to the customers, as instructed by the production instruction tool, Kanban. Therefore, JIT is also called the Kanban system.

However, when the amount of the parts that the following process receives from the preceding process is varied, the preceding process must prepare excessive stock, equipment, and personnel on time for the peak. To prevent this, the daily production volume of each product is averaged in the final assembly plant. This is known as "heijunka" (production leveling).

Small lot production and multi-item production will need to perform production leveling. For that purpose, flexible equipment, layout and organization is required. It is particularly important to perform a flexible work system organization, and the number of persons is increased or decreased as necessary without being fixed. This is called "shojinka".

The development of multi-task workers is required for flexible work organization. Toyota organizes about five workers into a work team (han), and unites about four teams to organize a work group (kumi) of about twenty workers. Multi-task worker development refers to having workers learn multiple jobs in the work team or group that they belong to. For that purpose, Toyota makes workers experience multiple jobs using job rotation. The multi-task workers make it possible not only to organize a work unit with the minimum number of workers, but to respond flexibly to variations in the production volume and product model.

If JIT production performs this way, cost reduction, improvement of productivity, and response to market changes are achieved.

Another core element of TPS is "jidoka". The Japanese word "jidoka" generally refers to automation. In the context of Toyota, jidoka means "to make the equipment or operation stop whenever an abnormal or defective condition arises".

At Toyota, problems on the production site are visualized by jidoka mechanism, leading to the online and offline solving of problems by workers. In online problem solving, workers rapidly solve the problem on the site where the problem is found to ensure high-quality factory output. This is called built-in quality. Offline problem solving is well-known for the small group activities including QC circles and suggestion systems.

In this way, jidoka encourages problem solving by multi-task workers, and functions to improve efficiency and quality at the same time.

3-2. Skill formation practice as TPS infrastructure

TPS is a system to enhance competitiveness by a flexible work organization based on workers' multi-task development and the promotion of problem solving. The knowledge and skills of workers are utilized sufficiently without relying on advanced automation technologies. These are the important features of TPS as well as Japanese production systems.

TPS is also a type of a mass production system. Therefore, the division of labor and standardization of work are ensured on production sites. However, it is not easy to foster a multi-task worker who can handle several jobs enough to work flexibly, and can propose improvement ideas in on site and off site QC activities. In this sense, the key factor to make TPS function effectively is promoting the skill formation of workers. Skill formation is the infrastructure of TPS.

Development of multi-task workers is achieved mainly by using on-the-job training (OJT) and job rotation. At Toyota, the supervisor (kumi-cho) makes plans for OJT and job-rotation, and also serves as a trainer. The supervisor is responsible for the training of workers as part of their work, rather than as a full-time trainer.[10]

Koike (1991), the representative study on the skill formation in Japanese companies points out that it is important to make workers experience a wide range of tasks that are technically related. Also, Koike, Chuma, and Ota (2001), the empirical study on Japanese auto manufacturer (Toyota-author) points out that it is important for the supervisor to understand the skill level of group members, plan the training and give them one-to-one training for effective skill formation. In other words, for the purpose of effective skill formation, it is necessary to give a trainee systematic tasks for training according to the plan.

As for OJT, work itself is training. As a result, the training cost reduction and practical training are enabled. It is hard, however, to differentiate production and training.[11] You must manage the training processes strategically. The work organization that workers belong to is a production unit and the "workplace as a learning environment" (Nakahara, 2012) at the same time. Arranging the learning environment to enhance the effectiveness of skill formation is a necessary condition to make TPS function.

---

10) See Suzuki (1980), Liker and Meier (2007), and Monden (2011).
11) Hiranuma and Kimura (2000) is mainly used as reference.

4. Employment management reform and skill formation: The Case of Toyota

The necessary condition to making the production system the source of Japanese manufacturers' competitiveness is the development of multi-task workers. Therefore, it is necessary to arrange the learning environment in work organization. What effects have the employment management reform had on the skill formation practices which are the infrastructure supporting the production system? Here, the case of Toyota in the early 2000s is analyzed to clarify the effects of the increase of non-regular employees upon the skill formation at the production site.

4-1. Non-regular employees at Toyota

Toyota, the world's largest auto manufacturer, has corresponded flexibly to variations in the production volume and product model by organizing work groups of the minimum number of regular employees (multi-task workers). On the other hand, non-regular employees have been utilized as the buffer against economic fluctuations. In the 2000s, Toyota boosted the number of non-regular employees.

The reason for the increase of non-regular employees is that the reduction of production costs and total labor costs has been required more than before, facing the long recession after Japan's economic bubble burst and global competition intensified.

According to Institute for Industrial Relations and Labor Policy, Chubu (2004), the top reasons for A company (Toyota-author) and A's group companies to utilize non-regular employees for the production department are "adjusting to economic/seasonal variation" and "labor cost saving". Also, according to Komatsu (2007), another reason is that regular employees travelling to overseas bases are increased, and substitute personnel have been required.[12]

For the above reasons, Toyota adopted the new employment management policy in the late 1990s. The policy consists of "a few talented regular employees" and "expanding the use of external manpower" (Toyota Motor Corporation Jinzai Kaihatsu Bu, 1997, p. 2). After the 2000s, seasonal workers

---

12) As Toyota increased overseas bases from the later 1990s to the 2000s, the employees assigned overseas and overseas business travelers have been increased. Comparing the numbers of 1998 and 2003, the number of employees assigned overseas increased from 988 to 1,360, and that of overseas business travelers increased from 13,700 to 17,160. See Komatsu (2007), p. 151.

were increased, and, after the revision of the worker dispatch law in the mid-2000s, dispatched workers began to be employed. Toyota surpassed General Motors in production volume around 2007, and grew to be the world's largest auto manufacturer. This growth was supported by the increasing use of non-regular employees.

According to *the Annual Securities Rreport* of Toyota, from 1990 to 2005, Toyota reduced the number of employees by approximately 10,000, and, on the other hand, the number of temporary employees (including seasonal workers and dispatched workers) was increased significantly.

This trend is distinguished in the production department. This is identified by the indicator called "juenritsu" that Toyota uses for employment management. This indicator is the ratio of the number of personnel (including seasonal workers, dispatched workers, and support personnel from another department of Toyota or affiliate companies) that the production department accepts from inside and outside the company to secure the number of employees required for production. Table 4 shows that juenritsu continued to increase in the early 2000s.

Table 4: Transition table of juenritsu : production department of Toyota

month	juenritsu (%)	month	juenritsu (%)
December, 2000	17.9	February, 2003	28.5
October, 2001	18.8	July, 2003	25.4
February, 2002	22.3	August, 2003	28.6
March, 2002	24.1	October, 2003	30.5
April, 2002	24.1	November, 2003	32.7
December, 2002	28.5	May, 2004	36.4
January, 2003	28.1	June, 2004	36.2

Source: The date contained in *Hyougikai News* (Published by Toyota Motor Workers'Union) author obtained is used as reference.

According to Toyota's "Personnel Plan" of June 2004 that the author obtained, Juenritsu was more than 36 percent. Of about 30,000 persons planned for the production department, about 9,000 persons were seasonal workers, and about 1,400 were external persons including dispatched workers and employees from affiliated companies (see Table 5).

The non-regular employees that were brought in during this period were low-wage workers with short-term contracts. The basic employment contract

Table 5: Employment of non-regular employees at Toyota production department

	Enrollment (Non-regular total : A+B)	Enrollment (A : Seasonal worker)	Enrollment (B : Dispatch worker, employee of affiliate company, etc)	Expiration of term (A+B)	Newly hired (A+B)
November, 2001	4,117	3,660	457	515	317
January, 2003	6,768	5,770	998	1,500	1,117
February, 2003	7,034	5,840	1,194	864	758
March, 2003	6,929	5,860	1,069	901	671
November, 2003	8,802	7,490	1,312	1,675	2,497
December, 2003	9,380	7,930	1,450	1,028	1,483
June, 2004	10,263	8,480	1,783	1,642	1,628
July, 2004	10,095	8,720	1,375	2,381	1,181

Source: The date of "Personnel Plan" of Toyota appeared in *Hyougikai News* (Published by Toyota Motor Workers' Union) author obtained is used as reference.

period of seasonal workers constituting the core of Toyota's non-regular employees was decided to be six months, and up to two years and eleven months if the contract is renewed. Also, the wage disparity exists between regular employees and seasonal workers. The monthly average wage for regular employees is 100 versus 57.6–65.9 for seasonal workers. A similar wage disparity is present for the annual income, with regular employees 100 versus seasonal workers 50.8–54.6 (see Table 6).

Table 6: The comparison of wages : regular employees and seasonal workers

		Monthly Wage Average (JPY)			Ratio (regular = 100) (%)	Annual Income (JPY)	Ratio (regular = 100) (%)
		Standard	surplus	Total			
Regular Employees		351,088	90,850	441,938	100.0	7,743,256	100.0
First year	First time	189,000	65,430	254,430	57.6	3,935,160	50.8
	Second time	199,500	69,070	268,570	60.8	4,124,840	53.3
	Third time	205,800	71,240	277,040	62.7	4,226,480	54.6
Second year		210,000	72,690	282,690	64.0	4,225,080	54.6
Third year		216,300	75,080	291,380	65.9	—	

Source: Sugiyama (2008), p. 99, Table 39 and 40.

4-2. Insufficient skill formation and quality degradation

Here, the effects of new employment policy of Toyota have had upon the skill formation practice on the production site are analyzed. The conclusion is that in Toyota's production sites in the early 2000s, the workload for regular employees was increased along with the combination of a few talented regular employees and increased non-regular employees. In addition, the OJT and job rotation became insufficient, which caused quality degradation.

In what follows, the way the skill formation on the production site became insufficient and the resulting quality problem are discussed.

4-2-1. Limitation to the works of non-regular employees

In Toyota, non-regular employees are given work that is subdivided, simplified, standardized, and can be learned in a short period. It is called "freshman process" (in Japanese, "shoshinsya kotei"[13]). The level and scope of the works that non-regular employees are responsible for are limited. Therefore, the use of non-regular employees does not contribute sufficiently to the multi-skill development infrastructure of TPS, although it is effective for cutting personnel costs and for flexible employment volume adjustment.

4-2-2. Short-term and liquidity of non-regular employment

Non-regular employees, such as seasonal workers, have a half-year short-term employment contract, as described above. As a result, the workers in work groups are replaced frequently. According to Toyota's "Personnel Plan" the author obtained, the seasonal workers and external workers (mainly dispatched workers) were replaced by about 500 to 2,000 persons per month. This number accounts for about 20 percent of the overall non-regular workers (see Table 5).

According to the plan of July 2004, it was expected that the contract term would expire for 2,381 non-regular employees in June, 1,181 non-regular employees would be deployed, and 10,095 non-regular employees in total would work.

4-2-3. Increased workload of regular employees

The work level and scope of non-regular employees is limited and the con-

---

13) This is according to the interview survey for several Toyota workers by author implemented from March to April, 2006. Respondent to author's survey are several regular employees of Toyota with introduction from Aichi Labor Institute. On this point, Komatsu (2007), p. 171, is used as reference too.

tract term is fixed and short. In addition, these workers are frequently replaced. If the ratio of non-regular employees increases, regular employees will have to undertake lots of work to manage work groups normally.

By the author's interview survey to several Toyota's workers, following has been revealed.[14] In the work group, the worker in charge of production line works and worker in charge of responding to rejected products and mechanical failures are placed separately. However, if non-regular employees whose work level and scope are limited are increased, regular employees will perform both these duties. Also, the supervisors and experienced workers must take charge of training non-regular employees.

According to Ihara (2007), non-regular employees often have not internalized the philosophy and disciplines of the company, and may have lower quality awareness compared to regular employees. Therefore, regular employees must communicate with many non-regular employees to detect and solve quality problems. Thus the workload for regular employees will be increased.

4-2-4. Insufficient skill formation on site

If the workload for regular employees is increased, it will be difficult to take time for training and select a person in charge of training, and OJT and job rotation will be insufficient.

Ihara (2003) reports on the real situation of skill formation at a Toyota production site based on the observation of participants for three months in 2001.[15] Job rotation is performed on site, and workers are able to take charge of various tasks. However, the report says, "The supervisor is allocating the works on a case-by-case basis, thinking only of achieving the norm for the day. On site, they have no room for taking a long-term view of human resource development". Rotation has become the "desperate means to manage the workplace". The work group (kumi) that he belonged to consisted of twenty-five workers, and the ratio of non-regular employees was 36 percent (nine seasonal employees).

Also, such an "unplanned rotation lacking in educational considerations" is observed in the changes of workers across work groups (this is called "ohen" in Japanese) as well. Many of the workers who are made to change to other groups for helping are "forced not only to make an irregular job shift, but to do the work irrelevant to their original one" . Mr A, a regular employee (fif-

---

14) The interview survey by author explained above.
15) This sentence and next sentence are written mainly based on Ihara (2003), chapter3.

teen years of service), who had been made to transfer to Group (X) from another group (Y), was made to transfer to a third group (Z) after about two-and-a-half months, and then he was made to return to X again. The following shows how the supervisor communicated with Mr A about the change.

"Hey, A. I am sorry to say, but I want you to transfer again. Only you can do so".

It is clear that the rotation of regular employees is not performed systematically based on educational considerations, but proceeded with as a short-term shift, leading to an increased workload for regular employees. These problems are considered to be caused mainly by the increase of non-regular employees.

The news published by Toyota Motor Workers' union points out as follows. On the production site, the acceptance ratio of persons from outside the workplace (juenritsu) is growing. Frequent personnel changes make the continuous development of human resources difficult. In each workplace, "the workers are too busy with their works to have any room for human resource development" (Toyota Motor Workers' Union, March 10, 2005).

4-2-5. Quality degradation

From the analyses of 4-2-1 to 4-2-4, it is revealed that the employment management policy combining fewer talented regular employees and increasing numbers of non-regular employees caused the workload for regular employees to be increased, and had negative effects on skill formation in the workplace. Here, we consider the performance of work organization under such circumstances.

According to Institute for Industrial Relation and Labor Policy, Chubu (2002), about 30 percent of the supervisors of the A company (Toyota-author) and A's group companies gave a negative reply to the question of whether the "skill succession and education/training are well performed" as the ratio of non-regular employees is increasing.

Also, as shown in Table 7, when the ratio of non-regular employees increases, various problems arise in managing the work groups on the production site. When the ratio of non-regular employees exceeds 30 percent, in particular, over 40 percent of the supervisors answered that, "The retention ratio is low, and the personnel management is difficult", "The accumulation of skills/techniques becomes difficult, and the improvement ability in the workplace is lowered", and over 50 percent of the supervisors reported that, "The rotation is hard to carry out at the workplace, and the development of regular employees is prevented", and "The quality maintenance and improvement are difficult".

Table 7: Increase of non-regular employees and Problem on production site

Ratio of non-regular employees	Less than 10%	10%- less than 20%	20%- less than 30%	30%-
The quality maintenance and improvement are difficult. (%)	44.5	47.3	55.8	56.1
The rotation is hard to carry out at the workplace, and the development of regular employees is prevented. (%)	41.8	47.3	55	51.7
The accumulation of skills/techniques becomes difficult, and the improvement ability in the workplace is lowered. (%)	32	34.9	38.3	44.4
The retention ratio is low, and the personnel management is difficult. (%)	24.1	30.1	36.7	42.4

Note: Respondent to the survey are 1,241 supervisors (in Japanese Hancho, Kumicho, etc.).
Source: The Institute for Industrial Relation and Labor Policy, Chubu (2002), p. 155, and Nakamura (2005), p. 160.

These problems were also investigated by the Toyota Motor Worker's union in 2006. As a result, the problems related to "safety", "quality", "work burden", "human resource development" are said to arise under high juenritsu. As the level and scope of works that non-regular employees (such as seasonal workers and dispatched workers) responsible for is limited, when juenritsu exceeds the proper level, the job rotation of regular employees becomes insufficient. Therefore, it is said that some of the regular employees, though they haven't acquired the basic skills yet, take charge of a higher level of tasks, which leads to poor quality (Toyota Motor Workers' Union, January 30, 2007) .

From 2009 to 2010, Toyota announced a large volume of recalls. One of the causes might be that the human resource development did not catch up with the rapid growth rate. Toyota expanded the production volume from about 6 million in 2002 to 9.5 million in 2007, and grew to be the world's largest auto manufacturer. But then, while the employment of regular employees was reduced on the production sites, non-regular employees were increased, resulting in the insufficient human resource development on site.

Mr. Akio Toyoda, Toyota president, speaking about the cause of the recall issue, stated that "the expansion of volume prevails over improving the quality", but actually, "the development of human resources did not catch up with the sudden expansion of business" (Nihon Keizai Shinbun, February 18, 2010, and March 18, 2010).

4-2-6. Summary

As described above, after the 2000s Toyota put effort into employment management to restrict the regular employees to fewer talented workers, while increasing their use of non-regular employees. However, as a result, the workload for regular employees became larger, and the time to perform effective skill formation was lost from the production site. To perform the skill formation effectively, it is necessary to systematize the works that workers experience from an educational viewpoint, and for the supervisory personnel to give sufficient training to employees. However, at Toyota, that was not necessarily sufficient. Therefore, the maintenance of quality, Toyota's lifeline, became difficult. The employment management reform in Toyota, and the introduction of EPM as the core, did damage to the skill formation practices—the infrastructure supporting TPS which was the source of competitiveness. This resulted in the degradation of the quality that was an important element of competitiveness.

5. Concluding remarks

After the 1990s, a number of Japanese companies reformed their employment management based on the concept of Employment Portfolio Management (EPM) proposed by Nikkeiren. Although Nikkeiren argued that the philosophy of "human-centered" and "long-term view" should be maintained firmly, the companies individually proceeded with EPM for the purposes of labor cost reduction and flexible employment adjustment, and regular employees were reduced to a smaller number of talented workers, while non regular employees were rapidly increased.

As a result, in Japan, the number of workers with unstable low wages has been increased, and the consumer demand supporting the success of corporate management has been decreased. Also, as shown from the case study of Toyota, the increase of non-regular employees caused the skill formation practice on the production site, that is the infrastructure supporting TPS the source of competitiveness, to become insufficient. As a result, quality, an important element of competitiveness, was degraded.

According to the results of the Health, Welfare and Labor Ministry's survey *"General Survey on Diversified Types of Employment"* (2014) that was published in November 2015, the ratio of the employees other than regular employees is nearly 40 percent. In this chapter, we focused on the increase of non-regular employees from the 1990s to the 2000s in particular, but EPM seems to have been affecting the employment management of Japanese companies after the 2010s as well.

Japanese companies need to recognize the problems arising from their own employment management reform and consider countermeasures so that they can develop. It is necessary to recognize that investing in human resources will enhance corporate competitiveness since the business models of Japanese manufacturers are supported by human resource development in many cases. Human resource investment will also be important for the stimulation of consumer demand, which is essential to the success of corporate management.

References

■ English

Arjan B. Keizer (2009), *Changes in Japanese Employment Practices : Beyond the Japanese model,* routledge: London and Newyork.

Fujimoto, Takahiro (1999), *Evolution of Manufacturing Systems at Toyota,* Oxford University Press: Newyork.

Jeffrey K. Liker, Fruin, W. Mark and Adler, Paul S. (eds.) (1999), *Remade in America : Transplanting and Transforming Japanese Management Systems,* Oxford University Press: Newyork.

Jeffrey K. Liker and Meier, David P. (2007), *Toyota Talent: Developing Your People,* McGraw-Hill.

Monden, Yasuhiro (2011), *Toyota Production System: An Integrated Approach to Just-In-Time,* 4th Edition, Productivity Press.

Ohno, Taiichi (1988), *Toyota Production System: Beyond Large-Scale Production,* Productivity Press.

Sugimori, Kusunoki, Cho, and Uchikawa (1977), "Toyota production system and Kanban system: materialization of just-in-time and respect-for-human system", in Shimokawa, Koichi and Fujimoto, Takahiro (eds.) (2001), *Toyota System no Genten,* Bunshindou.

■ Japanese

Hiranuma, Takashi and Kimura, Makoto (2000), "Nihon no Sangyo Kouzou no Henka to Syokugyo Kyoiku Kunren no Kadai to Tenbou", in Meiji University Kigyonai Kyoiku Kenkyukai (ed.), *Jinzai Katsuyou to Kigyonai Kyoiku,* Nihon Hyoron sya.

Ihara, Ryoji (2003), *Toyota no roudou genba : Dynamism to Context,* Sakurai Syoten.

── (2007), "Toyota no Roudougenba no Henyou to Genbakanri no Honshitsu:Post-fordism Ron kara Kakusasyakai Ron wo hete", *Gendai Shiso,* 35 (8), Seido Sya.

Japan Institute for Labor Policy and Training (2006), *Tayoka suru syuugyoukeitai no moto deno jinjisenryaku to roudousya no ishiki ni kansuru cyosa.*
Koike, Kazuo (1991), *Shigoto no Keizaigaku*, Toyokeizai.
Koike, Kazuo, Chuma Hiroyuki and Ota Soich (2001), *Monozukuri no ginou : Jidousya Sangyo no Syokuba de*, Toyokeizai.
Komatsu, Fumiaki (2007), "Toyota Seisan Hoshiki to Hitenkei Koyoka", in Tsuji Katsuji (ed.), *Kyaria no Syakaigaku:Syokugyo Nouryoku to syokugyo Keireki kara no Approach*, Mineruva.
Kumazawa, Makoto (2007), *Kakusa syakai Nippon de Hataraku toiukoto : koyou to roudou no yukue wo mitsumete*, Iwanami Syoten.
Ministry of Health, Labour and Welfare (2004) (2014), *General Survey on Diversified Types of Employment.*
— (2006), *Basic Survey on Wage Structure.*
— (2007), *Basic Survey of Human Resources Development.*
— (2009), *Hiseiki roudousya no yatoidometou no jyoukyou ni tsuite.* (July 21, 2009)
— (2013), *White Paper on the Labour Economy.*
Ministry of Internal Affairs and Communications (each year), *Family Income and Expenditure Survey.*
— (1994) (2004), *National Survey of Family Income and Expenditure.*
— (each year), *Special Labour Force Survey.*
— (each year), *Labour Force Survey (Detailed Tabulation).*
Nakahara, Jun (2012), "Gakusyu Kankyo toshiteno 'Syokuba':Keiei Kenkyu to Gakusyu Kenkyu no Kousa suru Basyo" (The Workplace as a Learning Environment : The Intersection between Management Research and Learning Research), *Nihon Rodo Kenkyu Zasshi* (The Japanese Journal of Labour Studies), 54 (1), Japan Institute for Labor Policy and Trainig.
Nakamura, Keisuke (2005), "Koyou System no Keizoku to Henka", in Institute of Social Science, The University of Tokyo (ed.), *'Ushinawareta 10 nen' wo Koete I : Keizai Kiki no Kyokun* (Beyond the 'Lost Decade' Volume 1 : The Lessons of Economic Crisis), University of Tokyo Press.
Nihon Keizai Shinbun, February 18, 2010.
Nihon Keizai Shinbun, March 18, 2010.
Nikkeiren shin nihonteki keiei kenkyu project (ed.) (1995), *Shinjidai no Nihonteki Keiei* (Japanese Management in the New Era).
Sugiyama, Naoshi (2008), "Toyota to Chingin Kakusa", in Saruta, Makaki (ed.), *Toyota Kigyo Shuudan to Kakusa Syakai*, Mineruva.
Suzuki, Yoshiji (1994), *Nihonteki Seisan System to Kigyo Syakai* (Japanese production system, management and workers), Hokkaido Daigaku Tosyo Kankoukai.
Suzuki, Yuzo (1980), "Tanoukouka to Job Rotation ni yoru jyunan na syokuba zukuri", *IE*, 22 (5), Japan Management Association (Nihon Nouritsu kyokai).
The Institute for Industrial Relation and Labor Policy, Chubu (2002), *Monozukuri no Densyo to Chukiteki na Roumuseisaku.*
— (2004), *Roudouryoku Tayouka no naka deno Atarashii Hatarakikata.*
Toyota Motor Corporation *Annual Securities Report* (each year).
Toyota Motor Corporation Jinzai Kaihatsu Bu (1997), *Ginoukei Shin Jinji Seido.*
Toyota Motor Workers' Union (2003), *Hyougikai Shiryo.* (November 27, 2003)
— (2004a), *Hyougikai Shiryo.* (June 28, 2004)
— (2004b), *Hyougikai Shiryo.* (June 9, 2004)
— (2005), *Hyougikai Shiryo.* (March 10, 2005)

― (2007), *Hyougikai Shiryo.* (January 30, 2007)
― (2005), *Hyougikai News.* (No.0767, March 10, 2005)
― (2007), *Hyougikai News.* (No.0831, January 30, 2007)
Womack, James P., Daniel Jones and Daniel Roos (1990), *The Machine That Changed the World*, Rawson Associates/Macmillan: New York.

VII.
How Lexus Has Utilized Culture in the Japanese Market: Content and Discourse Analysis of its Brochures

Takeshi SEGUCHI

1. Introduction

Contemporary multinational companies (MNCs) have to face intense global competition. To avoid commoditization and the consequent price competition, MNCs need effective market strategies that attribute an added value to their products. This value, however, should be distinct from a functional value, such as premium value,[1] emotional value,[2] cultural symbols,[3] and myths.[4]

This chapter focuses on the cultural meanings of the value mentioned above, and the market strategy that draws on this value. This strategy comprises of two meanings: utilizing "cultural factors" and creating a "cultural platform" for customers. Cultural factors add cultural signs to a product and articulates these factors to attract customers. The cultural platform forms a conceptual or interpretive framework for customers by adopting a diverse cultural apparatus. A brochure is a twofold media that, on the one hand, represents particular meanings and makes a product seem valuable; on the other hand, it becomes a cultural apparatus, providing a cultural platform for readers.

The purpose of this chapter is to understand how Lexus, the luxury brand of Toyota, has utilized Japanese culture in its market strategy through a con-

---
1) Endo (2007).
2) Nobeoka (2011).
3) Aoki (2008).
4) Holt (2004).

tent and discourse analysis of its brochures from 2006 to 2013. The reason for adopting content and discourse analysis is that, as we will discuss in Section 2, the representation or the process of constructing meanings inevitably involves the use of language from the perspective of cultural studies.

It is well known that Toyota built the Lexus brand for the American market in 1989. Later, it introduced the brand into the Japanese market in 2005 by integrating the existing car models into one brand. As we will discuss in Section 4, many studies argued that Lexus used Japanese culture as one of its competitive advantages. Various people involved with Lexus also confirmed to this fact. Therefore, we analyzed brochures in terms of the cultural factors that Lexus has utilized, how Lexus has represented aspects of its products, what differences exist in car models, and how its market strategy, which specifically refers to Japanese culture, has changed over time.

This chapter consists of five sections, organized as follows.

First, we illustrate the theoretical background of the present study in Section 2. In particular, we have drawn on the theory of representation, as developed by Stuart Hall in the context of cultural studies. Additionally, we introduce the concept of cultural apparatus.

Section 3 investigates the relations between MNCs and culture by addressing some of the theories that focus on these relations. We also propose the two key terms that guided this study: "cultural factors" and "cultural platform".

Section 4 outlines the introduction of Lexus into the Japanese market and clarifies the features of the market strategy of Lexus by using a variety of sources, including a hearing investigation. As we will argue, Lexus utilizes Japanese culture to compete against German automobile makers in the Japanese luxury car market. It is important to address the following questions: how has Lexus utilized Japanese culture? What factors have they used, and which aspects of their product do they combine with Japanese culture?

To examine these issues, we present the results of the content and discourse analysis, in Section 5. In the content analysis, we examine time trends and the difference among car models counting the frequency of appearance of cultural references and classifying their appearing place in the brochures. In discourse analysis, we extract words and expressions related to Japanese culture, and consider the questions mentioned above. In particular, we focus on the combination or articulation of expressions: in other words, which expression or words were selected and which factors explained the character of which products?

Finally, Section 6 summarizes our arguments,discusses the significance of this article in the broader field, and introduces issues that require further study.

2. Representation, meanings, and cultural apparatus

2-1. The theory of representation

It seems important to understand why and how culture can function through meanings or add value to a product. In order to consider these issues, we investigate the theory of representation proposed by Stuart Hall. As Hall noted, representation is "the production of meaning through language",[5] and "the link between concepts and language which enables us to refer to either the 'real' world of objects, people, events, or indeed to imaginary worlds of fictional objects, people, and events".[6] In other words, the theory of representation helps us understand how meanings are produced, why we need to address language, and how we perceive objects through concepts or language. The author argued that there are two systems of representation. Hall remarked that:

> "The first enables us to give meaning to the world by constructing a set of correspondences or a chain of equivalences between things—people, objects, events, abstract ideas, etc.—and our system of concepts, our conceptual maps. The second depends on constructing a set of correspondences between our conceptual map and a set of signs, arranged or organized into various languages which stand for or represent those concepts. The relation between 'things', concepts and signs lies at the heart of the production of meaning in language. The process which links these three elements together is what we call 'representation'".[7]

As mentioned above, the first system constitutes what we refer to as a conceptual map, which allows us to "make sense of or interpret the world in roughly similar ways". If this is the case, then "that is indeed what it means when we say we 'belong to the same culture'"[8]. Moreover, it is not a random collection of concepts, but concepts with complex mutual relations. These

---
5) Hall (2013), p. 2.
6) *Ibid.*, p. 3.
7) *Ibid.*, p. 5.
8) *Ibid.*, p. 4.

are the concepts that are organized, clustered, arranged, and classified: for instance, the principles of similarity and difference, sequence, or causality. The second system is also equivalent to signs that function and are organized into a language to represent or exchange meanings and concepts. These two systems need to be interpreted to produce meanings. Thus, encoding and decoding become indispensable processes in the production of meanings.

However, the tripartite relation between a sign, a concept, and an object is completely arbitrary. Codes construct and fix meanings temporarily, not permanently. On this matter, Hall argued:

> "Codes fix the relationships between concepts and signs. They stabilize meaning within different languages and cultures. They tell us which language to use to convey which idea. [. . .] Codes tell us which concepts are being referred to when we hear or read which signs. By arbitrarily fixing the relationships between our conceptual system and our linguistic systems [. . .], codes make it possible for us to speak and to hear intelligibly, and establish the translatability between our concepts and our languages which enables meaning to pass from speaker to hearer and be effectively communicated within a culture".[9]

Hall expanded the discussion further by using a semiotic approach that "concentrated on how language and signification (the use of signs in language) works to produce meanings" according to Saussure or Barthes, and a discursive approach which "concentrated on how discourse and discursive practices produce knowledge",[10] as developed by Foucault. As noted above, meaning is not permanently fixed. Thus a complex relationship between the sender and the receiver, including diverse interpretations, causes a "constant 'play' or slippage of meaning, to the constant production of new meaning, new interpretations".[11] Therefore, the functions of signs acquire not only denotation but also connotation.[12] On this point, the issue of power relations

---

9) *Ibid.*, p. 8.
10) *Ibid.*, pp. 45-46.
11) *Ibid.*, p. 17.
12) Concerning distinction denotation and connotation, we should pay attention to what Hall argued, as follows:
"Denotative meanings, of course, are not uncoded; they, too, entail systems of classification and recognition in much the same way as connotative meanings do; they are not natural but 'motivated' signs. [. . .] It suggested, only, that the connotative levels of language, being more open-ended and associative, were peculiarly vulnerable to contrary or contradictory ideological inflexions". (Hall (1982), p. 79).

arises.

This "wider meaning is no longer a descriptive level of obvious interpretation. Here, we are beginning to interpret the completed signs in terms of the wider realms of social ideology— the general beliefs, conceptual frameworks, and value systems of society".[13] In this way, discourse, representation, knowledge, and 'truth' are constructed within a specific historical context or discursive formation.[14] The constructed knowledge has 'the reality effect' that "regulate the conduct of others, entails constraint, regulation, and the disciplining of practices".[15] Then, "the relationship between knowledge and power, and how power operated within [...] an institutional apparatus and its technologies (techniques)",[16] which form "knowledge" or a conceptual framework, becomes critically important. Thus meanings are neither a reflection of what already exists in the world of objects, people, and events, nor the personal intention of the speaker, writer, or painter. Rather, meanings are constantly constructed in the various relations of power.

However, we should note that this relation of power is not unidirectional, or centrally mandated. Rather, it has the nature of "multi-accentuality", which includes "social struggle—a struggle for mastery in discourse—over which a kind of social accenting is to prevail and to win credibility". This accompanies "both the notion of 'differently oriented social interests' and a conception of the sign as 'arena of struggle' into the consideration of language and of signifying 'work'".[17] Then, in the next subsection, we turn our attention to the problem of the "apparatus", which includes tools or measures to form our knowledge, culture, conception, or interpretation.

2-2. Brochures as a cultural apparatus

The device or institution that produces, constructs, and forms our culture is called cultural apparatus. It is said that cultural apparatus was in earnest advocated by Mills. He explained:

"The apparatus is composed of all the organizations and *milieux* in which artistic, intellectual and scientific work goes on, and of the means by which such work is made available to circles, publics, and masses. In

---

13) Hall (2013), *op. cit.*, p. 24.
14) See Eagleton (1991) on ideology having the nature of discourse.
15) Hall (2013), *op. cit.*, p. 33.
16) *Ibid.*, p. 32.
17) Hall (2013), *op. cit.*, pp. 77-78.

the cultural apparatus art, science, and learning, entertainment, malarkey, and information are produced and distributed. In terms of it, these products are distributed and consumed. It contain[s] an elaborate set of institutions: of schools and theaters, newspapers and census bureaus, studios, laboratories, museums, little magazines, radio networks. [...] Inside this apparatus, standing between men and events, the images, meanings, slogans that define the worlds in which men live are organized and compared, maintained and revised, lost and cherished, hidden, debunked, celebrated. Taken as whole, the cultural apparatus is the lens of mankind through which men see: the medium by which they interpret and report what they see. It is the [semi-organized] source of their very identities and of their aspirations. It is the source of The Human Variety—of styles of living and ways to die".[18]

Ishida critically developed this viewpoint. She asserted that, although Mills regarded the masses as passive in the premise of the function of a cultural apparatus, we should not share this concept of passive masses of people, but limit this word to "the media that produces and reproduces our senses, meanings, conscious".[19] In short, also here, the notion of "multi-accentuality" can be applied.

We accept her perspective and believe that culture is constructed through various cultural apparatuses. Brochures of companies or products also are, in the broad sense, a form of cultural apparatus. A brochure is the medium through which a company provides information about its product or intention, and consumers receive information, such as the brand name, concept, image, character, and merit of a product through their code. MNCs attempt to utilize diverse cultural apparatuses to emphasize their inter-company market competition. That is, they use a cultural apparatus to be able to attribute signs or meanings to their products, induce consumers to interpret it meaningfully, and consequently build a strong brand and sell more products at a higher price. Therefore, they compete against rivals for making use of these apparatuses.

We do not intend to assert that a brochure alone influences the success or failure of MNCs, as it is only one of the many cultural apparatuses available. The present study attempts to interpret and "read" the activity of MNCs: they try to attribute cultural signs or meanings to their products, struggle to con-

---

18) Mills (1963), pp. 406–407.
19) Ishida (1998), p. 6.

struct a conceptual map that is desirable for them, utilize cultural factors, and form a cultural platform, which we describe in the next section, analyzing one apparatus, namely, the brochures.

3. Culture in the market strategy of MNCs

3-1. MNCs and culture

Culture has been thought to exist outside of MNCs in conventional research regarding the strategy of such companies. In earlier research, and often in present research, culture seemed to exist entirely independently of MNCs, be stable, and, therefore, measurable. Hofstede (1980), a classic and representative advocate of research on the relations between MNCs and culture, adopted this cultural concept and measured it through four indexes (though he added two indexes later): power distance, individualism versus collectivism, masculinity versus femininity, and uncertainty avoidance.

Researchers who consider culture as relatively homogeneous, stable, and measurable have tended to adopt the concept of culture before a "linguistic turn" or "cultural turn".[20] Therefore, these studies are based on cultural essentialism, which undoubtedly conceives that a nation, or an ethnic group, intrinsically has a culture, rather than taking the view of constructionism, which regards culture as being continually changing or reconstructed through the various relations of power. Thus it is generally thought that MNCs need to pay attention to the diversity of culture as an external environment in which business can be conducted smoothly. In this way, they seldom utilize or minimally alter culture to achieve their purpose, and this is the dominating perspective in many theories of international management or international marketing, but not in theories of cultural imperialism.[21] However, MNCs should be regarded as one of the agents that can exercise power and eventually influence culture, as well as a subject that makes efforts to overcome problems regarding the diversity of culture. We introduced the notion of a struggle for meanings through the relations of power in the previous section.

In recent years, several studies focused on MNCs that utilize culture. In terms of how MNCs can utilize culture to their competitive advantage, it is useful to investigate arbitrage strategy, as proposed by Ghemawat. Arbitrage strategy is used when MNCs acquire a competitive advantage utilizing various differences between nations, markets, or cultures. According to Ghe-

---

20) Yoshimi (2003).
21) See Thomlinson (1991) on the discussion about cultural imperialism.

mawat, the purpose of a global strategy is to "manage the large differences that arise at borders, whether those borders are defined geographically or otherwise". He further explained that "some companies are finding large opportunities for value creation in exploiting, rather than simply adjusting to or overcoming, the differences they encounter at the borders of their various markets".[22] Differences relating to competitive advantages of MNCs arise from four forms of distance: administrative, geographic, economic, and cultural distance. Ghemawat calls this cultural arbitrage, and explains that a competitive advantage is obtained through the successful management of cultural difference and distance. To explain cultural arbitrage, he used the example of French culture and noted that it "has long underpinned the international success of French haute couture, cuisine, wines, and perfumes". He also stated that "cultural arbitrage can also be applied to newer products and services",[23] as well as traditional products and services. Following this difinition, we infer that cultural arbitrage is at play when MNCs gain competitive advantage by making use of the cultural background of their home country. Cultural differences are, therefore, not a thorny problem for MNCs, but a resource that leads them to a favorable position.

We deal with the discussion from a different perspective, namely, that of cultural branding. Holt explained that cultural branding is needed to build a powerful brand.[24] This is important both for companies that expand business in one country and for MNCs. Holt et al. observed that:

> "Global branding should not be interpreted as a call to rid transnational brands of their national heritage, for two reasons. First, [. . .] consumers still prefer brands that hail from countries that are considered to have particular expertise: Switzerland in chocolates, Italy in clothing, France in cosmetics, Germany in cars, Japan in electronics, for example. More important, consumers expect global brands to tell their myths from the particular places that are associated with the brand. For Nestlé to spin a credible myth about food, the myth must be set in the Swiss mountains, because that is where people imagine the brand hails from. Likewise, if L'Oréal is to author a myth about beauty, it must do so from a particularly French viewpoint. Transnational companies would therefore to do well to manage their national identities as well as their

---

22) Ghemawat (2007), pp. 59-60.
23) Ghemawat (2003), p. 78.
24) Holt (2004), *op. sit.*

globalness".[25]

As shown by this quotation, they also emphasize the significance of cultural backgrounds for the marketing strategy of MNCs. MNCs are able to build a strong brand or attract consumers if they are to make a good use of the culture of their home country. However, a production of meaning, namely, a process of representation, contains two aspects: giving cultural signs or meanings, and constructing or influencing a conceptual framework. We, therefore, examine these two strategies more closely in the next subsection.

3-2. Cultural factors and cultural platform in market strategy

The strategy that MNCs use to make their products meaningful is based on two components: utilizing "cultural factors", and creating a "cultural platform".[26] These are the two key terms of the following sections, particularly Section 5. Cultural factors denote a set of factors related to cultural meanings or signs that are attributed to a product. To utilize cultural factors, MNCs must focus on several factors, starting from the cultural background constructed by the nationality, ethnicity, social class, generation, and simiar factors. In addition, they should create value, or a story, by using these factors as content, and attribute this value to their product. For example, Harley-Davidson has used cultural factors, such as the symbolic muscular white man with a mustache, the spirit of freedom embodied in a cowboy, or the nationalism associated with the Stars and Stripes.[27] Nike has used black cultural factors that symbolize physical ability and represent the image of "cool" individuas, the basketball courts of impoverished urban areas, and highly fashionable young people.[28] It is assumed that decision making related to which cultural factors MNCs select, the value or myth they choose to construct, or the wey they combine and articulate these factors with their products is different across companies, even across companies that share the same cultural background. Thus the ability to utilize cultural factors can become a significant cause their success or failure in the market.[29]

However, the strategy of utilizing cultural factors does not always work as a competitive advantage. Cultural factors cannot function efficiently without

---

25) Holt, Quelch and Taylor (2004), p. 75.
26) Seguchi (2012a), pp. 225-226.
27) *Ibid.*, pp. 245-252.
28) Klein (2000).
29) Seguchi (2012a), *op. sit.*, p.225.

being perceived to be fascinating for consumers, and occupy an indispensable position in their lives. Providing a cultural platform that is comparable to a conceptual framework, a way of interpretation, or the lifestyle of consumers is also needed. A cultural platform is the base, premise, or soil that creates great performance for cultural factors. In other words, consumers need to adequately perceive a cultural background, interpret cultural factors derived from this background as attractive, and incorporate a product that is combined with cultural factors into their lifestyle. Moreover, a cultural platform only focuses on the customer segment being targeted, not all consumers, and is created through various means of a cultural apparatus. Thus, MNCs need to consider which customer segment they intend to target, how to form a cultural platform that is desirable for them, and exploit cultural factors.

4. Lexus in the Japanese market

4-1. Introduction of the Lexus brand

Lexus was originally developed for the American market in 1989. The brand achieved fame as a luxury automobile brand that included a variety of models. In August 2005, Toyota introduced the Lexus brand into the Japanese market with three cars already sold in Japan—ARISTO, ALTEZZA, and SOARER—and renamed them GS, IS, and SC upon integration into the Lexus brand. In October 2006, Toyota introduced LS460, which was already being sold under the name of CELSIOR, as the flagship model of Lexus. In developing the Lexus brand in Japan, Toyota expressly separated it from the Toyota brand. Toyota aimed to supply "the supreme products with splendid service" and create a "'global premium brand' that pursued the essence of luxury in the twenty-first century".[30]

Toyota introduced the Lexus brand into the Japanese market for both global and domestic reasons. As part of its global strategy, Toyota aimed to capture the luxury segment of the global automobile market. The introduction of the Euro as a unified currency in 1999 and the abolition of voluntary export controls on automobiles from Japan made this especially true for the European market. Toyota constructed a dealer network for Lexus in 2000 and planned to increase its sales offices from 240 to 290 by 2003.[31] Likewise, it intended to sell 1,200,000 automobiles per year, including 100,000 in the European

---

30) *Toyota Annual Report* (2005), p. 25.
31) *Fourin's Monthly Report on the Global Automotive Industry* (2003), March, pp. 14–15.

market alone. In 2004, however, the number of Lexus cars sold in Europe only reached 25,000—one percent of the European luxury automobile market. To establish the Lexus brand in that market, Lexus needed to stress that the brand was not only valuable for Americans and to have "values and identity" that represent its home country; it needed to evolve into "an unshakable brand representing Japan".[32]

Emerging global markets also played a role. At that time, emerging markets like China, Russia, or India expected to expand their markets for luxury automobiles as well as passenger cars. To succeed in these countries, Lexus needed to, first, build a firm brand image in developed countries, including the European market, where the competition among many luxury brands is intense. Indeed, Toyota began to introduce the Lexus brand in Russia in 2005 and in China in 2008, locating sales offices in Changchun, Jilin province, and Shenyang, Liaoning province.

Toyota aimed to make a huge inroads into the luxury market in Japan. To understand this strategy, it is necessary to understand the bipolarizations of income and consumption that characterized this period;[33] namely, the aggrandizing of the luxury automobile market in Japan, because of economic and social reasons; the enlargement of the wealthy class due to income disparity and the emergence of consumers willing to pay more money for products they desire.

Toyota also struggled because it had not yet developed a way proper to market high-priced and high-grade cars that were made in Japan. In other words, most Japanese automobile companies, including Toyota, mainly targeted the market for cars that cost less than 5 million yen. The market for more expensive automobiles was dominated by European industries, particularly German companies, like Mercedes-Benz, BMW, Audi, and Porsche. In addition, among individuals with an annual income of more than 10 million yen, people younger than 30 tended to prefer imported cars, while older individuals (above 50) preferred Toyota. Therefore, if the younger generation was to buy luxury cars in the future, Toyota would have lost customers in the luxury automobile market. Thus, Toyota had complex and intertwining reasons for developing Lexus for the Japanese market.

Here, we discuss the current status of Lexus with some data. Figure 1 illustrates the shift in the number of newly registered luxury-brand cars in Japan. The figure includes only companies that sell over 10,000 cars per year.

---

32) Takagi (2007), p. 10 and Spennemann (2006), p. 52.
33) A hearing investigation at Lexus College, November 14, 2007.

Table 1: The Lexus models

Model Name	Type	Recommended Retail Price (Thousand Yen)		
LS	sedan	8,548	~	15,954
LS HYBRID	hybrid	10,811	~	15,954
LS F SPORT	sport	10,151	~	12,722
GS	sedan	5,517	~	8,463
GS F	sedan		11,000	
GS HYBRID	hybrid	6,153	~	8,463
GS F	sport		11,000	
GS F SPORT	sport	6,346	~	8,463
IS	sedan	4,544	~	6,278
IS HYBRID	hybrid	4,999	~	6,278
IS F SPORT	sport	5,092	~	6,278
RX	SUV	4,950	~	7,424
RX HYBRID	hybrid	6,025	~	7,425
RX F SPORT	sport	6,050	~	7,425
HS	sedan	4,244	~	5,705
HS HYBRID	hybrid	4,244	~	5,705
RC	coupe	5,210	~	6,787
RCF	coupe	9,540	~	10,310
RC HYBRID	hybrid	5,650	~	6,290
RC F	sport	9,540	~	10,310
RC F SPRT	sport	5,830	~	6,780
CT HYBRID	hybrid	3,662	~	4,608
CT F SPORT	sport		4,331	
NX	SUV	4,280	~	5,820
NX HYBRID	hybrid	4,920	~	5,820
NX F SPORT	sport	4,920	~	5,820
LX	SUV		11,000	

Source: Lexus homepage, http://lexus.jp/models/index.html (last access, July 10, 2016).

Figure 1: The number of newly registered luxury cars in Japan

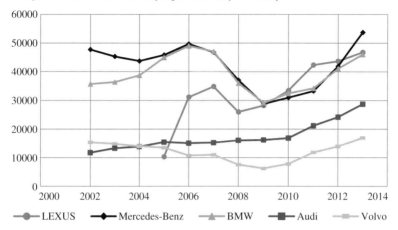

Source: Automobile Business Association of Japan and Nikkan Automobile Newspaper, *Automobile Yearbook*, each year.

As shown in this figure, Lexus is established firmly in that market, although we must also take into account the difference in the number of models each company sells. In particular, the figure assumes that Lexus directly competes with Mercedes-Benz and BMW.[34]

Table 1 shows the models that Lexus currently sells. In this table, we can see that Lexus develops products that generally sell from 4 million yen to more than 10 million yen. From this information, we can determine that, through the introduction of Lexus, Toyota overcame its inability to sell cars that cost more than 5 million yen.

4-2. The market strategy of Lexus

The cultural milieu surrounding the development of Lexus accounted for, global factors, such as Toyota's global strategy to build a brand identity based in its home country to establish the Lexus brand around the world, and domestic factors, such as the expectation that the luxury automobile market would expand and the enclosure of all potential future customers. Lexus needed to claim its identity as a Japanese brand, a culture that Europeans found attractive, in order to gain the European luxury automobile market. Lexus also needed to distingnish itself from other luxury automobile makers

---

34) *Ibid.*

to gain a competitive advantage and compete against companies that had first-mover-advantage and overwhelming predominance in the Japanese luxury automobile market.

Western luxury car manufacturers are mainly attractive because of "European" signs—a long history, tradition, heritage, or image of luxury—all of which provide their products with a strong brand personality.[35] In addition, these brands also have a cultural image or stereotype: for example, German products are perceived to have robustness or dignity; likewise, France has a stereotype of sophistication, and Italy is perceived as having superior design. Conversely, in Japan, Toyota's stereotype was good quality and durable products produced at a relatively lower cost; this was also true in the American market, where Lexus succeeded.[36]

To confront these issues, Lexus utilized two signs: "leading edge technology" and "traditional Japanese culture".[37] Of the two, the latter is considered more significant in the present study. Several other articles have referred to this point as well.

According to Takagi, this sign is most successfully expressed in the *Lfinesse*, a phrase that represents Lexus' brand identity. *L-finesse* is a coined word made up of *Leading-edge* and *finesse*. Combined, the term means "the new that illustrates the evolution of technique" and "the finesse that makes use of Japanese sensibility". Moreover, he argues that the most important factor to understand *L-finesse* is the *J-factor*,[38] or "the outcome that results from pointing to the spirit in the Japanese character and carefully researching the Japanese values that are acceptable to the world".[39] Likewise, Kaneko[40] and Hasegawa[41] describe how Lexus took advantage of Japanese culture for its brand identity, design, and employee education.

The fact that Lexus uses cultural factors derived from Japanese culture is not only referred to in the literature, as mentioned above. Lexus' staff have

---

35) Kaneko (2005), p. 26.
36) *Car Graphic* (2005), June, p. 53.
37) A hearing investigation at Lexus College, November 14, 2007.
38) On the *J-factor*, Yoshida, the managing officer of the Lexus development center, attests that the *J-factor* was devised by European staff employed by the design center in Nice. (*Navi* (2006), December, p. 59.). In other words, the cultural factor of the *J-factor* needs be considered from the perspective of Europe. This utterance proves the fact that Lexus intended to establish a cultural factor in order to attract not only the Japanese, but also the European.
39) Takagi (2007), *op. cit.*, p. 61.
40) Kaneko (2005), *op. cit.*, p. 24, p. 131.
41) Hasegawa (2005), pp. 40−42.

also confirmed so. For example, Akihiro Nagaya, the general manager of the Lexus brand-planning department, said that:

"Lexus has a great advantage in America, but is almost unknown in Europe. It is especially miserable in Germany. It is obvious that this is caused by consumer opinion: 'There is no reason to buy Japanese cars'. In other words, they are relatively expensive due to customs duties, although I know they are good in quality. Therefore, we must create a reason to buy. What is that reason? It is something local, in a word, having a firm identity—made in Japan. This message is irreplaceable and very significant".[42]

Shibata, Hidekazu, the group leader of Lexus design department, agreed:

"[In developing Lexus' design, I was affected by] the statue of *Kongo Rikishi* in the *Koufukuji* temple. It is smaller than that of the *Todaiji* temple. But the feelings of muscle condensation, the comparison of his elegant clothes, and his resolute expression with sharp eyes served as a useful reference, especially when I developed the design for the exterior".[43]

Based on various sources, including the above testimonies, Seguchi (2012b) points out that Lexus combines and articulates four Japanese cultural factors: the Japanese beauty of style; the Japanese traditional art of manufacturing of *takumi*; the Japanese spirit that regards contrasts or foreseeing as important; and the spirit of *omotenashi*.

Here, we want to explain two words that are going to be essential terms in the next section. *Takumi* means "the person who creates manufactured articles or buildings by handiwork or tools".[44] Although there are other words expressing this meaning, such as *shokunin* or *jukurenko*, *takumi* evokes the feeling of tradition or history, and a person who uses a specific technique. On the other hand, *omotenashi* is the polite expression of *motenashi* and means the Japanese spirit of selfless hospitality, welcome, reception, or service.[45]

---

42) *Car Graphic* (2006), June, p. 53.
43) *Motor Magazine* (2006), October, p. 152.
44) *Matsumura* (2006), p. 1537.
45) This word was also adopted as the key word in the presentation of the Tokyo Olympic 2020, a speech in French at 125th session of the International Olympic Committee held in Tokyo in September, 2013. This fact indicates that the Japanese tend to regard *omote-*

Keeping the above four aspects of Japanese culture in mind, we analyze brochures to determine what cultural factors Lexus has utilized, how Lexus has represented aspects of its products, what differences exist between car models, and how Lexus' cultural market strategy has changed through historical trends.

5. Content and discourse analysis of Lexus brochures

5-1. Content analysis: the historical trends and comparison by frequency and place of appearance

This section examines Lexus brochures from 2006 to 2013, both through content and discourse analysis, using the point of view we have already discussed in section 2 and 3. We count the frequency of cultural factors and the locations in which they appear by clearing the tendency of time trends and making an inter-model comparison.

Table 2 indicates the number of Japanese cultural factors found in Lexus brochures. The numbers in parentheses refer to expressions that do not precisely represent Japanese culture, although they do appeal to Japan. For example, "Lexus from Japan", "advanced Japanese technique", or "premium car from Japan".[46] Blank cells indicate that there was no change, or only a slight change that did not affect cultural factors, in the a brochure from the previous year.

First, the number of cultural factors have gradually reduced over time. In particular, these factors have decreased since 2009-2010, while many factors were used in 2006-2007. Second, as shown in this table, the different car models can be classified into three groups. The first group includes ISF, ISC, CT200h, and HS250h (Group A). This group's brochures contain few cultural factors, especially for ISC and ISF. The second group, introduced into the Japanese market in the beginning of 2005, includes GS, IS, SC, and RX (Group B). Although the brochures for these models featured many cultural factors in the early years, these factors have gradually reduced. The third group corresponds to the LS series (Group C). Both the brochures for LS460 and LS600 have reduced the number of cultural factors since 2010, in line with the brochures for other models. In 2013, these models were integrated into one version, the LS series. Although they featured a large number of cul-

---

nashi as the word standing for the Japanese original spirit and being able to appeal internationally.
46) *The Lexus GS brochure* (2006), p. 3.

tural factors at first, at the time of integration, the number of factors decreased. This group, however, utilized more cultural factors than others, even when their overall number decreased.

Table 3 through Table 5 show where cultural factors appear in the Lexus brochures. Along with frequency of appearance, the location is very important because it can reveal how much importance the author places on the word. The difference in location, therefore, can show the priority among factors, even if factors appear the same number of times. For instance, a title or subtitle usually expresses the concepts that an author wants to emphasize the most.

Here, we separate the locations into four categories: subtitle, subheading, front page, and main text. A Lexus brochure comprises titles, subtitles, subheadings, and several sentences on each page, in addition to the front page

Table 2: The number of factors related to Japanese culture in Lexus brochures over time, by model

	LS600	LS460	IS	ISC	ISF	GS	SC430	RX	CT200H	HS250H
2006			8 (4)			9 (5)	8 (3)			
2007	24 (1)	36 (2)	9 (1)				6 (1)			
2008					1	9 (1)				
2009		26 (2)	3 (1)	2			6 (1)	8		
2010	18	17	6	1	1	3		6		
2011			4	2						
2012						3		2		
2013	13		4						3	6

Table 3: The locations where cultural factors appear in brochures (Group A)

	Subtitle	Subheading	Front Page	Sentence
ISF 2008		1		
ISF 2010		1		
ISC 2009				2
ISC 2010				1
ISC 2011				2
CT200h		1		2
HS250h	1	1		4

Table 4: The locations where cultural factors appear in brochures (Group B)

	Subtitle	Subheading	Front Page	Sentence
GS 2006		2	2 (3)	5 (2)
GS 2008		1	2	6 (1)
GS 2010				3
GS 2012				3
IS 2006	1	1	3 (3)	3 (1)
IS 2007	1	2	2	4 (1)
IS 2009			1	2 (1)
IS 2010				6
IS 2011				4
IS 2013	1			3
SC 2006	2		4 (2)	2 (1)
SC 2007	2		2	2 (1)
SC 2009	2		2	2 (1)
RX 2009	1		1	6
RX 2010	1			5
RX 2012				2

Table 5: The locations where cultural factors appear in brochures (Group C)

	Subtitle	Subheading	Front Page	Sentence	Photo
LS460 2007	3	6	2	24 (2)	1
LS460 2009	2	4	2	17 (2)	1
LS460 2010	2	1		14	
LS600 2007	4	4	2	14 (1)	
LS600 2010	2	1		15	
LS series 2013	2	1		10	

(first and second pages) and, sometimes, a table of contents. In every Lexus brochure, each title is written very concisely in English: for example, "SERVICE", "LEXUS DESIGN", "ENGINE", or "GRACIOUS COMFORT". There is little possibility that Japanese cultural factors will appear in the title. A subtitle, which provides a supplementary explanation in one or two sentences, is written in Japanese, and it is where several cultural factors can be found. One page contains a few subheadings, and one subheading consists of several sentences. Each brochure has a front page that describes the features or concepts of each Lexus model. The front page also plays an important role conveying meanings or images of each model. Thus, we argue that cultural factors that appeared in a subtitle are considered to have a more important role. Likewise, those factors that are described in a subheading or on the front page are more significant than those in the main text. We further examine three groups that were classified through the result of Table 2 in terms of location.

There were not many cultural factors in Group A overall. The brochure for the ISF series has no sentences that contain cultural factors, in spite of their presence in a subheading. By contrast, the brochure for the ISC series only includes cultural factors in the main text. The brochure for the HS250h contains more cultural factors than any other in this group and puts them in places that we think are more important. The locations, as well as the frequency of appearance, of the factors in Group B have changed greatly over time. According to the brochures of the GS series, the cultural factors that could be found in subheadings and on the front page in the 2006 and 2008 editions have disappeared since 2010. The IS series has also reduced the cultural factors that could be found in important places of the brochure before 2009. The brochures of the SC and RX series reduced the number of cultural factors to a lesser extent. Last, the brochures for Group C still include cultural factors within the subtitle, subheading, and front page, although the number of these factors tended to decrease over time.

Thus, according to content analysis, we can summarize the main findings as follows: first, brochures apparently intended to vigorously utilize Japanese culture in the beginning. This intention has, however, seemed to progressively waver. Second, cultural factors representing traditional Japanese culture tend to be used more in the high-grade or flagship models. Third, we found a relationship between the frequency of cultural factors and the place in which they appeared. The models that use more cultural factors tend to situate them in more significant places, meaning that authors regarded these factors as particularly important.

5-2. Discourse analysis of each model

Here we examine brochures through discourse analysis, in terms of what factors Lexus has used, how it has utilized them, and how it has articulated its products and cultural factors, according to three groups from A to C, as discussed above.

5-2-1. Group A: the ISF, ISC, CT200h, and HS250h series

The brochure for the ISF contains the lowest amount of cultural factors among all Lexus models, as already discussed. It only reports one factor in each of its brochures. In both the 2008 and 2010 editions, the brochures describe in a subheading that "G-Link delivers the advanced *omotenashi* that is telematics service",[47] but there is no cultural factors within the main text. The ISC brochure quotes the second to least number of cultural factors. Although the front page of the 2009 edition of the brochure contains the phrase "a leading edge technology that looks ahead to people, society, and the future of the earth, and the art of *takumi* which put persistence to manufacturing", this expression disappears in 2010. Only one sentence remains to explain the painting process: "[. . .] pursue the highest quality by fusing together the manual work of *takumi* and leading edge technology".[48] In the 2011 edition, the brochure adds "Japanese culture" to the description of *Lfinesse*, the design philosophy of Lexus. The reason why the brochures for these two models contain few cultural factors is that both appeal to a different factor: being sporty. Instead of appealing to Japanese culture, the brochures use many words like "sports model", "motorsports technology", "a racing circuit", "high performance", and similar expressions.

Likewise, the CT200h features few cultural factors in its brochures. They use cultural factors to explain *L-finesse,* using exactly the same sentence as in the brochures of other models, and the expressions, "the sensibility and technique of the Japanese" and "the art of *takumi*" as an introduction to the painting process. Of this group, the HS250h brochure contains the largest number of cultural factors. However, the locations are restrictive: the same phrase as in the brochure for CT200h, in the explanation of *L-finesse*, and a factor related to the art or manual work of *takumi* in the description of the interior and painting process. The reason why the brochures for these two models have few cultural factors is similar to that stated in the previous paragraph: CT200h and HS250h are hybrid cars and, therefore, the brochures are intended to focus on this aspect. They contain the expressions, "environmental performance", "feelings towards the environment", and "thought for the future of the Earth".

5-2-2. Group B: the GS, IS, SC, and RX series

This group can be further classified into two parts: the former three mod-

---

47) *Lexus ISF brochures* (2008), p. 26, and (2010), p. 20. G-Link is a security system, including various services: for example, Help-net dials an emergency number on behalf of the driver in case of accident.
48) *Lexus ISC brochures* (2009), p. 15, and (2010), p. 15.

els and the latter model. In the former models, cultural factors had a strong importance and there were a lot of expressions regarding Japanese culture in their brochures, in the beginning. For example, in each 2006 edition of the brochures for these three models, there were sentences on the front page, as follows:

> "A new age of premium cars starts. Not only important are the values of profoundness or dignity, but being able to completely satisfy one's heart and harmonize with society or the earth are now just as important. Lexus from Japan changes the way of premium cars.
> The sensibility for beauty, the tenderness for nature, the spirit of *motenashi*, and the art of *takumi* in manufacturing, are all nurtured in this country. Traditional culture could carry new values for premium cars by uniting with Japanese advanced technology.
> The high performance that contends with the premium cars of the world and the technology to guard people and cherish the earth are infused with these thoughts".[49]

These sentences well represent the thought of Lexus in Japan during the early stage. As the first paragraph points out, what is profoundness and dignity, who has these values, who can surely satisfy Japanese customers, and who can harmonize our desires with the need to preserve the earth? It is assumed that the foreign luxury brands, centered on the German automobile manufacturers, which were, and still are today, a synonym for luxury cars in the Japanese market, have profoundness and dignity. However, Lexus combines Japanese culture, which satisfies customers in Japan, and leading edge technology, which contributes to society as a whole and to earth preservation. Indeed, in the second paragraph, the authors enumerate various Japanese cultural factors and cite both "traditional culture" and the "advanced technology" of Japan to "contend with the premium cars of the world".

Not only the front page, but also pages of the brochures introducing quality control ("the art of *takumi*", "the skilled art of *takumi*", "a careful consideration which is unique to the Japanese") and interior functions, such as the lighting system ("the art of *takumi*" and "*omotenashi*"), utilize cultural factors and an explanation of *L-finesse*, the design philosophy of Lexus. Furthermore, the brochures make use of cultural factors while commenting on their

---

49) *Lexus IS brochures* (2006), p. 3, *GS* (2006), p. 3, and *SC* (2006), p. 3.

environmental technology. For example, while referring to the Eco-Vehicle Assessment System, which monitors the environmental burden, the brochures says:

> "Further evolution for symbiosis with the earth is needed, so that automobiles may continue to be the vehicles that fascinate people hereafter.
> May the Japanese spirit that is tender for nature and the technology unique to Japan greatly contribute to this goal".[50]

Thus, a combination of Japanese culture and technology is seen in every description of the Lexus' concept, thought, technology, function, or quality of a car. A comparison with the brochures for ALTEZZA, the predecessor of IS, clearly reveals this character. The brochures of ALTEZZA and ALTEZZA Gita contain no cultural factors. Rather, there appear the expressions "driving pleasure" or "sporty car". Going even further, the words "Autobahn", "Switzerland", "Milano", and "Monaco" are found in an ALTEZZA Gita brochure. These cars have the same audio, ecological, and safety systems as the IS. Nevertheless, there are no cultural factors at all in their brochures. In short, although Lexus IS and ALTEZZA look almost identical, cultural factors did not appear in the brochures until the car was integrated into the Lexus brand. This means that, while their technology has been stressed before, cultural factors are a new and vital point for Lexus.

The brochures for the GS and IS series, however, report exponentially less cultural factors since 2009−2010. In a 2009 brochure for the IS series, only the phrase "the art of *takumi* which put persistence to manufacturing"— entirely identical to a sentence in the ISC brochure— remained on the front page. It had two factors: "a traditional Japanese value and leading edge unique to Japan" explaining *L-finesse*, and "through fusing the manual work of *takumi* and the leading edge technology", which appeared in the description of the painting process— this sentence was also identical to that in the brochure for ISC. Similarly, the number of cultural factors in the brochures for the GS series has rapidly decreased since 2010, and the factors that remain are identical to the phrasing of the brochures for other models. In other words, the personality of the GS and IS series disappeared, as far as cultural factors are concerned. The SC series also undergo a similar process, to a lesser

---

50) *Lexus GS brochures* (2006), p. 56, *IS* (2006), p. 50, and *SC* (2006), p. 42.

extent. Since Toyota announced end of production of the SC series in 2010, we cannot examine the shift of the SC series to cultural factors in recent years.

The RX series was introduced relatively recently, compared to these three models. However, the cultural factors in its brochures are similar to other models in this group. The first available edition includes many cultural factors, although some of these are duplicates: the front page ("the art of *takumi*"), the explanation of *L-finesse* ("finesse based on Japanese traditional values"), the description of the interior ("*omotenashi* of Lexus" and "the illuminated entry system which begins *omotenashi*"), the description of the painting process ("pursue the highest quality through fusing the manual work of *takumi* and leading edge technology"), and the description of the seats ("sewing done through the art of *takumi*"). However, by the 2012 edition, only two factors remained: the explanation of *L-finesse* and the description of the painting process, both featuring the same sentence as in other models' brochures.

5-2-3. Group C: the LS series

The LS series is the flagship model of Lexus. As we have confirmed in the content analysis, the brochures for this group contain more cultural factors than any other group. To turn our attention to individual brochures, only the brochures from 2006 to 2009 feature a photograph of a traditional Japanese garden, associated with *Karesansui* in Kyoto, on the front page. The 2007 LS460 brochure includes the largest number of cultural factors compared to any other model. In that brochure, several cultural factors are found: on the front page ("the art of *takumi*", "the characteristic sensitivity of Japan") and in the descriptions of the concept ("the art of *takumi*", "Japanese culture", "*omotenashi*"), manufacturing concept ("the art of *takumi*"), service concept ("*omotenashi*"), Lexus design ("the traditional values of Japan", "the sensitivity of Japan", "like a Japanese rock garden", "the spirit of manufacturing unique to Japan which puts our soul into a thing"), flagship design ("the art of *takumi*"), interior ("*omotenashi*", "the manner of opening and shutting in Japanese house"), engine ("by *takumi's* hand"), comfort ("*omotenashi*", "Japanese culture"), ecology ("the Japanese spirit that is tender for nature or the technology unique to Japan"), and body color variation ("the art of *takumi*", "the manual work by skilled *takumi*").

The 2007 brochure for the LS600 also reports several cultural factors. The main difference is that cultural factors were used to comment on the flagship model ("The elegance and nobility which the sensibility of Japan creates", "ultimate *omotenashi*", and "the spirit of *omotenashi* which arises from the careful sensibility that Japanese culture bore is alive in there"), and the long rear seat of LS600hl ("supreme *omotenashi* for the rear seat"). After all, Japanese culture represents, in this case, a sense of high-grade luxury that persuades customers to purchase.

While the mentions of cultural factors decreased in the 2010 brochure, they were still used in key positions: in the explanation of *L-finesse*, design concept, engine, interior, atmosphere inside the room, and painting process, which they distinguished on the front page. Even the 2013 brochure, which was integrated and involved fewer cultural factors, contained these factors at important points: on the front page, describing the flagship ("fuse creative sensibility and the art of *takumi*"), the explanation of *L-finesse* ("finesse means the sensibility or skillfulness which Japanese culture bore"), and descriptions of the wood panel ("the extremity of handwork by *takumi*"), engine ("a special *takumi* confirms any strange noise with a stethoscope"), the rear seat of the long body version ("heartily *omotenashi*" and "master *omotenashi* of the rear seat"), atmosphere inside cabin ("PRESTIGIOUS OMOTENASHI STYLE" serves as a noteworthy title), air conditioning ("the essence of this *omotenashi* of typically Japanese way"), painting process ("the art of *takumi*", "handwork of *takumi*", "Lexus color is a fruit of the art and sensibility of *takumi*"), and customization ("items of which the art of *takumi* make use").

Therefore, while the LS series' brochures reduce the number of cultural factors, the strong impression of the Japanese culture remains. From the above, we can read the obvious intention of Lexus LS to utilize cultural factors, even if some of the expressions are also seen in the brochures for other models.

6. Conclusion

Here, we review and summarize our discussion. To consider why and how culture functions in ways that associate meanings with products, we began our argument by investigating the theory of representation proposed by Stuart Hall. Hall insisted that there are two systems of representation: shared conceptual maps, and signs that work in a language. He also pointed out the significance of codes in the production of meanings. The relationships between concepts and signs contemporarily fixed by codes are arbitrary. Meanings are, therefore, constructed in the complex relationships of diverse powers.

Thus, the production of meanings has the same nature of politics. In this process, cultural apparatuses function as the devices or tools that help construct a culture. Brochures are a type of cultural apparatus because companies can use them to encode information that they would like consumers to read, while consumers can decode such information with their own codes. Therefore, brochures should be analyzed in terms of the production of meanings, and we need to focus on the function of language.

We proposed two key terms to analyze the function of language in brochures in Section 3: cultural factors and a cultural platform. Cultural factors are a set of cultural meanings or signs that are attributed to a product. To efficiently use cultural factors, a cultural platform is needed: it corresponds to a conceptual framework, a way of interpretation, or a lifestyle of consumers.

Section 4 explained how Toyota introduced the Lexus brand in the Japanese market, focusing on their market strategy. Lexus was introduced because Toyota needed to overcome global and domestic difficulties. In this process, Lexus used Japanese culture to create a brand identity representing home country to compete against strong foreign rivals that dominated the market for luxury cars in Japan.

In Section 5, we adopted content and discourse analysis in examining Lexus brochures. According to content analysis, we first found that the number of cultural factors had gradually decreased over time. Second, we found that we could classify models into three groups: the brochures for Group A almost had no cultural factors. Group B made use of a few cultural factors, though it originally used many, in the early stage. Group C utilized more cultural factors in its brochures. Third, we found that cultural factors have been primarily utilized for high-grade or flagship models. Fourth, we found a mutual relationship between the frequency of cultural factors and the location in which they appeared in brochures.

As a result of the discourse analysis on the above three groups, we also highlighted several important facts. The manner in which cultural factors are used in the three groups is distinct. Group A seemed to use cultural factors without explicit purposes. Group B used these factors eagerly; however, this interest declined with time. Group C utilized cultural factors to make its products seem more elegant, attractive, and luxurious. Discourse analysis also confirmed that "the art of *takumi*", "the spirit of *omotenashi*", and other expressions clearly representing traditional Japanese culture were frequently used. Cultural factors were utilized especially in explaining brand identity, elegance of the interiors, or the precision of the painting process, and, sometimes, to differentiate engines or designs from those of its rivals. In short, factors representing Japanese culture provided value added to a product.

Thus, Lexus regarded cultural factors as an important way to represent values that are unique to Japan, those that were not possessed by rival manufacturers. In this way, Lexus differentiated its products from its European competitors. This applied particularly to luxury models, as a way to justify higher costs.

This study concretely demonstrated how Lexus utilized Japanese culture in the Japanese market through content and discourse analysis. Consequently, we developed a comprehensive discussion, including diverse concepts that ordinary management or marketing theories seldom deal with, such as representation, the production of meanings, power relations, and cultural apparatuses. We also found a new issue: further research is needed to explain why Lexus has recently decreased its utilization of cultural factors. It is also necessary to analyze competitive relationships in the market for luxury cars in Japan, the strategy of the Toyota group as a whole, the development process for Lexus products, or shifting strategies and discourses to the automobile industry.

References

Journals, books and articles
■ **English**
Burr, V. (1995), *An Introduction to Social Constructionism*, Routledge: London and New York.
Du Gay, P. (ed.) (1997), *Doing Cultural Studies*, First Edition, The Open University: London.
Eagleton, T. (1991), *Ideology: An Introduction*, Verso: London.
Fairclough, N. (2003), *Analysing Discourse*, Routledge: Oxford.
Ghemawat, P. (2003), "The Forgotten Strategy", *Harvard Business Review*, Vol. 81, No. 11, pp. 84-95.
Ghemawat, P. (2007), "Managing Differences: The Central Challenge of Global Strategy", *Harvard Business Review*, Vol. 85, No. 3, pp. 58-68.
Turner, G. (1996), *British Cultural Studies: An Introduction*, Second Edition, Routledge: London.
Hall, S. (1982), "The Rediscovery of 'Ideology': Return of the Repressed in Media Studies", in Gurevitch, M., Bennet, T. and Woollacott, J. (eds.), *Culture, Society and the Media*, Methuen: London, pp. 56-90.
Hall, S. (2013), "The Work of Representation", in Hall, S., Evans, J. and Nixon, S. (eds.), *Representation*, Second Edition, Sage/The Open University: London, pp. 1-47.
Hofstede, G. (1980), *Culture's Consequences*, Sage: London.
Holt, D. B. (2004), *How Brands Become Icons*, Harvard Business School Press: New York.
Holt, D. B., Quelch, J. A. and Taylor, E. E. (2004), "How Global Brands Compete", *Harvard Business Review*, Vol. 82, No. 9, pp. 68-75.

Klein, N. (2000), *No Logo*, Vintage Canada: Toronto.
Mills, W. C. and Horowitz, L. (eds.) (1963), *Power, Politics, and People: the collected essays of C. Wright Miles*, Oxford University Press: New York.
Tomlinson, J. (1991), *Cultural Imperialism*, Pinter Publishers: London.

■ **Japanese**
Aoki, Sadashige (2008), *Bunka no Chikara* (*Power of Culture*), NTT Shuppan: Tokyo.
Endo, Isao (2007), *Premium Senryaku* (*Premium Business Strategy*), Toyo Keizai Shinposha: Tokyo.
Hasegawa, Yozo (2005), *Lexus: Toyota no Chosen* (*Lexus: the Challenge of Toyota*), Nihonkeizai Shinbunsha: Tokyo.
Ishida, Sawako (1998), *Yumeisei toiu Bunkasouchi* (*Cultural Apparatus as Fame*), Keiso Shobo: Tokyo.
Kaneko, Hirohisa (2005), *Lexus no Dilemma* (*The Dilemma of Lexus*), Gakushu Kenkyusha: Tokyo.
Matsumura, Akira (ed.) (2006), *Daijirin* (*Japanese Dictionary of Daijirin*), Sanseido: Tokyo.
Nobeoka, Kentaro (2011), *Kachizukuri Keiei no Ronri* (*Theory of Management to Create Value*), Nihon Keizai Shinbunsha: Tokyo.
Seguchi, Takeshi (2009), "Takokuseki-kigyo no Sijou-senryaku ni okeru Bunka no Katsuyou (Cultural Strategy of Multinational Corporations: How Multinational Corporations Utilize Culture in their Market Strategy)", *Hikaku Keiei Kenkyu* (*Comparative Studies of Management*), Vol. 33, pp. 142−161.
Seguchi, Takeshi (2012a), "Harley-Davidsonsha no Shijou-senryaku to Bukna no Kankei (The relation of Market Strategy of Harley-Davidson and Culture)", in Hayashi, Masaki (ed.), *Gendai Kigyo no Shakaisei* (*Sociality of Contemporary Companies*), Chuo University Press: Tokyo, pp. 221−257.
Seguchi, Takeshi (2012b), "Lexus no Shijou-senryaku ni okeru Bunka-teki Youso no Katsuyou (Utilizing cultural factors in market strategy of Lexus)", in Tokushige, Masashi and Hidaka, Kappei (eds.), *Kiro ni Tatsu Nihon Keizai Nihon Kigyo* (*Japanese Economy and Company Standing at the Crossroads*), Chuo University Press: Tokyo, pp. 177−201.
Spennemann, Kazuto (2006), "Doitsu ni okeru Lexus Jijou (The condition of Lexus in German)", *Navi*, December, p. 52.
Takagi, Haruo (2007), *Toyota wa Douyatte Lexus wo Tsukutta Noka* (*How Toyota created Lexus?*), Diamond: Tokyo.
Yoshimi, Shunya (2003), *Cultural Turn, Bunka no Seijigaku e* (*Cultural Turn, Toward the Politics of Culture*), Jinbunshoin: Kyoto.
Car Graphic, Nigensha: Tokyo.
Fourin's Monthly Report on the Global Automotive Industry, Fourin: Aichi.
Lexus Brochures, Toyota Motor Co. Ltd.: Aichi.
Motor Magazine, Motor Magazinsha: Tokyo.
Navi, Nigensha: Tokyo.
Toyota Annual Report, Toyota Motor Co. Ltd.: Aichi.

VIII.
Hyundai Motor Company's Alliance with Ford Motor Company in the Founding Period

Hyunjung JUNG

1. Introduction

Hyundai Motor Company (hereinafter HMC) was founded in 1976 as a late mover in the Korean market. After succeeding in manufacturing its first original model in 1973, HMC has made great strides, securing the number one spot in market share since 1977 up to the present. By 2010 it was among the top 5 automotive makers, and still continues to grow as a global maker.

How did HMC enter the automotive industry and acquire the necessary technology for automotive manufacturing? A large part comes from its alliance with Ford Motor Company (hereinafter Ford) at the time of the founding of HMC.

The purpose of this chapter is to discuss the effects of HMC-Ford alliance; how is the alliance related to HMC's operations at the outset and what did it gain from Ford? Research on these subjects is concentrated mainly on technical assistance from Ford. In other words, HMC was able to acquire basic level automobile assembly technology for automotive manufacturing including manuals for assembly, after-sales and the transfer of material relations, part plans, and samples.

However, cooperation with Ford was not confined to technological aspects. HMC was influenced by Ford not only in terms of technical assistance but also in terms of sales, and was able to establish its original sales system based on that influence. This chapter will analyze the results of the HMC-Ford alliance in terms of the two elements stated above.

This chapter will focus on the alliance with Ford at the time of HMC's founding, providing answers to the following questions. (1) How was HMC established? (2) Why did HMC ally with Ford? (3) What was Ford's role in the process of HMC's market entry? (4) How is the alliance related to the managerial foundation of HMC?

2. The Foundation of Hyundai Motor Company

2-1. Rapid growth and diversification strategy of Hyundai Engineering and Construction Corporation

HMC was founded by Hyundai Engineering and Construction Corporation (hereafter HECC)'s diversification strategy at a time of shift in the Korean automobile industry. HECC accomplished a rapid growth during the First Five Year Economic Development Plans in the 1960s when demand in construction industry was high. With the company's construction capacity being greatly improved especially in civil works, but also in architecture, machinery, electricity, etc., HECC was able to become the number one general contractor in Korea and accumulate huge capital in the cement industry, which was a growing industry with high potential at that time.

As shown in Table 1, the total capital increased by approximately twenty-fold from 1961 to 1966, and this capital growth led to HECC establishing

Table 1: Composition of HECC's Assets (1961-1966)

(Unit: Won, 1 million, %)

	1961		1962		1963	
	Amount	%	Amount	%	Amount	%
equity capital	76,234	54.3	255,183	67.4	341,613	35.7
borrowed capital	64,173	45.7	123,176	32.6	615,201	64.3
total capital	140,407	100	378,359	100	956,814	100
current asset	55,319	39.4	140,840	37.2	278,778	29.1
fixed asset	85,088	60.6	237,519	62.8	678,036	70.9
others						
	1964		1965		1966	
	Amount	%	Amount	%	Amount	%
equity capital	402,494	28.4	760,775	43.5	1,174,702	40.7
borrowed capital	967,499	70.6	986,862	56.5	1,713,301	59.3
total capital	1,369,933	100	1,746,937	100	2,888,003	100
current asset	374,938	27.4	482,971	27.7	920,633	31.9
fixed asset	905,371	66.1	1,161,151	66.5	1,390,420	48.1
others	89,684	6.5	102,815	5.9	570,950	19.8

Source: HECC (1997), *Hyundai Kunsul 50nyonsa (50-year history of Hyundai Engineering and Construction Corporation)*, p. 235.

diversification strategy. The point of this strategy was to expand the supply and demand of construction materials, expand overseas construction, and enter the field of manufacturing focusing on heavy chemical industry. The projects chosen in this diversification attempt were oil refining business, chemical pulp factory for paper-making, automobile industry, joint venture with OAK Electronics, hotel business, ship-making business, etc., and among these options, HECC decided to enter the auto market.

The technological foundation from auto-repairing business played a favorable role in the establishment of HMC. Juyung Chung, the first Chairman of HMC, already had experience in auto-repair business before the establishment of HMC. As shown in Table 2, Art Services was founded in 1940 and Hyundai Auto Service in 1946. He was able to learn basic structure and mechanism of automobiles while fixing the cars, and develop his potential for an entrepreneur that pioneers the auto industry in the future. Due to increased construction demand after the Korean War in 1950, he focuses on construction business, but this means that HECC was strengthening the foundation for HMC to enter the auto industry later on in full scale. Hattori (1988) points out about this matter as follows. "In a sense, entering the auto market could be considered a natural path as Juyung Chung was once in auto repair business and HECC's technology allowed them to freely use heavy machinery for construction and even repair them themselves".[1] As such, HECC was able to achieve phenomenal growth as the company realized the importance of mechanization, the core of development in construction business, as it had experience in auto repair business. According to Lee (1999), the close relationship in terms of technology between sectors is the basic characteristic of Hyundai Group's diversification, assessing that the group played a leading role in Korea's economic development.[2]

To summarize, the foundation of HMC became a key factor in HECC's capital and technological accumulation, and the starting line for entering heavy chemical industry through related diversification.[3]

---

1) Tamio Hattori, (1988), *Kankokuno Keiei Hatten (Management Development of Korea)*, Bunshindo, p. 262.
2) Kwangjong Lee, (1999), "Hyundai Group i Hankuk Kyunje Baljeone Michin Younghyang (A Study on the Influence of the Hyundai Group on Korean Economic Development)", *The Journal of Business, History*, 19, pp. 225-226.
3) After the foundation of HMC in 1967, Hyundai Heavy Industries was established in 1974. Hyundai Group developed its construction, heavy industries and auto businesses in a mutually beneficial way, pursuing the goal of 'One Heavy Industries Set' that aims to achieve economy of scale against the world, and eventually grew into the biggest Chaebol in Korea (Dongsung Cho (1990), *Hankuk Chaebol Yeongu (The study of Korean*

Table 2: Before the foundation of HMC

Date of Foundation	Company Name	Major Business Activities
Jan 1938	Kyungil Rice Store	Acquired and operated a rice mill called Bokheung Rice Store
Mar 1940	Art Service	Established an auto repair factory
Apr 1946	Hyundai Auto Service	Re-established an auto repair factory; major clients were the US Army and the government and business flourished to auto repair and improvement.
May 1947	Hyundai Togun	Started as a minor business into being in charge of US Army-related construction projects
Jan 1950	Hyundai Engineering and Construction Corporation	Was established by merging Hyundai Auto Service and Hyundai Togun. - In early 1950s, held a monopoly in US Army construction. - In April 1956, in order to import foreign equipment that US Army projects required in their specification, trade business was added to the business purposes. In 1962, Hyundai International Inc. was established. - Executed road paving projects from 1957 to 1962. - In late 1950s, focused on civil projects with high profitability. 50% profit on average. - In August 1958, established a daughter company, Kumgang Slate Industrial Co. Saw an annual growth of 80% until mid-1960s. - In June 1962, established Cement Factory in Danyang. - In September 1965, became the first Korean company to overseas market and executed 6 highway construction projects in Thailand.

Source: HECC (1997), HMC (1987), HMC (1992).

2-2. Juyung Chung's tenacity in auto business

There wouldn't be anyone who would deny the role that Hyundai Group's Chairman Juyung Chung played in Korea's economic development. Juyung Chung publicly said that 'the root of Hyundai was auto repair business' and played an important role in the foundation of HMC. Seyoung Chung, the first CEO of HMC and Juyung Chung's brother, said in an official interview about the reason why Hyundai chaebol entered the auto industry as follows. "It reminds me of around 1945 when Juyung Chung did not enter the construction business and instead ran an auto service factory in Seoul for several

---

Chaenol), Maeil Kyungje Shinmunsa, p. 234.).

years as his first business. That experience kept him interested in cars, and eventually became the motivation for entering automotive industry. (Maeil Business Newspaper, 10.08.1968)" Likewise, the determination of Juyung Chung, who has been involved in auto market since his twenties, to enter the auto industry resulted in the establishment of HMC.

At that time within HECC, many opposed entering the auto market, as it required a considerable amount of capital and technology. However, Juyung Chung mentioned in his autobiography as follows, "A long time ago I ran an auto repair business, fixing the cars myself with oily hands, so I feel unusually attached towards cars. So I've always wanted to run an auto business again. Also, I pride myself of having a deeper understanding than anyone in the mechanism of cars through my experience of running an auto repair factory and a heavy construction machinery factory. For the production technology, we need to receive help from an auto maker of an advanced country in the beginning anyways, so whether we're experienced or not is not an issue. Is there a country that started with experience? We can learn and do it".[4] and exhibited the "can-do" entrepreneurial spirit. Likewise, the experience in cars accumulated from auto repair business led to mechanization in construction business, and the comprehensive construction capacity led to success in the auto industry again.

In other words, HMC was born under the personal ambition of Hyundai's founder, Juyung Chung and his strong leadership with a unified and centralized management structure. Since the initial ownership structure was totally controlled by Juyung Chung and his family, its strategic goals and decision-making processes were dominated by the Chung family.[5]

Regarding this matter, Cho (1990) points out about Juyung Chung as follows. "Hyundai Group's exponential growth and determination towards overseas market, business areas that pursue production goods, and bold and risk-taking market entry strategy shown in the process of entering ship-making and electronics industry cannot be considered apart from entrepreneur and Hyundai Group Chairman Juyung Chung. He has had a decisive influence in shaping Hyundai's corporate culture, which can be summarized into controlling the organization and establishing business strategy, decisive business expansion and strong initiative".[6]

Such strong and bold influence of Juyung Chung on HMC was also exhib-

---

4) Juyung Chung (1998), *I Ttange Taeonaseo (Was born here)*, Sol, p. 133.
5) Barnett, W., March, J. and Rhee, M. (2003), *Hyundai Motor Company SM-122*, p. 4.
6) Dongsung Cho (1990), *op. sit.*, p. 225.

ited after the company was founded – when it entered the U. S. market. HMC entered the U. S. market in 1983, and an anonymous employee says as follows about the motivation.

"I would even say that Hyundai's entry to U. S. market was led by Chairman Chung's personal ambition. I agree that without Chung's strong drive, Hyundai's entry to U. S. could be delayed until its technology is comparable to the Japanese or European automakers".[7] As such, Juyung Chung have made bold decisions in important moments for HMC, while still focusing on construction and heavy industries business, and played an important role in the foundation of HMC.

2-3. Latecomer in Korean automobile industry, HMC

The Korean auto market before HMC had a government-led monopoly supply structure. In order to nurture the auto industry and achieve the goal of all-domestic production, Korean government deemed competition unnecessary.[8] Under such circumstances, Shinjin Motors (now GM Korea), a market leader, was granted a monopoly status by the Korean government, entered into alliance with Toyota Motor Corporation and produced their car model, *Corona*. That is, the auto industry was expected to grow by establishing a mass production system by realizing component systemization with Shinjin Motors in the center.

However, in order to meet the suddenly increased automobile demand, Shinjin Motors depended on import instead of using domestic components, drawing opposition from component makers. Shinjin Motors imported Knock Down (KD) components of Toyota Motor Corporation, assembled them and sold them to the domestic market at double to triple price, and this led to a major political issue. In other words, Shinjin Motors used its position in the market and neglected going domestic, and questions were raised about the government granting illegal privileges to Shinjin Motors. In the end, as the association effect between assembly companies and component makers was not realized in the monopoly production system, the growth of auto industry was rather undermined.[9]

---

7) Recited from Barnett, W., March, J. and Rhee, M. (2003), *op., sit*, p. 4.

8) The Korean government suggested a specific localization rate in order to replace imported components to domestic ones, but as Cho and Chu (1998) points out, it was an impractical plan that neither considered the growth rate of related industries nor reflected the opinions of the industry (Dongsung Cho and Woojin Chu (1998), *Hankuk ui Jadongcha Sanyeop, (Korean Automobile Industry),* Seoul University Press, p. 54.).

9) Kyunhyung Lee (2000), *Jadongcha Saneop Jungchak ui Yeokhalgwa Hankye (The Role*

Under the circumstances, Asia Motors takes Shinjin Motors's place and enter the auto market. In order to promote employment in the Honam region, which had comparatively less industrial benefits, Asia Motors claimed that there was a need to construct an automobile company there, and was successful in achieving the permit from the Korean government. In 1965, the company went in alliance with Renault, but as Renault Group changed its decision, the partnership failed and 2 years later, Asia Motors went in alliance with Fiat.[10] Also, Asia Motors received permit by the Korean government in order to respond to army and overseas demand, under the condition of avoiding competition with the former company, Shinjin Motors.[11] Likewise, Korean government's policy trend to limit competition by controlling the market from the production side did not change.

As seen above, HMC entered the market a latecomer when practically Shinjin Motors was in sole control of the market. When progress towards domestic production for automobile industry's growth became difficult, the Korean government gave permit to HECC to enter the market as well as Asia Motors. The grounds for permit was in the 'Automobile Plant Permission Standards (April 1967)' that Korean government presented. The major conditions are as follows.[12]

① A company with permit of introducing foreign currency with more than $7 million of facility machinery

② A company in technological alliance with an advanced country in automotive production and assembly and whose partner can guarantee the product's performance

③ A company with more than 991,736 m^2 of factory land and more than 33,058 m^2 of factory floor space

④ A company with more than $1 million worth of assembly and painting equipment

---

        & *Limitation of Automobile Industry Policies)*, Hyundai Kyungje Yeonguwon, pp. 8-9.

10) After receiving government permit in 1968, Asia Motors was going to complete the construction of its Gwangju assembly factory and produce Fiat 124, but as its business situation worsened dramatically, the company lost its control to Dongkuk Steel Co. the same year without being able to even begin the production (Korea Automobile Manufacturers Association (2005), *Hankuk Jadongcha Sanyeop 50nyunsa (50-year History of Korean Automobile Industry)*, pp. 137-138.). Afterwards, it continued to suffer and was merged by Kia Motors in 1976.

11) Korea Development Bank (1966), *Hankuk ui Sanyeop (Industries of Korea)*, p. 765.

12) Korea Institute for Industrial Economics & Trade (1997), *Hankuk Jadonchasaneope Paljunyeoksawha sungjangjamgaryok (Developmental history of Korean automobile industry and growth potential)*, pp. 34-35.

⑤ A company with more than $1 million worth of body frame production equipment

As shown above, a considerable amount of investment was required in order to enter the auto industry, so in a sense the government opened the entry way for emerging chaebols to automobile industry. In other words, HECC, which was emerging as a new chaebol at that time, was allowed to newly enter the auto market. The direct reason why HECC entered the auto market by going into partnership with Ford can also be identified here.

Likewise, HMC was founded in alliance with Ford at a time of change in Korean automobile industry. As you can see in Table 3, HMC laid its basic foundation as a new auto company by general alliance with Ford.

Table 3: Major Information on the Establishment of HMC

* Purpose: ① Automotive Production and Sales, ② General Machinery Production and Sales, ③ Various Vehicle Repair, ④ Army Supply, ⑤ Others, Business and Investment related to the above
* Capital: 100 million won
* Production Plan: As for first stage, annually produce 3,500 units and adjust production plan according to demand
* Supply Plan: As for the material for automobile production, purchase from Ford and Ford-related companies in Completely Knock Down (CKD)
* Localization Plan: In order to promote the level of domestic machine industry, seek effective localization with Ford providing technological guidance
* Factory Construction Plan: Plan to construct the factory in the seaside region within Ulsan City's industrial complex
* Roles & Responsibilities of HECC and Ford: HECC covers the necessary funds and plays a general role in operation. Ford is responsible of overall quality management in the production process.

Source: HMC (1987), pp. 40–43.

As latecomer HMC made its entry, Korean automobile industry finally pushed out of a monopoly and into a competitive system. At the same time, following Japanese and European automakers, US automakers also entered the Korean automobile industry, leading to expectations in acquiring technology comprehensively from automotive manufacturers of advanced countries.

3. How did HMC-Ford alliance get started?

We have focused on analyzing the establishment of HMC. It was the result of the growth of HECC, meanwhile the Founder Juyung Chung's leadership became an important factor for entering international market. In addition, it became a cornerstone for competitive Korean automobile industry and an opportunity to learn about vehicles in general from leading foreign automobile company, Ford. If so, we need to look into a couple of questions below to further analyze the alliance between HMC-Ford. Why did HMC ally with Ford and why Ford chose Hyundai?

3-1. Why did HMC ally with Ford?

As explained above, in order to enter Korean automobile industry as a late mover, HMC had to make "a technical alliance with advanced auto company". It was one of HMC's major concerns to choose the right foreign brand for future manufacturing plants. Official records state that it was the decision of the founder Juyung Chung and the other executives. In other words, in order to manufacture automobiles with its own technology in the future, they made a principle of "if technical alliance is required, the partner must be the pioneer of automobile industry with incomparable capacity".[13] Therefore, candidates narrowed into GM and Ford, the top two global players back then.

GM, the biggest brand then, was the first option for alliance. GM outran Ford in 1920's and became number one in the world. They quickly targeted the international market; they already owned nineteen manufacturing plants located in fifteen different countries. Traditionally, GM has entered foreign markets in the form of acquisitions existing auto makers, and if not possible, directly participated in capital and management.

However, this conflicted with Hyundai's independent management policies. In other words, GM's method of entering overseas market went straight against HMC's principle of 'no interruption in management'. Reminding himself with the past, Juyung Chung mentioned, "GM's level of production was much higher than that of Ford. Yet, I was not favorable of GM's way of performing international business. (omit) Such method of collaboration is hard to accept before and now. In a case of alliance with foreign company, even if the investment ratio is 50 to 50, in the end, it is highly likely to have the management initiatives taken away by the big company with their capital, productivity, and management know-hows. Then, creating goods and selling them in my way become very difficult. It would be very shameful to have foreign companies to control the company that I established".[14] Eventually, alliance with GM was called off in the beginning as management interruption

---

13) HMC (1997), *Dojun 30nyun Vision 21segi (30 years of challenge, twenty first century of vision)*, p. 109.
14) Juyung Chung (1998), *op. sit.*, pp. 133-134.

became an issue.

Next, they reviewed Ford for a potential alliance partner. Ford was especially centered in Europe and had fifteen affiliated companies to actively exchange technology and standardize production facility and compartments for international market. They did not stop establishing new affiliated companies to expand their way to overseas market. However, Ford negotiated rather flexibly when trying to enter Korea, under several conditions like moderate capital participation and lateral management support. Juyung Chung determined the conditions are worth for negotiations and aggressively searched the right alliance with Ford. As a result, HMC expressed their intention for partnership at the Ford Headquarters in Detroit when Seyoung Chung (then Director of HECC, later the first president of HMC) visited the United States due to an issue on cement factories.[15]

Also, Ford has thought to enter into the Korean Market. After mid 1960s, Ford aggressively pioneered overseas market and implemented international divisions; Korea was one of their targets with much potential. The size of the market may be small but the location was perfect to access China, the future giant market. They set up an investigation team in February 1967 to look into the potentials of the Korean automobile industry, and after the investigation, declared their will to establish an automobile plant in Korea. Eventually, both companies reached a partnership agreement in the same year.

So HMC made a following contract in accordance with the alliance with Ford. HMC officially signed Overseas Assembler Agreement with Ford U. S. and their affiliated companies, including Ford Motor Company, Ltd. and Ford Werke A. G.. Later on, Foreign Products Sales Agreement and Technological Assistance Agreement were added.[16]

3-2. Why did Ford ally with HMC?

We have looked into reasons why HMC allied with Ford. Then, why did Ford partner with HMC? There would be three reasons to that decision.

First, HECC was in the middle of avid construction and maintenance of roads. According to Ford, the key to expanding automobile demands in Korea was the modernization of road networks.[17] Responsively, HECC was focusing on road development as the leading construction company in Korea.

---

15) HMC (1997), *op. sit.*, p. 111.
16) HMC (1992), *Hyundai Jadongchasa (25-year history of Hyundai Motor Company)*, p. 276.
17) *Kyunghyang Sinmun (Kyunghyang newspaper)*, December 2, 1967.

As the Table 4 shows, it played a key role in the construction of major roads that penetrated Korea, including the Gyeongbu Expressway, Honam Expressway, Youngdong Expressway, Namhae Expressway and Jungbu Expressway in 1968.[18]

Table 4: Road Development by HECC (1968-1979)

Year	Road construction
1968	Gyeongbu Expressway (Seoul-Busan)
1968	Geyongin Expressway (Seoul-Incheon)
1969	Ulsan Expressway (Eonyang-Ulsan)
1971	Honam Expressway (Singal-Saemal)
1971	Honam · Namhae Expressway (Jeonju-Busan)
1972	Jungbu Expressway (Donong-Wangsookkyo)
1973	Expansion of expressway between Chungmoo-Jangseung
1974	Youngdong Expressway (Daegu-Masan)
1976	Buma Expressway (Daegu-Masan)
1979	Construction of roads at Yangji · Jincheon · Kwanghyewon

Source: HECC (1997).

Second, HMC already had experience in the auto repair business even before its foundation, which worked as an advantage. As noted, after establishing Art Services in 1940, Juyung Chung engaged in auto repair for 2 years (Table, 2). Following the foundation of Hyundai Auto Service in 1946, he went back to auto repair. He did focus his business mainly on construction, however, as there was a big boom in the construction business at the time. Such technology and expertise acquired from motor service experience indeed had an influence in partnership selection.

When Ford visited Korea to review the collaboration with HECC, Juyung Chung has left a record which made the story above much more persuasive. He said, "In February of 1967, Ford's vice president of international division visited Seoul with other representatives. They had a result of the highest credit. From automobile engine components to transmission, braking system,

---

18) HECC's achievement is especially outstanding when it comes to Gyeongbu Expressway. Gyeongbu Expressway was part of National Land Plan began at the behest of South Korean President Chunghee Park. It used a method of dividing a few lines of expressway into several regions and assign each to big corporations. Every national force, even ground, sea, and air forces, were deployed. Hyundai Construction Company was in charge of the first region, Seoul-Suwon, and completed two fifth of the entire road, which is 428km long in total (Wonchul Oh (1996), *Hankukhyung Kyungje Kunsul (Korean economic construction 4)*, Kia Kyungje Yeonguso, pp. 293-308.).

and ten thousands of parts, I had nothing but confidence. They believed I was more than just a car technician. Interview, which supposedly lasted 4 days, only went on for a couple of hours. After the interview, I drove them myself and served them to show that I am the best partner for their technological alliance.[19]

Third, it was closely related to Ford's global strategies. The great success of the Ford *Mustang* had the vehicle sell 2.37 million units in 1967 in the continental US, and Ford enjoyed an enormous boom in sales for over 10 billion dollars and a net profit of 700 million dollars. However, in 1967, (1) the 53 day long UAW ally strike, (2) the boycott of Ford cars in Arab nations, and (3) temporary recession caused car sales to drop to 1.85 million units and net profits to plummet to 84 million dollars.[20] Such management crisis forced Ford to look outside the US and hunt for new foreign markets.

However, Ford's foreign expansion shows a new set of characteristics. They changed their strategic focus from US and Europe to Japan and Southeast Asia, as they added Asia into their market. Whereas Ford valued overseas strategies, they continued to perceive the United States as a part of a global business, and attempted to adopt an international division of labor in the form of sharing parts through a domestic division and overseas affiliated company. In other words, they pursued an international division of labor at a global level centering on Asia, the US and Europe while integrating existing overseas businesses.[21]

Ford actually attempted to secure foothold in new markets including Korea and the Philippines, carrying out the above plans into action. Therefore, the partnership with HMC could be perceived as part of Ford's foreign strategies. In other words, it is part of Ford's Asian strategy. As such, it is important to understand the partnership of the two companies not only within the framework of the Korean market but also within the context of Ford's global strategy.

---

19) Juyung Chung (1998), *op. sit.*, p. 134.
20) HMC (1997), *op. sit.*, p. 113.
21) Koichi Shimokawa (1980), *Ford*, Tokyo Keizai, p. 168.

4. The entry of HMC to Korean automobile market and its sales strategy

4-1. Product strategy of HMC

The entry of HMC meant formation of competitive relation in automobile market of Korea. As noted, Shinjin Motors, a pioneering company, entered into an alliance with Toyota Motor Corporation and monopolized the market prior to that. However, without having a capital and technology to manufacture their own vehicles, they were selling assembled foreign models. For example for passenger cars, HMC was selling Ford *Cortina*, Shinjin Motors was selling Toyota *Corona*, and Asia Motors was selling *Fiat 124*, the exact alliance partner's model. Because of this, Korean automobile market became an arena of competition of Japanese, American, and European vehicles. Thus, the characteristic of competition then was dependent on the alliance with foreign automakers instead of promoting reinforcement of competitiveness based on the technical accumulation or economic scale. As a result, the significance of sales strategy emerged.

HMC, being a late starter, adopted the strategy to provide higher quality products and services by attracting customers with Ford cars which were a maker of higher rank than the partner company of pioneering company. They paid especially close attention to the selection of main model and selected *Cortina* of Ford England and *20M* of Ford Germany after a discussion with Ford.

Why did HMC selected European vehicles instead of models of Ford U. S.? The vehicles manufactured by the Ford US at that time were mostly extravagant full-sized vehicles or sports cars, and compact cars suitable to the actual condition in Korea were few. On the other hand, the European vehicles were durable and practical by comparison. HMC said that they focused on practicality and selected the vehicles of Ford England because the road condition of Korea was not good. Besides, Ford established Ford Europe in 1967 and generalized its affiliated company, and it was a period when standardization was aggressively executed by attempting the publication of manufacturing facility and parts through the mutual exchange of technology between Ford England and Ford Germany which were the axes, so, Hyundai chose European vehicles.[22]

Cortina, as a popular vehicle that recorded second place according to the

---

22) HMC (1992), *op. sit.*, p. 284.

number of sales in England after its release, had wider seat and larger engine displacement than *Corona* which was the main model of Shinjin Motors, and was superior in terms of safety and maximum speed. And, *20M* was the most suitable model for Korea where there were a lot of unpaved and narrow roads, and it was judged excellent compared to *Crown* of Shinjin Motors in terms of performance. That is, HMC chose to concentrate on models that can stand up to the competition with the pioneering company.

4-2. HMC and its own sales strategy

HMC was certain that the brand image of Ford would bring some advantages in Korean automobile market, but also knew that they need other innovative strategies to catch up and overtake Shinjin Motors. Therefore HMC established its own sales strategies to accelerate selling, based on the weaknesses of sales service from Shinjin Motors, which are as follows.

First, the principle of fair release was established. HMC, initially, decided to release the unit under the principle of giving priority to business use and following the order of application in order to resolve the complaints of consumers due to disorder of releasing under the exclusive system at that time. Especially in case of passenger cars, the considerable premium was adhered or the vehicles were released irrespective of the application order with the involvement of authority or brokers because the supply of the vehicle was insufficient under the exclusive system then. HMC set the fair release of units as its first principle in order to correct this negative effect.[23]

Second, HMC introduced the installment financing for the first time in Korea by using the new management system of Ford as reference.[24] An installment sales method, which has long period and low interest burden for the consumers while no financial stress for HMC, was invented after conducting studies. They persuaded Kookmin Bank that dealt with small-loan finance at that time, and agreed on the implementation of automobile loan according to the mutual premium of Kookmin Bank. Its composition was as follows. (1) The consumer enters into a mutual premium contract with a bank. (2) The bank lends auto sales loan and pays the loan to HMC. (3) The consumer pays monthly fees to the bank and repays the loan. (4) HMC enters into a guarantee insurance contract for the loan amount with an insurance company.[25] The

---

23) HMC (1992), *Ibid.*, p. 299.
24) Hyundai Motor Sevice (1999), *Hyundaijadongcha Service 25nyon (25-year history of Hyundai Motor Service)*, pp. 29-33.
25) HMC (1992), *op. sit.*, pp. 299-302.

Table 5: Sales & Production units of Passenger cars (1966~1973)

	1966	1967	1968	1969	1970	1971	1972	1973	1969~1973
Shinjin[1]	3,117[2]	4,983	11,016	13,152 11,855[3] (90.1)[4]	10,394 (8,057) (77.5)	7,161 (5,734) (80.0)	5,606 (4,242) (75.7)	6,696 (7,569) (113.0)	43,009 (37,957) (88.3)
HMC	–	–	614	6,242 (6,323) (101.3)	2,356 (2,212) (93.9)	2,398 (2,121) (88.4)	2,615 (2,387) (91.3)	5,426 (5,309) (97.8)	19,037 (8,352) (96.4)
Asia	–	–	–	–	1,737 (1,018) (58.6)	2,869 (2,517) (87.7)	1,731 (1,955) (112.9)	486 (456) (93.8)	6,826 (5,946) (87.1)
total	3,117	4,983	11,730	19,394 (18,178) (93.7)	14,487 (11,287) (77.9)	12,428 (10,372) (83.5)	9,952 (9,084) (91.3)	12,611 (13,334) (105.7)	68,872 (62,255) (90.4)

Notes:
1) After 1972, combined with GMK (GM Korea).
2) Production units
3) Sales units
4) Sales units／Production units = Percentage of sales. There might be percentage above 100%, because stock were included.
Source: Jahun Ryu (1990), *Hankuk Jabonjueiwha Jadongcha Sanyeop (Korean capitalism and automobile industry)*, Pulbit, p. 21.

implementation of this installment plan aimed to secure a sales appeal to reduce the financial burden of consumers than Shinjin Motors.

It was a result of decision made from HMC executives. Seyoung Chung, the president, explains the background of coming up with the innovative sales strategies as this. "One though I had when I decided to start the installment plan was that all I need is the trust and faith. Consumers who buy cars at that time were considered as a middle-high class, and I had a faith in them as economic activists who are the core force to lead the credit community".[26] As we can see, the executives of HMC at that time were deeply influenced by the sales system with installment plan in advanced countries, and tried to bring it to Korean market. Based on the official record, HMC stated that they expected "By starting the advanced installment financing, the brand image would be improved as the customers recognize us as the company trying to provide the most convenience to them. It would lead us to absorb the costumers who were complaining about the monopoly system". as a result.[27]

---

26) Seyoung Chung (2000), *Miraenun Mandunun Gusida (The future is something we create)*, Hangrim Chulpansa, pp. 138-139.
27) HMC (1992), *op. sit.*, p. 302.

The sales strategy like this worked well and HMC successfully entered the Korean automobile market (Table 5). In the early days, the publicity of Ford demonstrated its effect that there was no inventory due to preorders. In other words, the latecomer HMC was able to enter the market smoothly by providing more excellent products and services using the alliance with Ford. Also, HMC was able to raise its market share immediately as they absorb consumers who had been having complaints in a monopolistic market by establishing own sales strategy.

5. The results of the alliance

HMC succeeded to enter into Korean automobile market based on the brand value of Ford and its unique sales strategies. If so, how the alliance related to the managerial foundation of HMC?

5-1. Technical assistance from Ford

HMC, as a late competitor in the auto industry, recognized the importance of foreign technologies, and in 1968 entered into an Overseas Assembler Agreement with Ford. The agreement consisted of six main points as follows; (1) When necessary, Ford can cooperate with and give advice to assembler on equipment placement of the assembly plant, the selection, purchase and installation of equipment, the purchase of parts supplied from Korea and automobile assembly. (2) Ford designates KD materials to be procured for assembler and assembler uses only the materials and parts approved by Ford when assembling automobiles. (3) Automobiles must be assembled so they are in accordance with Ford's quality standards. (4) The assembler sells automobiles to dealers approved by Ford and purchasers agreed by Ford. (5) HMC cooperates in the designation of domestic automobile parts suppliers, and provides reasonable counsel and cooperation to suppliers so that their parts' performance and quality satisfy Ford's standards. (6) Ford provides specifications, plans or other materials for the production of localization products.[28]

With the cooperation of Ford, HMC organized an assembly line and was able to learn assembly skills through repeated practice under the supervision of Ford technicians. As soon as the agreement was signed, Ford sent Hyundai manuals, parts plans and samples required for assembly and dispatched tech-

---

28) HMC (1992), *Ibid.*, pp. 274-275.

nicians for each specific field in accordance to the progress of production preparation. As FASPAC (Ford of Asia & Pacific) was in charge of the affiliates west to Hawaii and technical problems of technical partners, most Ford technicians coming to HMC were from Australia. With instructions and manuals from Ford technicians, HMC was able to master various work related to production technology.

HMC secured an excellent pool of human resources to master technology from Ford. The main pool from which individuals were drafted was HECC. Of employees with excellent entrance scores and work performance, individuals who had mastered automobile related technology such as having backgrounds in heavy equipment factories and machinery department were selected. There were also scouting from outside the group, including three from Shinjin Motors and few others with military vehicle background. Back then, when cars were not common in Korea, the only place to acquire high quality manpower with automotive experience, apart from existing automobile companies, was military organizations. There were also open calls for employees, putting stress on fair procedure and English conversation skills, and required employees to continue to cultivate their English speaking skills even after entering the company. Behind this requirement was the strategy that immediately had to cooperate with technicians and managers from Ford and prepare for overseas expansion in future. Based on human resources acquired as stated above, HMC started to cooperate with Ford across all sectors.

HMC actively dispatched trainees overseas for the technology transfer from Ford. Trainees acquired production technology from Australia where the Ford Asia Technology Headquarters was located, AS from Ford Japan, and sales training from dealers in Ford America. It was a financially tight period for Hyundai, but the management pushed forth strongly with the decision to aggressively learn from the beginning the expertise and technology of industry leaders. Especially what Seyoung Chung, the first CEO of the HMC, said was very noticeable. He commented about his thought of overseas training, "It wasn't easy thing to do when the financial situation wasn't stable. But the decision came out from the thought I had at that moment that it needed to be started over from the beginning", well represents his aggressive desire to learn.[29] Chairman Juyung Chung also positively evaluated this by saying "It was all my brother's decision to dispatch employees to overseas, when other automobile company didn't even consider doing it, and the result tells us that

---

29) Seyoung Chung (2000), *op. sit.*, p. 132.

he was right about it".[30] Since all capacity available was concentrated on production, training took place chiefly in Australia.

HMC abode by all terms and conditions put forth by Ford and strictly followed Ford rules. All processes and procedures, from production, material operation systems, customs and storage management, thoroughly adapted the Ford system. Specific procedures according to the Ford system came to be accepted as natural and fair to employees of HMC.

Moreover, in order to meet the 21% localization rate required by the Korean government, HMC selected parts suppliers with the cooperation of Ford. HMC discussed and agreed with Ford to procure from Korea parts, mainly batteries, and visited each aspiring supplier with parts development technicians dispatched by Ford. Together, they evaluated productivity to 50 suppliers and had them make prototypes according to the part plans and technical instruction provided. Certain parts had to be sent to Ford Australia for validation, and only approved parts were able to be mass produced. Initially, even parts manufactured according to design plans had to be approved by the Ford inspector dispatched to Korea before proceeding to mass production. [31]

Responding to the cooperation on overall automobile industry from Ford, HMC's engineers, technicians and construction workers lived together in a makeshift structure at the plant site and worked 16 hours a day, seven days a week by sharing ambitious goal to acquire a production capability in the shortest possible time. While plant construction was underway, production teams rehearsed production operations by disassembling and reassembling cars over and over to routinize the production procedures, internalizing transferred production manuals. As a result, HMC was able to achieve its first commercial production in a span of six months from groundbreaking. This was the shortest time among the 118 Ford assembly plants in the world.[32]

Consequently, HMC gained experience needed to adopt these technologies through technical assistance from Ford. [33] HMC regarded the technical collaboration with Ford as a stepping stone, accumulating technical capabilities.[34] HMC developed its indigenous model based on accumulated technology. Therefore, *Pony* of HMC created. It was very noticeable because it was

---

30) Juyung Chung (1998), *op. sit.*, p. 139.
31) Byungjae Park (2012), *New Brilliant Company,* Maeil kyungje Shinmunsa, pp. 17–20.
32) Linsu Kim (1998), "Crisis Construction and Organizational Learning: Capability Building in Catching-up at Hyundai Motor", *Organization Science*, 9 (4), pp. 510–511.
33) Alice, H. Amsden (1989), *Asia's next giant*, Oxford University Press, p. 175.
34) Young-suk Hyun and Jinjoo Lee (1989), "Can Hyundai Go It Alone?", *Long Range Planning*, 22 (2), p. 65.

the sixteenth in the world, the second in Asia following after Japan.

5-2. Limitation on the technological assistance from Ford

On the other hand, no matter how great foreign technical assistance was, when assistance reached its limit, the nontrivial matter remained of mastering technologies.

One example would be the Unitization Trolley System, a method of supplying material from Ford. The Unitization Trolley System categorizes KD parts into mini boxes, places the boxes on the trolley, and repeats each procedure to put necessary parts in the same process. Specifically, it (1) Stores KD boxes according to storage plans (2) Categorizes all parts according to processes (3) For each process, puts parts for one vehicle into one mini box. (4) Load mini boxes on the trolley according to the order of procedures.[35] This is a simple system in which one vehicle is complete once a trolley provides the mini boxes to all necessary procedures. There should be no problem in automobile production if each process receives parts smoothly like the steps above.

However, shortages and defective parts would result into trouble. If shortages were not followed up quick enough, the process that required the parts would stop, which eventually led to the halt of the entire factory. Such problems were fixed by contacting the materials team during times of shortages or defective parts and receiving the necessary parts directly from the storage. However, limitations of the Unitization Trolley System continued to appear.

Nevertheless, the Unitization Trolley System is still in use. The reasons are first, making changes to the trolley system required the authorization from Ford. Ford opposed to changing the trolley system. Second, employees were also skeptical to the new part supplying method. They believed that the method proposed by a leading global company, albeit inconvenient, should still be adopted. This limited further learning.[36]

5-3. Establishment of initial sales system

HMC's after-sales service system building was propelled well before the car assembling factories were constructed based on the strong recommendation of Ford. Ford pointed out based on their experience of being engaged in

---

35) HMC (1992), *op. sit.*, pp. 292-293.
36) Hong Lee (2007), "Hyundaijadongcha Sungjanggwajunge Chujukkwa Eoimihesuk (Tracking of growth of Hyundai automobile and its significance)", *The Korean Academy of Organization and Management*, 31 (3), pp. 1-25.

car industry for long that HMC should be able to carry out smooth maintenance and part supply at the same time as car sale by being fully equipped with after-sales service system before the car production. Accordingly, they required HMC to establish the sale system before producing new cars as stated below. (1) Build the after-sales service center first. (2) Build more than 5 direct management maintenance shops across the nation. (3) Organize the nationwide part sale network. (4) Spread the maintenance skills. Selling agencies must include maintenance and part sale certainly.[37]

With this, Ford put out a business plan about complete building of after-sales service system. The amount of this plan was larger than entire plan of car industry and it required them to input the factory construction-matching fund to after-sales service system building. In western automobile market, selling parts and after-sales services was systemically combined, as dealers were involved from selling vehicles to maintenance, and even to the part supply. Because of this, Ford asked for the each branch to be responsible for the maintenance and the component supply.[38] Ford required them to put after-sales service system building before the production system building or put the same portion to it at least. This requirement showed how much stress Ford put on after-sales service.

However, HMC responded to this assignment inactively. As HMC had just taken the first step toward the car industry, they concentrated every power and capital on the production so they couldn't afford to care even after-sales service for customers. Also, the supply was always insufficient compared to the demand during that time which looked as if HMC distributed cars to customers so Ford's request was not persuasive to HMC. Moreover, considering the Korean situation in 1960s, it was very difficult to find dealers with the capital power and management ability to handle sales of new cars, maintenance, and part sale comprehensively in local areas.[39]

Relating to this, Youngwook Park who worked as an auditor from 1974 to 1979 explained the situation at that time. "At that time, Ford doubted the ability of HMC. We realized that market environment in Korea was very inadequate to start the automobile business, after discussing several months with Ford. In other word, we realized that it is impossible for necessary footholds such as dealer, after service network, and sales finance to be preceded

---

37) HMC (1992), *op. sit.*, pp. 304-305.
38) Hyundai Motor Sevice (1999), *op. sit.*, p. 36.
39) Hiromi Shioji (2002), *Jidosha Ryutsuuno Kokusai Hikaku (The Structure of Automobile Distribution: An International Comparison)*, Yuhikaku, pp. 187-188.

in Korea. It was the problem that only can be solved from macroscopic approach, such as the flow of national economy, the size of market, or the flow of money. Even though those problems needed to be resolved prior to start the automobile business, we concluded to start it without dealers, after service network, and sales finance. (omit) As a result, the Korean automobile industry (HMC) had to start in abnormal way".[40]

Therefore, HMC accepted Ford's requirement partially and built direct management after-sales service centers in Seoul and Busan, other major cities, and built selling agencies in local areas, one in each province and built the sale channels via the part agencies. It is similar with Ford's initial sale channel.[41] Ford built a huge sale facility in Detroit and built sale channels through independent dealers in suburban areas. The center of sale system was Seoul Business Place which not only sold as Ford's requirement but also included the maintenance and part sale. HMC asked Ford to design the maintenance factory of Seoul Business Place and Ford designed a two-story maintenance factory in accordance with their own typical format. Also, general matters including sale education, administrative procedures, and paper forms were done according to Ford system.

In short, the beginning of a sales system of Hyundai shows that the sales system was constructed with sales rather than after sales service as its center despite of strong recommendation by Ford.

5-4. Management crisis of HMC and strategy change to direct sales system

However, the demand for after sales service of HMC jumped along with the sales of *Cortina* and a long period of time was consumed for repairs as a result of the inability to provide the parts on time. It was because HMC, being dependent on Ford for most of the parts, always lacked the parts inventory especially for repair. Since it was beginning of the business, they couldn't predict accurately the quantity demand per month for each part. Even though they made advance orders, there were many cases of lack of stock because the shipment was delayed due to situations of the providers from England or Germany.[42] Moreover, Ford provided the parts for repair in sets whereas

---

40) Recited from Hyundai Motor Service (1999), pp. 29-30.
41) Hyukki Kwon (1998), *Kokusai Hikaku Kara Mita Kankokuno Jidosha Ryutsu System (International comparison of automobile distribution)*, Ph. D dissertation, Kyoto University, p. 25.
42) HMC (1992), *op. sit.*, p. 276.

Toyota Motor Corporation provided parts to Shinjin Motors by piece such that the unit price of parts of HMC was expensive than other rival companies. Finally, the customers started to have dissatisfaction to this action and this led to a situation where they refuse to repay the installments. As a result, HMC faced a severe financial difficulty despite of high sales they derived and it became an impetus to think about the importance of the sales system.

HMC constructed an emergency management system to deal with this crisis. In other words, a task force team was organized around the sales department in order to resolve the problem on after sales service and the collection of the overdue payments. This, as an organization of crisis management expanded and reformed from the existing sales department, carried out 5 functions (sales management, installments management, recollection of overdue payment, repair, and parts). It gathered the competent employees from the whole organization and devoted their strength in overcoming the financial difficulty by linking all functions. The sales department had 206 employees that was equivalent to 57% of all employees.[43]

Finally, Hyundai changed to the sales system emphasized on after-sales service in this process. Indeed, with the management policy to concentrate thoroughly on the after-sales service of one unit sold instead of trying to sell 100 units, 5 operation guidelines of following were formed. (1) Have a smooth supply of the parts. (2) Expand the network of repairs. (3) Take responsibility for the defective chassis. (4) Operate circulating maintenance teams. (5) Disseminate the driving skills.[44]

Especially, the bench stock system of Ford was adapted that hardware stocks like bolts, nuts, and washer were stored in different places and the private tools were provided to all mechanics, thus, the work efficiency rose higher at the same time the repair system improved. Moreover, the performance based pay system of Ford was introduced and the salaries were paid according to the standard working hours (after sales service time) set for every repair items.[45] In this way, HMC actively dealt with regards to the recommendation about after sales service by the Ford only after they had experienced the financial difficulty.

However, HMC did not adhere to the initial sales system model of Ford with this kind of measure. In an economic depression accompanied by financial difficulty, the dealers couldn't create demands with their sales capacity

---

43) HMC (1992), *Ibid.*, pp. 344-346.
44) *Ibid.*, pp. 347-349.
45) *Ibid.*, pp. 349-350.

and they couldn't resolve the distressed-debt they made. In the end, HMC decided to expand the direct sales system which was practiced only in Seoul and Busan to all over the nation.

The direct sales system was constructed based on the activities by the overdue payment recollection team of sales management department. They not only recollected of the overdue payment but they checked the real condition of the sales management of dealers and expanded the area of activity to the sales of vehicles. Therefore, HMC cancelled the contract with the dealers by association since 1971, and replaced gradually to directly managed stores. This store was based on the liaison office installed with recollection of overdue payments as its goal.[46]

Consequently, the sales system of Hyundai was influenced by the Ford, but formed and adjusted to the actual condition in Korea depending on the feature of Korean market and sales environment as it can be seen through the process of establishing direct sales system.

6. Summary and discussion

In terms of content of this chapter, it focused on the alliance of HMC with Ford. The main contents are as follows.

First, The background of HMC and its establishment was analyzed. HMC was founded by the alliance with Ford amidst changes in the Korean auto industry. The significance of the foundation of HMC was both the realization of founder Juyung Chung's personal wish to expand into the auto industry and the start of the expansion into the heavy chemical industry. Also, the Korean auto industry started the transition from a competition-limited monopoly to a full-fledged competition system as HMC emerged as a new player in the market. Simultaneously, the introduction of an American auto maker to the Korean market meant a new unraveling of the auto scene.

Second, the reason why HMC partnered with Ford was analyzed from the standpoint of domestic and global auto industries. It revealed the intention of HMC pursuing its entry into the auto industry, combined with the global expansion strategies of Ford.

Third, the alliance between HMC and Ford was an effective tool for Hyundai to enter the domestic auto industry, which was becoming competitive.

Fourth, how the alliance with Ford was related to the business manage-

---

46) Kwon (1998), *op. sit.*, pp. 30-33.

ment of Hyundai as a start-up was analyzed. Also, the results of the alliance in terms of building a management basis of HMC were analyzed. As for benefits, Hyundai was able to acquire auto assembly technologies promptly, thanks to its vigorous efforts to learn packaged technologies and systems of Ford, which also cooperated by transferring these technologies actively. Amazingly, HMC was able to begin manufacturing cars in a relatively short period of time. However, some of the systems transferred from Ford didn't fit the circumstances of Korea and made it difficult for Hyundai to acquire them, due to no modification.

While HMC was striving to solve its management crisis arising from its after-sales service and overdue payment recovery, the automaker realized the importance of effective sales system. It prompted HMC to switch to 'direct sales system'. Although it was influenced by the sales system of Ford, it was remodeled to adapt to the situation in Korea. That's when the current direct sales system of HMC, which is known as a rare system in the global community, was formed.

The analysis provides the following implications in terms of alliance of HMC with Ford as a start-up automaker.

First, the alliance with advanced automakers does not ensure successful technical learning and acquisition. Successful utilization of technology depends on the strategies of the learner, as HMC has illustrated. Therefore, the biggest success factor is as follows: how effectively the learner (automaker introducing a new technology) incorporates new technologies into its own technology and learning efforts, based on its alliance. In case of HMC, although it stimulated its technical learning through alliance with Ford, it had the following problem: HMC didn't make sufficient efforts to find and utilize new technologies to overcome its technical limitations and achieve greater outcomes.

Second, HMC recognized the importance of integrating production and sales, amid its severe management crisis. Unfortunately, the alliance intention of HMC, as well as the Korean government, only focused on technical assistance for establishing production capabilities. However, a solid sales system is essential for manufacturing, as demonstrated by the direct sales system created by HMC.

＊Contents above were written based on the presentation at 2014 IFSAM.

IX.
Multinational Enterprises' Global Supply Chain: Study of the Global Reporting Initiative and United Nations Global Compact

Kanako NEGISHI

1. Introduction

Multinational enterprises (MNEs) from advanced countries often reinforce their competitive advantage through complex supply chains in developing and less developed countries. While this is seen as the engine for economic growth in host countries, it sometimes triggers social issues, such as environment, human rights, and poverty, in the target communities (Jones, 2005; Bardy et al., 2012). The gap between the home country and host country in regulations, customs, culture which differences is well-known. For example, child labor for those below 15 is allowed in some developing and less developed countries, while it is banned in most of advanced ones.

According to Umeda (2011), there is a gap between the negative aspects created by economic actors such as MNEs and the ability of control global each society have. To bridge the gap, Umeda (2011) suggests two approaches. One is to give firms more responsibility, suggesting that the key to solve such issues lies in firms' independency. The other approach is to reinforce national regulations, which suggests the limitations of corporate social responsibility (CSR). Therefore, not depending on firms' independency, regulations would be the solution to these problems.

Although the second approach is important, we explore the first one in this paper. As such, one of the purposes of this study is to analyze MNEs' global supply chains and how they affect the societies in developing countries.

MNEs often use the gaps between home and host countries to obtain competitive advantage, trends shared by CSR and creating shared value (CSV) recently. MNEs have CSR and/or CSV policies and strategies adapted to various countries' laws, level of income, etc.

However, there are trends to integrate worldwide guidelines and principles. Sustainable Japan comprises institutions which lead the guidelines of sustainable reports, connecting entities such as non-governmental organizations (NGOs) and international institutions.[1] It looks quite complex but there are mainly 3 points focusing on the relationships; GRI, UNGC and Integrated Reporting (IR).

Nowadays sustainability is one of the important issue for firms, especially for MNEs. However, these public institutions and NGOs mainly makes the environment for firms' sustainability reporting. The reports appear the result of the firms' sustainability. Therefore, it strongly relates to disclosure.

Public institutions and NGOs recognized important stakeholders (Sakurai, 2010), although not the same ones firms' have, as there are no suppliers or consumers, except for specific cases.

To identify the features of the environment regarding MNEs' sustainability, this paper is organized in three parts: first, we review previous literature; subsequently, we use surveys and analysis of GRI and UNGC to clarify how firms use these reporting guidelines and participate in them; finally, the findings, implications, and scope for further research are explained.

2. Literature review

Vogel (2005) notes the complex and specific environment of MNEs sustainability.

He explains that 'Since the 1990s, many major American and European manufacturers and retailers headquartered in United States and Europe have adopted voluntary standards for labor conditions, environmental practices, and human rights. These new commitments have been institutionalized in corporate and industry codes, multi-stakeholder initiatives, and private standard-setting bodies.

He describes these new commitment as 'complex web of "soft" law' and it has constructed new social norms for several important dimensions of business conduct.'[2]

---

1) Sustainable Japan homepage, http://sustainablejapan.jp/2015/04/28/reporting-guideline-chaos-map/14933 (last access, July 4, 2016).
2) Vogel, D. (2005), *The Market for Virtue: the potential and limits of corporate social re-*

As described in the introduction, sustainability is an important agenda for MNEs. However, new commitments have been made by institutions such as UNGC and GRI.

GRI is an international organization that helps businesses, governments and the other organizations understand and communicate the impact of business on critical sustainability issues such as climate change, human rights, corruption and many others.[3]

UNGC is 'the world's largest corporate sustainability initiative. A call to align strategies and operations with universal principles on human rights, labour, environment and anti- corruption, and take actions that advance social goals.'[4]

The questions that arise are as follows. What is the content of the complex web of soft law? How does it relate to firms' sustainability? Is there any possibility to change firm's strategy?

One of the purposes of this paper is to determine the specific environment. As such, we choose the representatives of this environment as firms, GRI, and UNGC.

Vogel noted the American and European firms are pressured to behave more responsible. In the same time, they are also competitive pressured from the firms in developing countries.

Subsequently, do the Japanese firms which are not American or European, and firms in developing countries use the sustainability guideline and participate in the UNGC?

Although he suggests Japanese firms' CSRs features, the international relationship between the firms and the global institutions it is not clear (Vogel, 2014).

Additionally, these guidelines and principles are criticized for their nationalistic influence and cannot be eliminated from the global standards. Fukukawa and Teramoto (2009) note: ". . . nevertheless, despite CSR's apparent all-pervasiveness, the underlying definition and development of the concept has arguably been based upon a predominantly Western-led discourse".[5]

The effect has been examined and the gap between the practice and reports

---

sponsibility, Brookings Institution Press: Washington D. C.
3) GRI homepage, https://www.globalreporting.org/information/about-gri/Pages/default. aspx (last access, June 14, 2016).
4) UN Global Compact homepage, https://www.unglobalcompact.org/what-is-gc (last access, May 23, 2016).
5) Fukukawa, K. and Teramoto, Y. (2009), "Understanding Japanese CSR: The reflections of managers in the field of global operations", *Journal of Business Ethics*, 85: 133-146.

by each institution criticized (Fukukawa K and Teramoto, Y., 2009).

Focusing on each guideline and principle, literature suggests the gap between reporting and action (Fortanier, F., Kolk, A. & Pinkse, J., 2011).

Knundsen (2011) focuses on delisting firms by UNGC. According to the paper, it is appeared that a strengthening of domestic governance institutions is crucial to assist companies in fulfilling UN Global Compact requirement; furthermore, it is likely that the UN Global Compact has a stronger appeal to international oriented firms than to domestically oriented firms.[6]

Particularly internationally oriented firms, MNEs, are sensitive about criticism of their behavior. Their strategy reflects their complex global supply chain.

Certain studies note the issue of labor in the supply chain (Kawaguchi, 2005; Gugler and Shi, 2008; Suzuki and Yokozuka, 2012).

Literature also discusses that CSR spreads from the headquarter to suppliers, including outsourcing on their global supply chain.[7] For example, MNEs meet their suppliers, take surveys, monitor, inspect, and provide them with training.

In some cases, firms create a common platform to spread their sustainability practices in the electric industry.

However, the flow regarding MNEs sustainability to their suppliers is not clear, particularly when suppliers are not MNEs subsidiaries.

Vogel noted that for the suppliers, the business case for CSR is problematic. Behaving more responsibly may help them maintain their contracts with Western firms, but it does not permit them to charge higher prices. While noncompliance may reduce their sales, compliance does not necessarily increase them. Adding to this tension is that the cost of compliance are borne primarily by developing country producers, the benefits accrue primarily to Western firms.[8]

Therefore, this study explores how CSR/CSV practices spread from MNEs to Small and Medium Sized Enterprises (SMEs) in developing countries.

---

6) Knudsen, J. S. (2011), "Company Delistings from the UN Global Compact: Limited Business Demand or Domestic Governance Failure?", *Journal of Business Ethics*, 103, pp. 331-349.
7) Bardy, R., Drew, S. and Kennedy, T. F. (2012), "Foreign Investment and Ethics: How to Contribute to Social Responsibility by Doing Business in Less- Developed Countries", *Journal of Business Ethics*, pp. 267-282.
8) Vogel (2005), *op. cit.,* p. 95.

2-1. Deffinition

The definition of developing countries in this paper is a country whose economic growth ratio is higher than the world average and the per capita GDP levels are lower than world average. Based on this definition, developing countries are as follows: Bangladesh, Myanmar, Malaysia, Philippine, Thailand, Laos, Viet Nam, Egypt, Morocco, Chili, Colombia, Bulgaria, Romania, China, India, Brazil, Russia, Indonesia, Iran, Turkey, South Africa, Argentina (Mori, 2012).

GRI defines firms in three categories: MNEs that have over 250 employees and undertake overseas business; large firms have over 250 employees without overseas business, and SMEs have under 250 employees.

According to GC, companies are divided into those with over 250 employees and SMEs with less than 250.

In the subsequent section, we use the system of delisting from UNGC, which means that new participants must submit their first Communication on Progress (COP) one year after joining the initiative. Existing participants are required to submit their COPs yearly. For example, if the last submission took place on April 1, 2015, the next COP will be due on April 1, 2016 (UNGC, 2013).

Breaching the deadline leads to the company being delisted. GC office upload the "expulsion companies and organizations list" on the (New York headquarters) web site, will be a very tough situation where companies and organizations name continues to be published (Global Compact Network Japan).

All data that used in the subsequent section about GRI is from GRI database[9], and UNGC is based on the participants database.[10]

2-2. Results
2-2-1. GRI

Figure 1 shows the transition of the firms' users, including MNEs, large companies, and SMEs. The number of GRI users has been increasing with an average of 1.31, except between 1999 and 2000; if including these years, the average is 3.82. From 2003 to 2008 the average is exceeded, but falls below it after 2010. This suggests that the CSR reporting boom has settled worldwide. Subsequently, the growth rate of new users reduced, because interested

---

9) GRI homepage, http://database.globalreporting.org/ (last access, July 13, 2016).
10) UNGC homepage, https://www.unglobalcompact.org/what-is-gc/participants (last access, July 13, 2016).

firms already use it.

The average increase is 1.16 in Japan, except between 1999 and 2000; if including these years, the average is 1.29. The increasing trend above average has been continued from 2003 to 2010. As such, we can consider 2003 as the first year of CSR in Japan.

Table 1 shows the ratio of regional location of user firms and the percentage of user's size. The number of firms by size is as follows; MNEs are 1,347, large firms number 2,456, and SMEs 429 (June 6, 2016).

From this table, large companies, whose number of employees is over 250 but have no overseas business, are the most common in every region. In Asia and North America, the ratio of MNEs tends to be higher than in other regions and that of SMEs lower. European, Latin American and Caribbean, and Oceania firms exhibit a similar trend. However, the ratios for SMEs are relatively higher than for the other regions above.

Table 2 is detailed in Table 3, the ranking of users by countries. Although CSR/CSV have progressed further in advanced countries, especially USA and European countries, both advanced and developing countries are in the top 20.

Considering which firm sizes use GRI guidelines, Table 3 is the ranking of SMEs in the top 20 countries. The ranking changes from Table 2, particularly from the first to the seventh positions, occupied by developing countries and relatively smaller advanced countries. Additionally, Peru, India, Belgium, and Indonesia are introduced in Table 3, while Japan, United Kingdom, South Africa, France, and Argentina are excluded.

Table 5 is largely different from Tables 3 and 4, as in Asian countries occupy the first two positions. There is a large gap between the third and fourth positions, and advanced countries are occupy top 10 based as opposed to Table 3, which ranks several developing countries. Taiwan and Japan tend to have similar. The larger the size of firms, the more firms use the guideline. In particular, Japanese MNEs are ranked second, whereas its SMEs are not listed in table 3.

From Tables 3, 4, and 5, developing countries India, Brazil, China, Indonesia, South Africa, and Argentina do not exhibit any correlation. However, Indonesia, China, and India show that SMEs are most common. Large firms and MNEs are not ranked in Figure 2.

For advanced countries, Japan, the United Kingdom, Germany, and USA show similar trends (Figure 3)

Table 6 shows each ratio by firm sizes. The ranking is based on the number of all firms.

Top three countries, Taiwan, USA, and Japan, and Finland and France's MNEs ratio is higher than for large companies, focusing on advanced countries. Only China's ratio of MNEs is a one-digit figure.

The Japanese SME's ratio is the lowest in this ranking, followed by the United Kingdom. As the ratio of MNEs is higher, SMEs ratio tends to be lower.

From these results, not only advanced countries, but several developing countries' SMEs use GRI guidelines, the most common guideline worldwide, to publish their sustainability reports.

Subsequently, Table 7 shows the ranking of all users by sector.

The discussion on CSR and/or CSV was based on manufacturing, resources, and agriculture and food industries because of their large impact on developing countries.

However, financial services hold the first position, which affects largely host countries, especially their environment and human rights.

Positions 2, 5, 7, and 19 are related to natural resources. Food industry is ranked third and manufacture related industries are ranked on positions 6, 10,11, 13, 14, and 17.

The results suggest that not all firms that have strong effects on developing countries' sustainability are ranked in the table. However, they tend to be ranked higher by sector.

Table 8 focuses on MNE users and Table 9 on SMEs. The sector of financial services is ranked first in both MNEs and SMEs. The sectors roughly resemble those in Tables 7 and 8, whereas there are settled differences between Tables 7, 8, and 9.

The sectors of waste management, media, water utilities, agriculture, textiles and apparel, and tourism/leisure are only ranked in Table 9.

On the other hand, financial services, energy, food and beverages, chemical, energy utilities, automotive, logistics, commercial services, and metal products are ranked in all tables.

Technology hardware is ranked higher in Tables 7 and 8, but does not feature in Table 9.

Focusing on Japanese MNEs, financial services are ranked seventh and technology hardware fourth, while equipment is the first. For example, AISIN SEIKI Co., Ltd. and ALPS ELECTRIC CO., LTD. are in the equipment sector. Including this sector, the sectors related to resources and manufacturing occupy top 10.

This is reflected in the Japanese industry structure. Similar to other advanced countries, financial service are placed second in the USA, as well as healthcare products, while technology hardware is fourth. At the same time, technology hardware is the first in Taiwan. Some resources are well ranked in China as well (first is metal products and mining).

Additionally, the Japanese SME users of GRI guidelines are only four as follows.

2-2-2. UNGC

GC noted about firm's supply chain that a company's entire supply chain can have a significant impact in promoting human rights, fair labor practices, environmental progress, and anti-corruption policies. However, UNGC participants rank supply chain practices as the biggest challenge in improving their sustainability performance. Extending the UNGC's Ten Principles into the supply chain can be difficult because of its scale and complexity.

To assist this agenda, they propose that doing so promotes a broader understanding within an organization of how decisions made beyond procurement can affect the supply chain. For example, legal staff, product developers, and marketing can all have an impact. Additionally, companies must look at their supply chain as a whole, and consider the suppliers that may have the most significant challenges to address.[11]

To undertake suppliers in developing countries by MNEs in advanced countries, GC is not only a way to promote social responsibility, but tool to assist the agenda of suppliers and the Ten Principle as a symbol of social responsibility worldwide.

Based on the GC database, 16,469 firms joined, including companies, SMEs, and micro enterprises; the number of companies is 6,134 and SMEs number 10,122 (May 23, 2016).

Table 12 shows the ranking of Global Compact Top 20 countries by the total number of participants. Literature suggests CSR and/or CSV is preceded by advanced countries. However, the result is different from the above tables. In the top 20 countries, not all countries are advanced, some being developing countries.

Tables 13 and 14 show the ranking by companies and SMEs. Several countries' order was changed, but the same countries rank in both tables.

For Japanese firms, more SMEs participate in GC than companies. One of

---

11) UNGC homepage, Supply Chain Sustainability, https://www.unglobalcompact.org/what-is-gc/our-work/supply-chain (last access, June 22, 2016).

the reason is that the share of SMEs is 99.2% in Japan (The Small and Medium Enterprises Agency)

Compared to GRI, the countries in GC are not largely different in top 10, because GRI and UNGC are both for sustainable reporting of firms.

Additionally, the UNGC and GRI are complementary initiatives that can help companies of all sizes, and in all locations and sectors, work towards sustainable development and transparently report progress towards this goal. The UNGC and GRI renewed their Memorandum of Understanding in May 2013. The renewed agreement affirms a long-standing collaboration and alliance between the two organizations, and also marks the beginning of a number of innovative collaborations, in particular on the UN Post-2015 Development Agenda (UNGC and GRI, 2013).

They have co-operated to achieve each agenda. Recently, the reports which firms use reflect these guideline and principles because of their comparability.

Sectors are different between GRI and GC.

However, the trend that not only the sector which has been discussed long time but the sector which less strongly effect on MNEs and developing countries' sustainability is the same as GRI. Particularly the resource industry is not ranked in the top 10, although discussed deeply in the 1960s and 1970s in the UN.

For example, firms in support services in industrial goods and services in Japan is Deloitte Tohmatsu Consulting LLC, Mitsubishi Research Institute, INC. and West Nippon Expressway Company Limited.

Compared to Table 17, only the banking sector is not in Table 16. Other sectors ranked are the same in Tables 16 and 17.

However, MNEs and SMEs show a different trend from GRI. The sectors below 14 in Table 16 are not ranked in Table 17. On the other hand, media, pharmaceuticals and biotechnology, fixed line telecommunication, real estate investment trust, aerospace and defense, and electricity sectors are not ranked in Table 16.

Table 18, 19, and 20 focus on Japanese firms. In the Japanese GRI users, there are different sectors ranked in each table. These tables do not show the same trend as GRI.

As previously noted, UNGC have the system for expelling firms which fail to submit their reports (COP).

Table 21 shows 10 countries which are ranked in Table 13, both advanced and developing countries by status and size. Except for China, SMEs delisted ratio is higher than for companies.

Additionally, the average ratio of SMEs delisted in advanced countries is slightly higher than in developing countries (61.56% and 57.13%), although it is assumed that SMEs in advanced countries have better financial conditions than in developing countries.

The largest gap is between Japanese companies and SMEs: 2.91% and 84.19%.

3. Conclusion and further research

The relationship between MNEs and environment on sustainability has changed over the last decade. MNEs still strongly affect developing countries' societies through their global supply chain, which sometimes improves working conditions and/or income levels, whereas it involves the firms in developing countries in global competition.

To identify the environment features and determine how of CSR/CSV spread from MNEs in advanced countries to developing countries, this paper explored GRI and UNGC data.

First, the finding is that not all MNEs in advanced countries, in particular American and European firms, Asian firms and SMEs in developing countries are using GRI guideline and participate in UNGC.

The SME GRI users by home country are mainly developing countries, whereas MNEs' home countries are advanced countries. This is different from UNGC which mixes both types of countries.

Second, focusing on GRI, while MNEs' home countries are mainly advanced countries, SMEs are from developing countries. It is assumed that there are not any obligation of MNEs in advanced countries to SMEs in developing countries, as Vogel (2005) noted. To clarify this, more research and case studies are needed by sector.

Third, focusing on UNGC, the average ratio of SME delisting in advanced countries is slightly higher than in developing countries, although SMEs in advanced countries have better financial conditions.

In particular, Japanese companies' delisting ratio is the lowest in the table, while Japanese SMEs ratio is the highest, although Knudsen (2011) shows that domestic governance institutions are crucial in assisting companies in fulfilling the UNGC requirement. More research is required to clarify the reasons for these results as well.

References

Journals, books and articles
■ English

Fortanier, F., Kolk, A. and Pinkse, J. (2011), "Harmonization in CSR reporting", *Management International Review*, Vol. 51 (5), pp. 665–696.

Fukukawa, K. and Teramoto, Y. (2009), "Understanding Japanese CSR: The reflections of managers in the field of global operations", *Journal of Business Ethics*, 85, pp. 133–146.

Geoffrey, J. (2005), *Multinationals and Global Capitalism from the Nineteenth to the Twenty First Century*, Oxford University Press: West Sussex.

Janney, J. J., Greg, D. and Victor, F. (2009), "Glass Houses? Market Reactions to Firms Joining the UN Global Compact", *Journal of Business Ethics*, 90, pp. 407–423.

Knudsen, J. S. (2011), "Company Delistings from the UN Global Compact: Limited Business Demand or Domestic Governance Failure?", *Journal of Business Ethics*, 103, pp. 331–349.

Philippe, G. and Shi, Jacylyn Y. (2009), "Corporate Social Responsibility for Developing Country Multinational Corporations: Lost War in Pertaining Global Competitiveness?", *Journal of Business Ethics*, 87, pp. 3–24.

Roland, B., Stephen, D. and Kennedy, T. F. (2012), "Foreign Investment and Ethics: How to Contribute to Social Responsibility by Doing Business in Less- Developed Countries", *Journal of Business Ethics*, 106 (3), pp. 267–282.

Sethi, S. P. and Schepers, D. H. (2014), "United Nations Global Compact: The Promise-Performance Gap", *Journal of Business Ethics*, 122, pp. 193–208.

Vogel, David (2005) *The Market for Virtue: the potential and limits of corporate social responsibility*, Brookings Institution Press: Washington D. C.

Vogel, David (2008), "Private Global Business Regulation", *Annual Review of Political Science*, 11, pp. 261–282.

Vogel, David (2014), "Global Corporate Responsibility and Business Ethics", *Japan Society for Business Ethics Study*, 21, pp. 329–333.

UNGC and GRI (2013), *Making the Connection: Using the GRI G4 Guidelines to Communicate Progress on the UN Global Compact Principles*.

■ Japsnese

Kawaguchi, Mariko (2005), "Global keizainiokeru Roudoumondai to CSR", *DIR Keieisenryaku kenkyu*, Vol. 5, pp. 18–49.

Mori, Takeshi (2013) *Shinkoukoku towa Nanika (Navigation and Solution)*, Nomura Research Institute, pp. 58–69.

Sakurai, Michiharu (2010), "Characteristics of Stakeholders from the Standpoint of Stakeholder Theory: Identification of Stakeholders in the Discussion of Corporate Reputation", *Business Review of the Senshu University*, No. 101, pp. 99–112.

Suzuki, Yutaka and Hitoshi, Yokozuka (2012), *Bijinesu to Jinken wo meguru Kokusaidoukou to Kigyoukeiei eno Eikyou*, Daiwasouken Cyousakihou, Vol. 5, pp. 38–53.

Umeda, Toru (2011), "An Approach to 'Protect, Respect and Remedy' framework: voluntary corporate efforts or tighter legal and other regulations", *Journal of International Law and Diplomacy*, vol. 110(1), pp. 1–29.

Websites

Global compact network Japan FAQ, http://ungcjn.org/faq/index.html#q10 (last access, June 21, 2016).

Global Repoting Initiative homepage, http://www.globalreporting.org/services/analysis/Report_list/Pages/default.aspx (last access, June 3, 2016).

The Small and Medium Enterprises Agency homepage, http://www.chusho.meti.go.jp/faq/faq26.html (last access, June 28, 2016).

UNGC (2013), 'UN Global Compact Policy on Communicating Progress', https://www.unglobalcompact.org/docs/communication_on_progress/COP_Policy.pdf (last access, June 21, 2016).

UNGC Explore our library, https://www.unglobalcompact.org/library/306 (last access, June 21, 2016).

Figure 1: Transition of GRI guideline User organizations

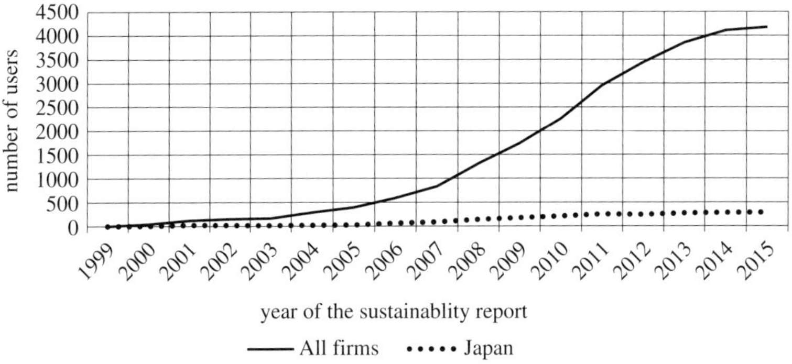

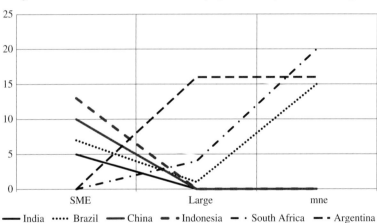

Source: GRI homepage, http://database.globalreporting.org/ (last access, July 13, 2016).

Figure 2: Transition of GRI Users in Developing Countries by Size and Ranking

Source: GRI homepage, http://database.globalreporting.org/ (last access, July 13, 2016).

Figure 3: Change of GRI Users in Advanced Countries by Size and Ranking

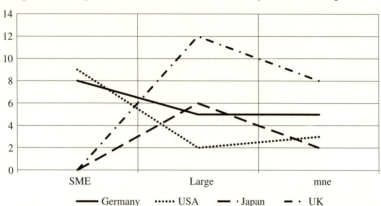

Source: GRI homepage, http://database.globalreporting.org/ (last access, July 13, 2016).

Table 1: Ratio of GRI user firms' size and regions in 2015

		Size of firms		
		MNE	Large	SME
Region	Africa	13.51%	79.73%	6.76%
	Asia	42.72%	50.83%	6.45%
	Europe	28.03%	58.62%	13.36%
	Latin America and the Caribbean	15.12%	69.25%	15.63%
	North America	41.96%	50.44%	7.60%
	Oceania	31.32%	53.30%	15.38%
	All regions	31.34%	57.93%	10.72%

Source: GRI homepage, http://database.globalreporting.org/ (last access, July 13, 2016).

Table 2: Ranking of GRI users

	Country	All size firms
1	Taiwan	377
2	USA	350
3	Japan	283
4	Brazil	223
5	Spain	176
6	Germany	171
7	China	164
8	France	149
9	Colombia	148
10	Finland	134
11	Sweden	127
12	South Africa	126
13	Netherlands	113
14	Switzerland	106
15	Canada	99
16	UK	95
17	Australia	90
18	Mexico	86
19	Argentina	84
20	Italy	83

Source: GRI homepage, http://database.globalreporting.org/ (last access, July 13, 2016).

Table 3: Ranking of GRI guidelines SME users

	Country	Number of SMEs
1	Colombia	39
2	Spain	37
3	Sweden	24
4	Peru	24
5	India	21
6	Belgium	20
7	Brazil	18
8	Germany	18
9	USA	17
10	China	17
11	Switzerland	17
12	Italy	17
13	Indonesia	14
14	Taiwan	13
15	Netherlands	12
16	Australia	11
17	Austria	9
18	Finland	8
19	Canada	8
20	Mexico	7

Source: GRI homepage, http://database.globalreporting.org/ (last access, July 13, 2016).

Table 4: Ranking of GRI guidelines large users

	Country	Large firms
1	Brazil	182
2	USA	166
3	Spain	113
4	South Africa	107
5	Germany	100
6	Japan	98
7	Taiwan	94
8	Colombia	82
9	Finland	76
10	Sweden	75
11	Netherlands	69
12	UK	60
13	Mexico	60
14	Korean Republic	60
15	Canada	59
16	Argentina	59
17	Switzerland	58
18	France	57
19	Australia	41
20	Singapore	11

Source: GRI homepage, http://database.globalreporting.org/ (last access, July 13, 2016).

Table 5: Ranking of GRI guidelines MNE users

	Country	MNE
1	Taiwan	270
2	Japan	181
3	USA	167
4	France	86
5	Germany	53
6	Finland	50
7	Australia	38
8	UK	34
9	Netherlands	32
10	Canada	32
11	Switzerland	31
12	Sweden	28
13	Colombia	27
14	Spain	26
15	Brazil	23
16	Argentina	20
17	Mexico	19
18	Korean Republic	19
19	Singapore	18
20	South Africa	15

Source: GRI homepage, http://database.globalreporting.org/ (last access, July 13, 2016).

Table 6 : The ranking of ratios for all sizes In GRI

		SME/All	Large/All	MNE/All	All
1	Taiwan	3.45%	24.93%	71.62%	377
2	USA	4.86%	47.43%	47.71%	350
3	Japan	1.41%	34.63%	63.96%	283
4	Brazil	8.07%	81.61%	10.31%	223
5	Spain	21.02%	64.20%	14.77%	176
6	Germany	10.53%	58.48%	30.99%	171
7	China	10.37%	82.93%	6.71%	164
8	France	4.03%	38.26%	57.72%	149
9	Colombia	26.35%	55.41%	18.24%	148
10	Finland	5.97%	56.72%	37.31%	134
11	Sweden	18.90%	59.06%	22.05%	127
12	South Africa	3.17%	84.92%	11.90%	126
13	Netherlands	10.62%	61.06%	28.32%	113
14	Switzerland	16.04%	54.72%	29.25%	106
15	Canada	8.08%	59.60%	32.32%	99
16	UK	1.05%	63.16%	35.79%	95
17	Australia	12.22%	45.56%	42.22%	90
18	Mexico	8.14%	69.77%	22.09%	86
19	Argentina	5.95%	70.24%	23.81%	84
20	Italy	20.48%	62.65%	16.87%	83

Source: GRI homepage, http://database.globalreporting.org/ (last access, July 13, 2016).

Table 7: Ranking of GRI users by sector in 2015

	Sector	Number of all users
1	Financial services	548
2	Energy	308
3	Food and beverages	254
4	Chemicals	197
5	Energy utilities	167
6	Technology hardware	153
7	Mining	144
8	Real estate	133
9	Telecommunication	129
10	Construction	125
11	Equipment	123
12	Conglomerate	120
13	Automotive	105
14	Construction materials	102
15	Logistics	95
16	Commercial services	91
17	Health care products	90
18	Retailers	87
19	Metal products	83
20	Aviation	75

Source: GRI homepage, http://database.globalreporting.org/ (last access, July 13, 2016).

Table 8: Ranking of MNE GRI users by sector

	Sector	Number of MNEs
1	Financial services	132
2	Technology hardware	110
3	Chemicals	96
4	Food and beverages	85
5	Equipment	66
6	Energy	58
7	Conglomerate	45
8	Mining	44
9	Health care products	38
10	Computers	37
11	Real estate	37
12	Automotive	35
13	Commercial services	35
14	Construction	34
15	Construction materials	34
16	Telecommunication	32
17	Retailers	31
18	Metal products	28
19	Logistics	26
20	Energy utilities	25

Source: GRI homepage, http://database.globalreporting.org/ (last access, July 13, 2016).

Table 9: Ranking of SME GRI users by sector

	Sector	Number of SMEs
1	Financial services	34
2	Energy	25
3	Food and beverages	25
4	Real estate	19
5	Waste management	17
6	Chemicals	14
7	Construction	14
8	Commercial services	14
9	Media	10
10	Agriculture	10
11	Water utilities	10
12	Energy utilities	9
13	Automotive	9
14	Logistics	9
15	Health care services	9
16	Metal products	8
17	Construction materials	7
18	Textiles and apparel	7
19	Equipment	6
20	Tourism/leisure	6

Source: GRI homepage, http://database.globalreporting.org/ (last access, July 13, 2016).

Table 10: Ranking of Japanese MNEs by sector In GRI

	Sector	Number of companies
1	Equipment	39
2	Chemicals	27
3	Others	18
4	Technology Hardware	17
5	Conglomerate	12
6	Automotive	10
7	Financial services	10
8	Construction	8
9	Food and beverages	8
10	Energy	6
11	Health care products	6
12	Metal products	6
13	Real estate	5
14	Household and personal products	4
15	Logistics	4
16	Retailers	4
17	Computers	3
18	Consumer durables	3
19	Commercial services	2
20	Construction materials	2
20	Energy utilities	2
20	Telecommunication	2
20	Textiles and apparel	2
20	Tobacco	2

Source: GRI homepage, http://database.globalreporting.org/ (last access, July 13, 2016).

Table 11: List of Japanese SME GRI users in 2015

Firm name	Sector
Joshin	Retailer
Pasco Shikishima Corporation	Food and beverages
Revacs Corporation	Waste management
SoftBank	Telecommunication

Source: GRI homepage, http://database.globalreporting.org/ (last access, July 13, 2016).

Table 12: Ranking of GC participants by country

	Country	Number of all size firms
1	Spain	2,169
2	France	1,775
3	Mexico	821
4	Brazil	722
5	USA	672
6	Colombia	503
7	China	502
8	Germany	443
9	JAPAN	434
10	UK	423
11	Denmark	394
12	Argentina	389
13	Myanmar	338
14	Turkey	321
15	India	310
16	Italy	274
17	Sweden	260
18	Korean Republic	247
19	Netherlands	129
20	Iraq	119

Source: UNGC homepage, https://www.unglobalcompact.org/what-is-gc/participants (last access, July 13, 2016).

Table 13: Ranking of GC participant countries by number of companies

	Country	Number of companies
1	France	638
2	Spain	563
3	Brazil	319
4	China	273
5	Mexico	256
6	USA	214
7	Colombia	206
8	Germany	192
9	Japan	177
10	Argentina	166
11	Korean Republic	155
12	India	148
13	UK	138
14	Denmark	133
15	Sweden	125
16	Turkey	108
17	Italy	95
18	Myanmar	70
19	Netherlands	69
20	Iraq	11

Source: UNGC homepage, https://www.unglobalcompact.org/what-is-gc/participants (last access, July 13, 2016).

Table 14: Ranking of GC participant countries by number of SMEs

	Country	Number of SMEs
1	Spain	1,606
2	France	1,137
3	Mexico	565
4	USA	458
5	Brazil	403
6	Colombia	297
7	United Kingdom	285
8	Myanmar	268
9	Denmark	261
10	Japan	257
11	Germany	251
12	China	229
13	Argentina	223
14	Turkey	213
15	Italy	179
16	India	162
17	Sweden	135
18	Iraq	108
19	Korean Republic	92
20	Netherlands	60

Source: UNGC homepage, https://www.unglobalcompact.org/what-is-gc/participants (last access, July 13, 2016).

Table 15: Ranking of the number of firms of all sizes by sector

	Sector	Number of firms of all sizes
1	Support services	2,659
2	Construction and materials	1,387
3	General industrials	1,331
4	Software and computer services	939
5	Financial services	854
6	Media	709
7	General retailers	683
8	Food producers	651
9	Travel and leisure	524
10	Industrial transportation	429
11	Electronic and electrical equipment	422
12	Technology hardware and equipment	405
13	Beverages	382
14	Automobiles and parts	373
15	Health care equipment and services	356
16	Personal goods	349
17	Industrial metals and mining	309
18	Chemicals	306
19	Gas, water, and multiutilities	288
20	Oil and gas producers	266

Source: UNGC homepage, https://www.unglobalcompact.org/what-is-gc/participants (last access, July 13, 2016).

Table 16: Ranking of MNE participants by sector

	Sector	Number of companies
1	Support services	651
2	General industrials	477
3	Financial services	469
4	Construction and materials	392
5	Food producers	309
6	General retailers	259
7	Software and computer services	228
8	Beverages	192
9	Automobiles and parts	183
10	Industrial transportation	182
11	Travel and leisure	179
12	Industrial metals & mining	176
13	Gas, water, and multiutilities	170
14	Personal goods	165
15	Oil and gas producers	154
16	Technology hardware and equipment	151
17	Chemicals	149
18	Electronic and electrical equipment	148
19	Health care equipment and services	145
20	Banks	145

Source: UNGC homepage, https://www.unglobalcompact.org/what-is-gc/participants (last access, July 13, 2016).

Table 17: Ranking of SME participants by sector

	Sector	Number of SMEs
1	General retailers	2,008
2	Software and computer services	995
3	Support services	854
4	Gas, water, and multiutilities	711
5	Industrial metals and mining	575
6	Beverages	424
7	Food producers	385
8	Media	345
9	Automobiles and parts	342
10	General industrials	274
11	Financial services	254
12	Pharmaceuticals and biotechnology	247
13	Travel and leisure	211
14	Oil and gas producers	190
15	Fixed line telecommunications	190
16	Industrial transportation	184
17	Real estate investment trust	173
18	Construction and materials	157
19	Aerospace and defense	137
20	Electricity	133

Source: UNGC homepage, https://www.unglobalcompact.org/what-is-gc/participants (last access, July 13, 2016).

Table 18: Ranking of Japanese UNGC participants of all sizes

	Sector	Number of firms by all sizes
1	General retailers	84
2	Software and computer services	42
3	Support services	32
4	Beverages	29
5	General industrials	28
6	Financial services	16
7	Technology hardware and equipment	15
7	Chemicals	15
9	Automobiles and parts	14
9	Gas, water, and multiutilities	14
9	Fixed line telecommunications	14
12	Construction and materials	13
12	Oil and gas producers	13
14	Food producers	12
14	Pharmaceuticals and biotechnology	12
16	Real estate investment trust	10
17	Industrial metals and mining	9
17	Electricity	9
17	Household goods and home	9
20	Personal goods	7

Source: UNGC homepage, https://www.unglobalcompact.org/what-is-gc/participants (last access, July 13, 2016).

Table 19: Ranking of Japanese UNGC company participants

	Sector	Number of Japanese companies
1	Support services	23
1	General industrials	23
3	Financial services	15
4	Construction and materials	12
4	Food producers	12
6	General retailers	8
7	Software and computer services	7
7	Pharmaceuticals and biotechnology	7
9	Beverages	6
9	Gas, water, and multiutilities	6
11	Automobiles and parts	5
11	Industrial transportation	5
11	Travel and leisure	5
11	Industrial metals and mining	5
15	Personal goods	4
15	Oil and gas producers	4
15	Technology hardware and equipment	4
15	Chemicals	4
15	Electronic and electrical equipment	4
15	Health care equipment and services	4

Source: UNGC homepage, https://www.unglobalcompact.org/what-is-gc/participants (last access, July 13, 2016).

Table 20: Ranking of Japanese SME participants

	Sector	Number of Japanese SMEs
1	General retailers	76
2	Software and computer services	35
3	Beverages	23
4	Fixed line telecommunications	12
5	Technology hardware and equipment	11
5	Chemicals	11
7	Real estate investment trust	10
8	Support services	9
8	Automobile and parts	9
8	Oil and gas producers	9
11	Gas, water, and multiutilities	8
12	Household goods and home	7
13	Electricity	6
13	Real estate investment and services	6
15	General industrials	5
15	Pharmaceuticals and biotechnology	5
17	Industrial metals and mining	4
17	Leisure goods	4
19	Personal goods	3
20	Health care equipment and services	2

Source: UNGC homepage, https://www.unglobalcompact.org/what-is-gc/participants (last access, July 13, 2016).

Table 21: Rating of delisting

		Active	Delisted	Total	Ratio of delisted
Spain	company	308	219	527	41.56%
	SME	574	866	1440	60.14%
France	company	373	204	577	35.36%
	SME	415	559	974	57.39%
USA	company	127	73	200	36.50%
	SME	139	276	415	66.51%
Germany	company	154	35	189	18.52%
	SME	139	91	230	39.57%
Japan	company	167	5	172	2.91%
	SME	40	213	253	84.19%
Brazil	company	199	94	293	32.08%
	SME	175	182	357	50.98%
China	company	82	252	334	75.45%
	SME	69	138	207	66.67%
Mexico	company	134	94	228	41.23%
	SME	224	277	501	55.29%
Colombia	company	155	35	190	18.42%
	SME	147	119	266	44.74%
Argentina	company	96	59	155	38.06%
	SME	66	140	206	67.96%

Source: UNGC homepage, https://www.unglobalcompact.org/what-is-gc/participants (last access, July 13, 2016).